MEXICO

AND HER

MILITARY CHIEFTAINS,

Litho by Walsworth Pub. Co., Inc., Marceline, Mo.

MEXICO

AND HER

MILITARY CHIEFTAINS,

FROM THE REVOLUTION OF HIDALGO TO THE PRESENT TIME.

COMPRISING SKETCHES OF THE LIVES

OF

HIDALGO, MORELOS, ITURBIDE, SANTA ANNA, GOMEZ FARIAS, BUSTAMENTE, PAREDES, ALMONTE, ARISTA, ALAMAN, AMPUDIA, HERRERA, AND DE LA VEGA.

BY FAY. ROBINSON.

Illustrated by Twelve Portraits and Engravings.

GLORIETA, NEW MEXICO · 87535

First edition from which this edition was
reproduced was supplied by
ZIMMERMAN LIBRARY
University of New Mexico
Albuquerque, N. M.

A RIO GRANDE CLASSIC
First published in 1847

LIBRARY OF CONGRESS CARD CATALOG 77-13726
I.S.B.N. 87380-069-9

First Printing 1970

GLORIETA, NEW MEXICO · 87535

Publisher's Preface

Some years ago we were in Silver City, New Mexico, where in an antique shop we chanced upon a tattered and torn two-volume set of books entitled *History of the Organization of the Army of the United States 1776 to 1848*. The author was Fayette Robinson. We bought the books without a second's hesitation, and in 1971 we will reprint them as a new title in our line of beautiful Rio Grande Classics.

In our research on the biography of author Fayette Robinson, we discovered he had also written other books, one of them being this one. For years we have tried to buy a copy of *Mexico and Her Military Chieftans 1800-1847* on the rare book market. We could find no dealer who had ever even seen a copy, let alone sold one. Naturally, the library at West Point had a copy, but the legions of Julius Caesar could not pry it loose from the Academy's special collections. We finally located a copy in the Zimmerman Library of the University of New Mexico (next door, so to speak!). Thanks to the kind cooperation of Director David Otis Kelley, we were able to obtain from that copy the offset printing negatives from which this edition was reproduced.

We were most anxious to reprint this title because it is so little-known while still a highly authentic contemporary account of the men and events that led to the war with Mexico (1846-1848). We consider this period in time our special field of interest, and we have reprinted a number of major items documenting the American viewpoint contemporary with the conflict. Author Robinson was an American, true enough, but he was able nevertheless to write fairly objectively about a subject that did not lend itself well to objectivity.

The author writes well, but not necessarily accurately, of the men who make up the pantheon of early Mexican heroes. He writes here of Hidalgo, Morales, Iturbide, Santa Anna, Gomez, Farias, Bustamente, Paredes, Almonte, Arista, Alaman, Ampudia, Herrera and De la Vega. Most of the vital statistics kept in Mexico at that time were kept by church records, and those were highly fallible. Robinson could obviously not obtain the exact and precise biographical data about the great men of Mexico, especially during war time. It is possible, and even probable, that such information did not then exist and perhaps does not exist even now.

Whether Robinson's biographical data is one hundred per cent accurate or not, the information he sets forth in this book is better than nothing, and nothing in the way of biographical data for these giants of Mexican history is what scholars have mostly had heretofore. In all of our research, we have found no other one book that provides the information Robinson provides.

Thus *Mexico and Her Military Chieftans* fills a considerable gap that has heretofore existed in the history of the Mexican War. We consider this indexed reprint edition of this exceptionally rare title to be a major contribution to the renewed and developing body of historical literature about the "...war that nobody knows."

According to *List of Officers of the Army of the United States from 1779 to 1900,* by Col. Wm. H. Powell (New York 1900; repr. Detroit 1967), Fayette Robinson was born in Virginia, with no date given. We could obtain no birthdate from the Library of Congress or the Old Military Records Division of the Army. But if one assumes he was about 20 years old when he received an appointment as second lieutenant on February 1, 1837 (to rank from January 25, 1837), Robinson may have been born during or about the year 1817. He died in New York City March 26, 1859.

The Old Military Records Division of the National Archives and Records Service, in Washington, furnished us this information:

> "...We searched the records of The Adjutant General's Office and found that Fayette Robinson was appointed a 2nd Lieutenant on February 1, 1837, to rank from January 25, 1837. A letter dated January 27, 1837, informing him of his appointment, was sent under cover to his father in Richmond, Vir-

ginia.

"He accepted the appointment on February 1, 1837, at Richmond. The records indicate he reported to Fort Leavenworth, Kansas, on March 24, 1837, and was assigned to Company D, 1st Regiment U. S. Dragoons on March 28, 1837. He was promoted to 1st Lieutenant on February 3, 1839, and assigned to Company G, same regiment, at Fort Wayne, C. N. From November 1839 to March 1840 he was on leave of absence, at the end of which time he was reported as being on recruiting duty at Carlisle Barracks, Pennsylvania. He joined his company May 23, 1840, at Fort Gibson, C. N., and was again reported on leave of absence in November 1841. His resignation was tendered on November 11, 1841, and accepted to take effect on December 31, 1841."

What we have written here of the author is the extent of the information we have been able to develop. When we republish Robinson's military work early in 1971, it may be we can add more biographical data than we have accumulated here.

The first edition of this exceedingly rare book had no index. We turned to our friend and colleague, William H. Farrington, of Santa Fe, who promptly read the book, prepared the index and wrote a brief commentary for us. We considered the note so good we have inserted it following these words and just preceding the formal introduction. Mr. Farrington indexed the book mostly to proper names—names of people and places, but to a lesser extent, also to events. The result is a most comprehensive index which should be very helpful to those using the book.

We were delighted when Dr. D. E. Livingston-Little, Professor of History at Los Angeles Valley College in Van Nuys, Calif., agreed to write a formal introduction to the book. Dr. Livingston-Little is a recognized authority on the history of the Mexican War period. He is one of those talented historians who can write twice as much as most can in half the space. In our several telephone conversations, he expressed real pleasure that the book was being reprinted. He regards it as a most useful reference source for the scholar, researcher and the student.

Dr. Livingston-Little makes a reference to the author's personal prejudices, evident from time to time throughout the work. Fayette Robinson was a product of his generational milieu; the mid-19th century was in America a time of social and intellectual roughness. Pride and prejudice were the rule, not the exception. Our reprinting of this book in no way reflects the author's opinions. We have visited Mexico many times. We like the country. We like and respect the people of Mexico. We only wish our fellow-Americans were as universally courteous and friendly as our Latin cousins across the border. Few gringos today share the views of many of the men of author Robinson's generation.

Finally, we should mention that the first edition of *Mexico and Her Military Chieftans* is a small, pocket-size book measuring 4" in width by 7" in height. The print is very cramped and small in the first edition. The page margins are skimpy, the sulphite paper yellowed and brittle with age. In the copy we used, some reader during the last 120 years penciled underlines to remember something he deemed significant. The art is coarse and badly printed—the plate between page 152 and page 153, for instance, is chopped off at the top in the first edition, and consequently in ours. There are brown age stains on page after page throughout the book.

All the skill and craftsmanship of the graphic arts has been brought to bear to improve, insofar as possible, upon the original. To that end, we have enlarged the book's dimensions from 4" x 7" to 6" x 9". This automatically enlarges the type, making it far easier for us old dogs to read. But with this technical improvement comes the inevitable enhancement of the first edition printing defects. In enlargement the faulty typefaces (originally the type was handset) become clearly evident, the penciled underlines could not be totally obliterated, and even with brown filters not all of the age stains could be eliminated entirely. We have done the best we could to improve upon the original. If perchance some rascally reader deems our effort poor, he should compare our edition with a first edition. We have no apologies to make for our edition.

We are truly proud to resurrect and restore to usefulness this important—even if relatively unknown—historical document. *Mexico and Her Military Chieftans* is the 65th title in our continuing line of beautiful Rio Grande Classics. We usually call our reprints source books of American history. In this instance, we can also call this book a source book of Mexican history.

Robert B. McCoy

La Casa Escuela
Glorieta, N. M.
October 1970

Foreword

Recently while I was reading Robinson's *Mexico and Her Military Chieftans,* prior to preparing an index, some auxiliary tanks on spaceship Apollo 13 exploded. Everything went by the boards while I sat glued to radio and/or television, talking, thinking, praying and just *willing* those three astronauts back safely to earth. I am not at all sure that I was *entirely* responsible for their safe return, because billions of others were doing the same thing, but I did feel it important that I watch their news conference and get the full details of what I considered their highly perilous flight.

During the flight the garbled messages from Apollo, the split-second decisions, the atmosphere of calm men in great danger fairly crackled with reality; these incredible events were happening, *now!* The news conference, planned and programmed when the astronauts were home again, allowed for second thoughts, clearer heads and that bane of historians...hindsight. All of which brings us in a roundabout way to Mr. Fayette Robinson and his book.

He wrote *Mexico and Her Military Chieftans* because the United States was then at war with Mexico. His observations on her leaders and her people are not tempered by the cool, clear thoughts and the historian's 20/20 hindsight vision. He wrote to give information about, and understanding of, the "enemy" to a nation at war. He did not have our advantage of time-distance to view both sides of the question. He could not, in the heat of battle (so to speak), realize that across the border the Mexican War was the United States' War. It is amazing that author Robinson could be as objective as he was.

During the past few years I have had occasion to read a number of books written during the war years about World War II. I was surprised to find so much emotionalism and prejudice, so much unintended (and intended!) propaganda in the works of supposedly enlightened researchers and scholars. In time of war there is always a tendency to underrate the enemy, to ignore his strengths and to magnify his weaknesses. In time of non-war (but not peace) we can admit that an enemy has a few attributes, too, and just possibly might be as smart as we are.

Author Robinson managed to write a narrow line and even gave credit where credit was due. He was not, however, above a little chauvinism. He may have hinted from time to time that ten American soldiers were equal to a regiment of Mexican soldiers, but mostly he did try to be fair. Santa Anna and several other Mexican chieftans may be presented here with something less than sympathy (their nature did not invite sympathy, really), but it should be remembered that Robinson wrote in the mid-19th century when few shades of gray existed. Most Americans of the time thought Santa Anna was a raging beast; few were willing to admit, as Robinson did, that the man was also a brilliant politician and an extraordinary leader.

The historical accuracy of this work is not the main point here. Where, anyway, is the history that does not contain some glaring mistakes—usually discovered and gleefully evaluated by the author's colleagues? Though his facts are for the most part true, the importance of this work does not lie in the field of history. This is a contemporary account of Mexico at war, and at war with the Colossus of the North; it is this contemporary viewpoint so well elucidated, and his nearly single-handed attempt to create a better understanding of the war and its ramifications, that makes this book highly relevant today. Would that some writer could write about the Viet Nam war today with Robinson's dispassionate aloofness.

The literature of the Mexican War period is very sparse compared to that of other conflict periods. Each new or re-found work like this is precious, and rightfully should be restored to current usage. The Mexican War was a tragedy unique in American history, really a war of territorial conquest, and as such deserves study to see if such a thing can be prevented from ever happening again. The Rio Grande Press has once more made a wise choice for its ever-expanding collection of Western Americana; they have not abided by the standard, the tried and true works of the past—they have been willing to reprint the contemporary account (viz., *A Complete History of the Mexican War* by Nathan Covington Brooks, and others), even the controversial, when they felt it important to the understanding of the emergence of the American West.

I suppose it is a truism, or even a sophistry, that succeeding generations never learn the lessons of history. The United States is scarcely 200 years old, but has fought eight bloody wars and is now reeling from the ninth. Nine wars in 200 years computes to an average of one war every 22 years, or a war every generation. Each war, from the revolution of 1775 to the horror of Viet Nam, has yielded up countless lessons for the oncoming generation to ponder and reflect upon. Every lesson, every single lesson of history, has not prevented the next war. No doubt, this is the way it will be forever. But what a shame that a nation of such immense human resources can never use those resources for its own good, only its own harm. The lessons of history go unheeded, and on the vast wall of time the moving finger writes in letters of fire:

"Mene, mene, tekel upharsin."

You are weighed in the balance, and found wanting.

William H. Farrington

Santa Fe, N. M.
October 1970

Introduction

Mexico and Her Military Chieftans, from the Revolution of Hidalgo to the Present Time, is a unique book in several ways. The author, Fayette Robinson, had gathered data on all the leading figures of the Mexican fight for independence and planned to write a book about the struggle, but had been deterred by changing circumstances. When the Mexican War started, he attempted to weave this timely and pertinent information together as useful background material for all of the Americans interested or involved in that war. The writing was completed by early 1847, and since Zachary Taylor had by then scored all his military triumphs in northern Mexico, and Scott had captured Vera Cruz and defeated Santa Anna at Cerro Gordo, Robinson included that much of the war as an "additional chapter" to this book.

It is there, however, that the narrative ends. It was apparently the author's plan to get the book published as early in the war as possible. Some delays in publication were encountered, and the book did not reach the public until 1851—three years after the signing of the Treaty of Guadalupe Hidalgo.

Unlike the half dozen or more books written by Robinson's contemporaries, his book devoted little space to the actual war itself. Also, by contrast to the other works which make only passing reference to the top Mexican leaders, Robinson devoted most of this book to career biographies of a baker's dozen of the leading military and political personages of Mexico, prominent during the period 1800 to 1847. He explains that he had researched the data for another book, which was never written; thus he was ready with information in hand to provide the background of Mexico's war with the United States. Robinson's five years of service as an officer in the First Dragoons gave him much of the background to write knowledgeably concerning the purely military matters and events which complement the biographical data.

One final comment needs to be made about this book. The author voiced a number of prejudices and rather harsh criticisms of Mexican politics, culture, race and religion. He was perfectly aware that he was doing so, for he remarked about it in his preface. The readers of today who might be offended by the author's views should remember two things: First of all, this was written well over a century ago when prejudices were so common that no one attempted to hide them, and second, Robinson was writing about an enemy with whom his country was at war. Evaluated in this context, his views and opinions should be easier to understand.

Mexico and Her Military Chieftans, which obviously offers information not found in other contemporary works, has been out of print for well over a century. Copies have naturally become very scarce and much sought after. With the current upsurge of interest in the Mexican War, the reprinting of Robinson's book at this time will make it available to generations of scholars who have never seen a copy, and who may fine it most valuable and interesting. The few who have handled copies of Robinson's book before will be delighted to find it readily available again.

D. E. Livingston-Little
Professor of History
Los Angeles Valley College
Van Nuys, California

* Publisher's note: D. E. Livingston-Little, Ph.D., is also an Associate Editor of *Journal of the West,* an important historical quarterly published in Los Angeles by Lorrin Morrison.

Don Antonio Lopez de Santa Anna.

MEXICO

AND HER

MILITARY CHIEFTAINS,

FROM THE REVOLUTION OF HIDALGO TO THE PRESENT TIME.

COMPRISING SKETCHES OF THE LIVES

OF

HIDALGO, MORELOS, ITURBIDE, SANTA ANNA, GOMEZ FARIAS,
BUSTAMENTE, PAREDES, ALMONTE, ARISTA, ALAMAN,
AMPUDIA, HERRERA, AND DE LA VEGA.

BY FAY. ROBINSON.

Illustrated by Twelve Portraits and Engravings.

HARTFORD, CONN.:
SILAS ANDRUS & SON.
1851.

PREFACE.

WHILE an invalid several years ago, and resident of more than one of the ports of the "American Mediterranean," I whiled away many weary hours in collecting materials for a far more elaborate work than this, on the history and the revolutions, not only of Mexico, but of the states of the southern continent. With this view I searched several conventual libraries, and found curious documents, which amply recompensed me for the time and labor thus expended.

Circumstances which it is now unnecessary to refer to more particularly, had made me almost forget, and for a time entirely neglect this scheme; when it was suggested to me, that for want of some such book as this, the peculiar policy of Mexico and its men was almost unintelligible. Such was the occasion of this work, in which I have sought to present a fair view of the past condition of the self-named republic, and to trace the origin of that series of events which have made it the victim of successive revolutions, each of which has left the country in a worse condition than when the tenor of circumstances was interrupted by the preceding convulsion.

I once knew a person who had passed the greater part of a long life in the neighborhood of Niagara, without having seen it, and was ultimately induced to visit the great cataract, because a foot-race took place in its immediate vicinity. Similar in many respects seems the neglect by the people of the United States of the history of our neighbors, who have presented to the world as many pure self-sacrificing men as any other nation, at the same time that they have perhaps exhibited in a short period more despicable characters than have disgraced the annals of any other people. Recent events have, however, rendered all that relates to Mexico important, and absolve me from any apology of this kind.

I might make many acknowledgments of the sources whence I have drawn information of things, which occurred too long ago for me to have been a contemporary, or at least to have remembered them. Among the facts I have thus been enabled to present to the reader, are included no small portion of the life of General Guadalupe Victoria, from Ward's "Mexico," and a part of the history of the castle of San Juan de Ulua, from the "Life in Mexico" of Madame Calderon de la Barca.

I have carefully read all the books of travels I could obtain, and also many minor sketches, for the most part anonymous; a sheaf of letters in French and German, I have also been kindly permitted to examine, and from them have drawn many hints.

The additional chapter will be found principally a collation of official documents, which it was believed would give a better idea of the present war than any sketch which could be crowded into so small a space as I was restricted to, when the course of my story had brought me to the days in which they occurred.

Many of the opinions inculcated in this book, especially in relation to the peculiar ecclesiastical position of Mexico, may seem paradoxical; and it may not, therefore, be improper to state distinctly and precisely the idea sought to be conveyed. I have wished to show that it would not be less reasonable for the Roman Catholic to attribute to the Reformed churches the dogmatism and the crudities of many of the current *isms* of the day, which fritter away most of the essentials of faith, than is a disposition sometimes evinced to hold the Roman Catholic church responsible for the countless Indian superstitions engrafted in Mexico on its traditions.

There are many other points to which I would be pleased to refer, but as it is impossible to touch on all, I will end at once, dedicating to my countrymen these records of their enemies.

F. R.

CONTENTS.

NOTE.

As the words *pronunciar*, *pronunciamento*, and *pronunciados* are frequently used in the following pages, it may not be improper to define precisely their meanings. When any body of men, civil or military, declare their opposition to the government, and their intention to support any particular chief or principle, they are said *pronunciar*, to pronounce; they are called *pronunciados*, persons who have pronounced; and their act is styled a *pronunciamento* or pronunciation.

The two or three days' talk or *powwowing* which precedes the pronunciamento, is called *el grito*, or cry; and when the whole is complete, the result announced to the world is said to be a *plan*.

Such things are common in Mexico, where an obscure priest, the *alcalde* of an Indian *puebla*, and a non-commissioned officer of *civicos* or national guard, have more than once proclaimed a system or *plan* for the regeneration of the world.

ERRATUM.—P. 65, 9th line from foot, for *I have* read *they*.

MEXICO

AND

HER MILITARY CHIEFTAINS.

CHAPTER I.

MEXICO UNDER THE VICEROYS.

Extent of the viceroyalty of Mexico—Form of goverment—Taxes—The clergy—Education—Classes of the people—Topography—Political divisions.

By far the most beautiful portion of all the possessions of Spain in America, which extended from the mouth of the Sabine, with but few interruptions, except the Brazils, to the fortieth degree of south latitude on the Atlantic, and on the Pacific from the forty-second degree north to the fortieth south, was the viceroyalty of Mexico. It occupied a portion of the globe, towards which nature has been peculiarly beneficent, where every mountain was the seat of mines, and where in contradiction of the rule which condemns to sterility regions which abound in mineral wealth, every fruit of every clime grew in proximity. It was strewn with vast and venerable ruins, which even now astonish the traveller and reveal to him the monumental history of a bygone people, the great resources and peculiar civilization of whom constituted but a portion of its power. The vice-kingdom of Mexico was of far greater extent than the old Aztec Empire, and Galvez and Iturrigaray ruled over nations and countries of the existence of which Montezuma and his ancestors were ignorant. It embraced people of many languages and habits, originally with different laws and peculiar creeds, all of which had been annihilated by a long series of oppression and reduced to one level, that of slavery and degradation. How this vast region passed under the dominion of Spain, is an important point in the history of the world, to the elucidation of which some of the most skilful pens and brightest intellects of the age have been employed; but interesting as it is, scarcely comports with the plan marked out for this sketch—though from that conquest resulted the fearful peculiarities of the ante-revolutionary rule, and indirectly the long series of atrocities which finally subsided into the present unsettled *mis*-government, which so far has borne but the ashes and dust of turmoil and strife, instead of the wholesome fruit of order and free institutions. As it is, however, it seems indispensable to refer to the condition of Mexico under the Spanish rule, and to the events of its first revolution, before we touch upon the men who have influenced its subsequent destinies.

It is the greatest curse of misgovernment that it destroys not only the present happiness of a people, but its future capacities; and it is true that rarely has any people, which has been long oppressed, been able to establish a good government, until it had learned by a series of calamities, that freedom is not an absence of restraint, but a rule, the correct administration of which requires as many sacrifices, or as passive obedience, as the purest monarchy. This is obvious, when we remember that the difference between the freest and most absolute governments is but that in the first, the wishes of the individual must be sacrificed to the interests of a community, in the second, the interests of a community to the wishes of an individual. The one is not more exacting than the other, though few are able to think this is the case, and hence originates not a few of the errors so fatal to new governments, in the establishment of which it has been necessary to beware of the example of the past not to take advantage of accumulations of its experience. The history of all the revolutions which have yet occurred also teach, that those nations which have been most oppressed have had most difficulty in perceiving what course true wisdom prescribed to them; a more striking evidence of the truth of this can no where be found than in the annals of the Mexican Republic.

Mexico, Peru, Buenos Ayres, Chili, Cuba, and the other Spanish possessions in America were never known as colonies, in the sense attached to that term by England and France. They were not subject to the law of Spain, but were governed by codes prepared to suit what were considered their respective exigencies, and reference was made to the Roman law only in cases for which no provision was made in the several systems ordained for them. Each and all were in fact separate kingdoms, and were called such, with the exception of Cuba, and united formed that empire which enabled the successors of Ferdinand and Isabella to call themselves Kings of Spain and the Indies. At the head of each of these realms, except Chili and Cuba, which were governed by Captains-General, and Quito, at the head of which was always a Presidente, was a Viceroy, representative of royal authority, and, as far as the people were concerned, entirely irresponsible. They were appointed by the *real audiencia de las Indias*, representing the imperial power, residing in Spain, and in many respects the most peculiar body which ever existed. It was established in 1511, consequently very soon after the discovery of the American continent, and under the *Rois Faineants* of the house of Bourbon gradually usurped exclusive control of the Indies. As a legislature, it issued all laws and regulations for the government of the Indies; in the exercise of its executive faculties, it made or confirmed all appointments, civil, military, and even ecclesiastical, and ordered or instructed the higher officers, with regard to the performance of their duties; lastly, it was a supreme court of judicature, to which causes involving important questions might be submitted for their final determination. It thus possessed all the powers of the government over these extensive realms. The assent of the monarch was, indeed, necessary to give authority to its proceedings, yet that assent was rarely, if ever, withheld; and as vacancies in its own body were always filled agreeably to its own recommendation, the whole period of its existence might be viewed as the reign of one absolute sovereign, ever sagacious, and ever adding to his stores of experience. The viceroy was but their creature, responsible only to them, and by a most tyrannical provision could only be proceeded against within a very short time after the expiration of the term for which he was appointed—five years. The viceroys were almost always nobles and courtiers, who came to Mexico to restore dilapidated fortunes, and generally returned effete with wealth wrung from the American subjects of their master. It sometimes happened they were willing to remain for longer terms. As these officers could scarcely be presumed familiar with the administration of justice, they were provided with *Fiscales* or administrators of various kinds, whom they were obliged to consult before taking any important step ; each might act contrary to the opinion of his *Fiscal*, but the latter had the right to enter his protest, which might afterwards be submitted to the Supreme Council. Such a system carried out correctly would be bad enough, but in its appointments the *real audiencia* seems to have forgotten that they owed any obligation to the people of Mexico, thinking them only beasts of burden bound to eternal vassalage, not only to the Spanish monarch, but to every Spaniard. Long, long after the establishment of this system, scarcely more than thirty years ago, it was gravely asserted in a Spanish legislative assemblage, that "as long as one man lived in Spain, he had a right to the obedience of every American," a paradox more ridiculous than any of the grave sayings of Sir Robert Filmer. In the long list of viceroys appointed to all the Indies (one hundred and sixty in America), but four were born on this side the Atlantic, and the proportion of other officers was quite as small. In 1785 the minister Galvez referred to the fact that a few Mexicans held office in their own country as an abuse. The conduct of the audiencia and the officers they sent to America fully authorized the maxim which seems to have actuated the one in their forgetfulness of all humanity, and the other in the hopeless submission to the rule, that GOD IS IN HEAVEN AND THE KING IN SPAIN: from one they inferred there was no limit to their power, from the other no remedy for their wrongs. When we look at this state of things, can we be astonished at the condition of Mexico at the present time? When oppression does not force from its victims the fierce spirit of resistance, it evidently degrades those on whom it weighs; when violence does not struggle with injustice, man is driven to cunning and subterfuge, and habits of fraud take pos session of the whole mind, and those who have suffered from the tyranny of others are ever most prone to exhibit their own haughtiness and arrogance. Thus it is, that after expelling the Spanish oppressors, so few Mexicans are found worthy of the power they have won.

As a check on the power of the viceroy, to secure the royal privileges, another officer was appointed an Intendente, the duty of whom it was to take care of the collection and application of the taxes, of the revenue of the mines, and the imposts, which were many and vexatious. Subordinate to these in each province was an officer, usually a military commander, called *Intendente de Provincia*, the powers of whom were those of a governor, and who was responsible to the viceroy. The provinces were divided into districts, each of which was superintended by a board called *El Cabildo* or *Ayuntamiento*, the power of appointing which, either rested with, or was controlled by the higher authorities.

The most serious check upon the absoluteness or the ambition of all the executive officers, were the *Audiencias* or high courts of justice, of which one or two were established in every kingdom. They consisted each of a small number, generally between three and eight, of *Oidores* or judges, aided by *Fiscales*, chancellors, notaries, *Alguaziles* or sheriffs, and other officers or agents. On ordinary occasions they were presided over by one of their own number, styled a Regent; the viceroy was, however, *ex-officio*, the President of the Audiencia established in his capital.

The taxes we have said were vexatious, and it is a matter of mystery and surprise, how any people submitted so long to such extortion. The chief of these, independent of the odious capitation tax or tribute, levied on the Indians, whether rich or poor, were the *almojarifazgo*, or import duty; the *alcabala*, on all sales of estates; the *millione*, on the articles of daily use; and monopolies of all necessaries, whether of life or of industry, as salt, tobacco, quicksilver used in mines, &c. That under such a system, so crushing to energy and industry, the people became idle and nerveless, is not to be wondered at; the wonder is, that they existed at all. The worst features of the two worst governments in the world, the Gothic rule, and that of the Spanish Moors, had been combined to form the government of the mother-country, and its worst features had been carefully preserved to oppress the native population of Mexico, in the code sent out to them by the supreme council of the Indies. Why they did not resist centuries before, we cannot imagine, since the military force consisting of regulars, were nearly all Spaniards, and of native militia, neither class, however, at any time very numerous; the government appearing to have but little dread of foreign attacks, and to place full confidence in the organization of its civil powers, for preventing internal disturbances.

The ecclesiastical establishment was an important branch of the government of America, where it was maintained in great splendor and dignity. The clergy presented the same characteristics there, as in other countries where the Roman Catholic religion prevailed exclusively; the inferior members being generally honest, kind, and simple-minded persons, loving and loved by their parishioners, while the high dignitaries were, for the most part, arrogant, intriguing, and tyrannical. The Inquisition exercised its detestable sway, unchecked, in every part of the dominions; occasionally exhibiting to the people of the great cities, the edifying spectacle of an *auto da fe*, in which human victims were sacrificed, to confirm the faith of the beholders in the power of the archbishop and the viceroy.

Before the revolution, the diffusion of knowledge was studiously prevented. The charge of keeping them in ignorance was committed to the priests, who, with the exception of the Jesuits, executed it with fidelity; the few schools and colleges were directed solely by ecclesiastics, who excluded from the course of instruction every branch of study, and from the public and private libraries every book calculated to strengthen the mental faculties, or to elevate the feelings. In the year 1806, there was but one printing-press at Mexico, from which a newspaper was published, under the immediate direction of the government; and as the Spanish newspapers, the only ones allowed to be imported, were devoted almost wholly to the movements of the court or the church, the inhabitants remained in absolute ignorance of all that transpired elsewhere. A few poems and plays, none of any value, and some works on natural history, or speculations, generally wild and baseless, on the antiquities of those countries, form nearly the whole of their original literature.

The incomplete outline here given of the system by which Mexico was governed, at the time when that system was the most liberal, and perhaps, in general, the most liberally administered, may serve to afford some idea of the evils to which it was subjected before its separation from Spain—evils by no means productive of proportional advantage to the oppressors. A more minute review of the history of Spanish supremacy in America, would serve to show that, throughout the whole period of its existence, the wishes and welfare of the inhabitants were sacrificed to the interests, real or supposed, of the monarch or of his European subjects.

To secure these interests permanently was the great object of the government, and, unfortunately for America, they were considered as being confined within very narrow limits; in fact, it had long been established as a principle, that to supply Spain with the greatest quantity of the precious metals, and to gratify her nobility and influential persons with lucrative situations for themselves or their dependants, were the only purposes for which these countries could be rendered available without endangering the perpetuity of the dominion over them.

The people were divided into seven great classes; 1st, The old Spaniards, known as Guachupines in the history of the civil wars; 2d, the Creoles, or whites of pure European race but born in America; 3d, the Indigenos, or Indians; 4th, the Mestizos, of mixed breeds of whites and Indians, gradually merging into Creoles as the Indian parentage became more and more remote; 5th, the Mulattoes, or descendants of whites and negroes, and 7th, the African Negroes; of these classes, the last named was very small, and the others were intermingled, so as to produce crosses, to be defined by no possible degree of anthropological science. The white population was chiefly collected in the table land, near the centre of which the Indian race also concentrated (near Puebla, Oaxaca, Mexico, Guanajuato, and Valladolid); while the northern frontier was inhabited almost entirely by whites, the Indian population having retired before them. In Durango, New Mexico, and the interior provinces, the true Indian breed was almost unknown. In Sonora it again appears. The coasts both of the Gulf and the Pacific, to the south, were inhabited by a race, in which there was a great mixture of African blood, from the fact, that to these unhealthy provinces, the few slaves imported into Mexico were sent.

There they have multipled with the fecundity peculiar to the descendants of African parentage, and now form a mixed breed, peculiar to the *tierra caliente*, and unlike any other in the world. The mestizos are found every where, from the fact that but few Spanish women emigrated early to America, and the great mass of the population is of this class; and now too that a connexion with the aboriginal race confers no disadvantage, few pretend to deny it. The pure Indians in 1803 exceeded two millions and and a half, and next to them are the mestizos. At the time of the revolution the pure whites were estimated at one million two hundred thousand, of whom eighty thousand only were Europeans. These distinctions were, however, soon annihilated, and at an early day in the revolution the only distinction known was of Americans and Europeans.

The events of the present war have so universally directed attention to Mexico, that its geography and topography are well known, and will excuse any more minute allusion to it than the following. The Cordillera of the Andes, after passing along the whole western coast of South America and through the Isthmus of Panama, immediately on entering the northern continent is divided into two branches, which leave between them an immense *plateau*, the central point of which is seven thousand feet above the level of the sea. This elevation towards the eastern coast gradually subsides to a level with the ocean, but on the west maintains itself in its stern rigidity till it becomes lost in the ices of the north. This table land presents some rare vegetable phenomena. On the coast its tropical latitude exhibits itself in its productions, but the rarefaction of the air attendant on elevation gradually neutralizes this, until at the central points we find growing the productions of colder climes.

Thus Mexico, Guanajuato, and Zacatecas, enjoy a far different temperature from that of Vera Cruz, Tampico, and other cities on the coast. On the ascent from Vera Cruz to Mexico, Humboldt says that climates succeed each other by stories, and in the course of forty-eight hours we pass through every variety of vegetation. The tropical plants are succeeded by the oak, and the salubrious air of Jalapa replaces the deadly atmosphere of Vera Cruz. The sky is generally cloudless and without rain, and a succession of hills, seemingly at some remote day the boundaries of lakes, are now the limits of extensive plains or *llanos*. The country is barren because it is dry, and every stream is accompanied with fertility. The first of these stories is called the *tierra caliente*, or hot, where the fruits and diseases of the tropics are produced; the *tierra templada*, or temperate, a term needing no explanation; while far beyond the city is the *tierra fria*, where the vegetation is alpine and the hills are covered with eternal snow.

The present states of Mexico are nineteen in number: Yucatan, Tabasco, Chiapas, and Oaxaca, Vera Cruz, Tamaulipas, St. Luis de Potosi, New Leon, Coahuila, Puebla, Mexico, Valladolid, Guadalajara, Sonora, Sinaloa, Guanajuato, Queretaro, Zacatecas, Durango, Chihuahua, New Mexico, and the Californias. In several instances two of these are united to form one state. Thus was the country divided previous to the revolution, and so it has continued; with the exception only, that the governments of the *Intendentes de provincias* have now become states, and that some of the southern provinces have (as now they may) occupied a position difficult to define, now claiming to belong to Central America, now to Mexico, and again to be independent.

CHAPTER II.

THE REVOLUTION.

Abdication of the Bourbons in Spain—Effects in Spain—Effects in Mexico—Supreme central junta resigns—Change in the Spadish constitution—Insurrections in America—Vanegas appointed viceroy—Hidalgo.

On the 5th of May, 1808, by means of a series of fraud, and treason, which recalls to us the annals of that prince whom Machiavelli immortalized, Charles IV. of Spain, his son and rival Ferdinand VII., and the male members of his family, were induced to place themselves in the power of Napoleon at Bayonne, and to surrender, for themselves and their heirs, all right to the crown of Spain. Joseph Bonaparte, the elder brother of the emperor of the French, was immediately placed in the vacant throne, and a constitution promulgated for the government of the Spanish empire, by which the subjects of the American colonies were to enjoy all the privileges of the mother country, and to be represented by deputies in the Cortes or General Congress at Madrid. The nobles of Spain, effete with luxury and forgetful of the chivalry which had made them the admiration of Europe, submitted to the new authorities imposed by fraud and violence on the nation, while the great mass of the people rejected the rule with scorn. Insurrections broke out every where in the kingdom, and *Juntas* or boards of direction were formed in every place for the support of the national cause.

Success attends all popular movements. When a people rises in its might it is sure of success. The attacks of the French were repelled with great valor; at Baylen a whole army was forced to surrender, and those who kept the field began gradually to waste away, under the influence of what might be considered assassination, were not all things justifiable in a people fighting for its liberty and integrity. The country was at last partially freed from the pollution of the French, and a supreme *junta* established at Seville, to watch over the interests of Ferdinand VII., yet a prisoner, which claimed from every Spanish subject the same obedience due the monarch.

The news of the captivity of the monarch and the abdication of the princes they had been so faithful to, produced in Mexico and in all the Spanish colonies a feeling of the greatest dismay. It shook loose the whole social system, it broke all the links of society, and revealed to all the necessity of some provision against the effects of convulsion not to be influenced or controlled by the action of persons on this side of the Atlantic. The feelings called forth were, however, various in character, and the only universal sentiment seemed that of opposition to the French.

The dethronement of the Spanish Bourbons was first proclaimed to the people of Mexico on the 20th of July, 1808, by the viceroy, who declared himself determined to sustain their interest in his government. This seemed a general determination throughout all Spanish America. In Havana the captain-general Somruelos decided on this course, in which he was sustained by the people, the ecclesiastical authority, and the army. In Buenos Ayres, Liniers, an officer of French extraction, who had been made viceroy in consequence of the valor displayed in resisting the English invasion under Sir Home Popham, having exhibited some disposition to favor King Joseph, or at least to remain neutral until the difficulties of the peninsula should be settled, insisting that Buenos Ayres should be a dependency of the Spanish crown, was at once displaced, and Don Baltasar de Cisneros was sent to replace him by the junta. So it was in Grenada, where war was declared by the audiencia against all the partisans of Bonaparte, and at Popayan and Quito. Iturrigaray, the viceroy, soon after made known the establishment of the junta, and required the ayuntamiento to submit to its orders. The seed had now begun to ripen: they were yet faithful to Ferdinand; he was still their monarch; but they recollected that Mexico and Spain were two kingdoms, that the Junta had no authority, either direct or by implication, in Mexico, and refused it obedience, at the same time recommending the establishment of a similar body, to be composed of deputies from all the local *cabildos*, in Mexico, to take care of the interests of Ferdinand VII. in his Mexican possessions. Iturrigaray was inclined to give his assent to this scheme; and judging from this fact and his great popularity, it is probable he was a kind, sensible man, too good for those with whom he had to deal. We may here state that in the ayuntamiento of Mexico there chanced to be a majority of natives of the soil. This action of Iturrigaray was of course opposed by the audiencia, composed as it will be remembered of *oidores*, *fiscales* and the military and civil officers sent out from Spain, erected into a species of oligarchy and forbidden by law to marry with the children of the soil. Finding their remonstrances vain, the audiencia arrested the viceroy in his palace, and confided his functions temporarily to the archbishop of Lizana. The audiencia, by a system of bold and oppressive action, drowned all opposition to the authority of the central junta, which, on its becoming evident that the archbishop was incompetent, endowed it with all the viceroy's authority, until some noble could be found in Spain on whom it might confer the vacant appointment. Thus things continued during 1809, a year of great distress in Spain, the French having overrun the whole country and the junta being driven to Cadiz, its last foothold, from Seville. The junta was now evidently incompetent, and it laid down its power. It however previously summoned a Cortes, or council of the whole nation, which was to convene at Cadiz on the 1st of March, 1810, and in which the American kingdoms were to be represented as integral portions of the empire. As they could not be notified in time, the places of American deputies were to be filled temporarily by persons chosen in Spain. The supreme central junta having appointed a regency of five to administer the government until the meeting of the cortes in February, 1810, disappeared from history. The regency immediately addressed a circular decree to the different provinces of the Indies, calling upon them without delay to elect their deputies, who were to be in number twenty-six; this decree was accompanied by an appeal to the people, reminding them that "*they were now raised to the dignity of freemen*," and imploring those who would be called on to vote for the deputies, to remember that "*their lot no longer depended upon the will of kings, viceroys, or governors, but would be determined by themselves*." There was now no withdrawal; the die was cast, the collars were cast from the necks of the slaves, and no event which could occur would rivet them again. Thus it seemed to the governing class in America, and to those who had so long submitted. The feeling of the former was that the existing government was subverted; of the latter, that joy those only could know who had been taught that *"while one Spaniard remained, he had a right to govern the Americans."*

The reverses sustained by the Spanish arms had taught the Mexicans to hope they would be able to free themselves from the control of the audiencia, the idea of popular rights not seeming to have entered their minds, while even the Spanish office-holders seemed to be divided, a large party wishing to remain neutrals, as had been done in the dispute between the first Bourbon king and the house of Austria. The people took advantage of this; parties were formed, and it become evident that a slight spark would produce a general conflagration. Rebellion had taken place in La Plata, which was suppressed, and in Quito, where the people overawed the presidente, and a confederation of the provinces of Guayaquil, Popayan, Panama and Quito arose, which professed obedience to Ferdinand VII. at the same time that it denounced the authority of the central junta. In all the American dominions, except Mexico, there had been difficulties; and there, too, the match was burning slowly but surely. As the news of the Spanish disasters became known through Mexico, associations were formed far and wide to further the general scheme of independence of the Spanish junta or audiencia. The exertions of these, however, a watchful government contrived to foil, and by prompt action prevented more than one attempt at revolution; as at Vallodolid, in May, 1810, where the conspirators were arrested, and we need not say, executed just as all had been prepared for action.

At this crisis came Don Francisco Xavier Vanegas to assume the viceroyalty. He was the last man to whom, at this crisis, authority should have been confided; he was brave, and valor was needed to enable him to fulfil the duties of ruler of a realm on the eve of convulsion, but he was passionate when he should have been careful, and hasty when every word should have been uttered with consideration and reflection. The mild Iturrigaray might have restored quiet. Vanegas but hurried on the outbreak. He most imprudently continued, with greater vigor, the course marked out by the audiencia, and left to the people no hopes, but of resistance, or doing what never yet people did, resuming duties from which they had been released. The insurrection had been suppressed at Valladolid, the capital of Michoacan, but broke out in Guanajuato, where a remarkable man appeared on the stage.

HIDALGO.

Don Miguel Hidalgo y Costilla was the *Cura*, or parish priest of Dolores, a quiet and secluded town in the state, or as it was then called, intendencia of Guanajuato, midway between San Luis de Potosi and Guanajuato. He was a man of undeniable acquirements, who had read much and thought more, who was devoted to his duties and evidently anxious to promote a knowledge of the branches of industry then almost unknown in Mexico. He had introduced the silk-worm, in the rearing of which in 1810 his people had made much progress, and had turned his attention to the cultivation of the vine, seeing, as all must who look at the peculiarities of the soil and climate of Mexico, that it was calculated to become a great source of wealth. Hidalgo was a man of books; a mighty revolution had taken place on the American continent, of which he could not be ignorant, and the events of later date in Europe officially promulgated had awakened a deep feeling in the whole people, to which he was no stranger. A quiet, unambitious, meditative man, he was far in advance of the most of his countrymen, but might have continued to dream of freedom, yet restricted his sphere of action to his own cure, had he not been called forth by one of those personal wrongs, in all cases found to be the most powerful means of awakening man to a perception of the sufferings of his neighbour.

It had ever been the policy of Spain not only to wring from Mexico and the other Indies the produce of their mines and peculiar wealth, but to prohibit them from the pursuit of all industry which would conflict with the interests of the mother country. Therefore, except in one remote part of the country whence it could never be brought to a market, the production of wine and the cultivation of vineyards had always been prohibited in New Spain or Mexico. Hidalgo had planted around his modest curacy a vineyard, which he was, by a positive order from the audiencia at Mexico, ordered to destroy. The quiet student had planted his vines in his leisure hours. In his lonely life they had been to him as children. He would not obey, and soldiers were sent to enforce the order. The fruits of his labor were destroyed; the vines were cut down and burned; but from their ashes arose a more maddening spirit than possibly even the vine had previously given birth to.

This private wrong, added to the many oppressions to which he was subjected together with the mass of his countrymen, animated him, and may account for the stern, dogged, almost Saxon perseverance with which he began this contest, in which every chance was against him personally, and in favor of his country, in the result. The dark spirit of the Spanish rule had met the only feeling which could contend with it, the resolution of a man who knew his country's rights and was determined to maintain them. The whole people thought as he did, and it was not difficult to form a party to sustain him. It has been said that the pulpit and confessional were used by him to promote his views; and if so, never were the powers which are sheltered by it, applied to a purpose against which so little can be said with justice. Certain it is, that he used so little concealment that Allende, Aldama, and Abasolo, three Mexican officers in garrison at Guanajuato, and the first to whom he imparted his plans, were ordered by the superior powers of *Intendencia* to be arrested. This mischance did not destroy the confidence of Hidalgo, who, having been joined by Allende on the 13th of September, 1810, three days after, on the anniversary almost of the arrest of Iturrigaray two years before, commenced the revolt by seizing on seven Europeans living in Dolores, and the confiscation of their property, which he immediately distributed among his parishoners.

There is a hackneyed proverb, that no man is a hero to his *valet-de-chambre*, and that a prophet is without honor in his own country. This may be so generally; but if so, it enhances the merit of Hidalgo, who was followed by all his parishioners. The news of his enterprise spread wide among the people, who had evidently been waiting long for the signal to act; so that within twenty-four hours, the patriot-priest was at the head of a force powerful enough to enable him, on the 17th of September, to occupy San Felipé, and on the next day San Miguel el Grande; of which places the united population was more than thirty thousand. The property of the Spaniards was confiscated, and enabled him to add yet more to his numbers. In this enterprise Hidalgo had unfurled a rude copy of the picture of our Lady of Guadelupe, whose shrine has ever been looked on with peculiar reverence in Mexico, and gave to his undertaking the air more of crusade than a civil war. Unfortunately, the worst features of crusades and pilgrimages were imitated by his followers.

He wished to attack Guanajuato, the capital of the province, and the depot of the wealth of the Spaniards in that country. The chief of the province, Riañon, a great favorite in Mexico, and a man universally respected for his courage and humanity, was in command of a large body of troops; and as the population, seventy-five thousand men, had not as yet pronounced; Hidalgo was afraid to risk the attempt. The people, however, began at last to give evidence of a disposition to take sides with Hidalgo. Riañon determined not to defend the city, but shut himself up with all the Europeans, and the gold, silver, and quicksilver in the *Alhondega* or granary, a strong building and amply provisioned, in which he evidently intended to defend himself. On the morning of September 28th, Don Mariano Abasolo, one of the Mexican officers before referred to as partisans of Hidalgo, appeared before the town in the uniform of the insurgents, and presented a letter from the cura Hidalgo, "announcing that he had been elected captain-general of America," by the unanimous choice of his followers, and been recognised by the ayuntamientos of the towns of Celaya, San Muguel, San Felipé, &c. That he had proclaimed the independence of the country, the only difficulty in the way of which was the presence of the Europeans, whom it was necessary to banish, and whose property, obtained by the authority of oppressive laws, injurious to the people, should be confiscated. He promised, however, protection to the Spainards if they would submit, and that their persons should be conveyed to a place of safety. Riañon replied modestly, but decidedly; and as he declined to capitulate, Hidalgo at once marched to the attack. His army consisted of twenty thousand men, but the mass of them were Indians, armed with bows, arrows, slings, *machetes*, and lances. Arms of *obsidian*, the volcanic glass so constantly referred to by the early historians of Mexico, which lay neglected since the days of Cortez, were now brought out; and a stranger contrast can scarcely be imagined than that presented by the Aztec levies, and the beautiful regiment of La Reina and a portion of the troops of Celaya, which had joined Hidalgo on his march to Guanajuato. The army of Hidalgo immediately occupied numerous eminences, which commanded the Alhondega, and with their slings kept up such a rain of stones that scarcely a person could appear on the fortifications. The musketry, however, did great execution, scarcely a single ball being lost, so dense was the crowd around the building. The whole population of the town declared in favor of Hidalgo, and the fate of the garrison was sealed; though Riañon still persisted in his defence, which he prolonged by means of shells formed by filling with powder the iron flasks in which the quicksilver was contained, which were thrown by hand among the besiegers. The Spaniards at last, however, became confused, and resistance was given up. The great gate was forced open, and Riañon fell dead as all was lost.

The number of persons who fell in the defence and after it, is not known, and among them were many Mexican families connected by marriage with the obnoxious Spaniards. One family alone is said to have lost seventeen members; and the obstinate and prolonged defence could only have been made by a considerable number. We wish we could close our eyes to what followed; but justice requires us to mention that *all* in the Alhondega were slain. The Indians seemed to delight in repaying on their victims the grudges of three centuries; a matter of surprise to all, for they had lain so long dormant and submissive that it was supposed they had forgotten or become regardless of their former distinct nationality. This is not, however, astonishing, for the history of that people which has been enslaved and forgotten its lost freedom is yet to be written. In the Alhondega was found a vast sum, estimated at five millions of dollars, the possession of which materially altered Hidalgo's views, and promised success to what had seemed at first to all but a premature attempt. The property of the Spaniards or Guachupines was surrendered to Hidalgo's troops; and so diligent were they in the lesson of rapine, that the Mexican troops of to-day, after thirty-six years of civil war, have scarcely improved on them. The action terminated on Friday night only, and on the next morning not one building belonging to a European was left standing. The greatest scenes of outrage were committed, which Hidalgo certainly could not prevent. He, too, was a Mexican, with the blood of the aborigines in his veins; though a priest, human, and smarting under recent wrongs, and it is doubtful if he wished to. Policy, too, may have influenced him. He himself, if unsuccessful, was doomed, and he may have wished all around him should so deeply dye their hands in blood, they would be compelled to abide by him in the contest which had begun. The siege of the Alhondega of Guanajuato was the Bunker-hill of Mexico, and deserves the attention bestowed on it.

Hidalgo did not remain long at Guanajuato, but while there established a mint and a foundry of cannon, for which he made use of all the bells found in the houses of the Spaniards. On the 10th of October he left Guanajuato for Valladolid, which he entered on the 17th without resistance, the bishop and the old Spaniards flying before him. The news of his successes had spread far and wide, and recruits joined him from all parts of the country. By universal consent he was looked on as the head of the revolution, and distributed commissions and organized boards, which yet more extensively diffused his schemes and augmented the number of his partisans.

The city of Mexico was taken aghast at the capture of Guanajuato, in which, besides the mere town, much more had been lost. The *prestige* of tacit obedience had been broken, the whole country was in arms, and the depot of one of the mining districts had been sacked. Vanegas, the new viceroy, who had been installed but two days previous to the outbreak, displayed great firmness and prudence, in spite of the persuasions of his counsellors, who utterly contemned the Mexican people, and maintained that the first tuck of the drum would put them to flight. This was but natural; they had been long obedient, and persons who submit are always despised. It will be remembered that during the American Revolution, after more than one collision had taken place, persons quite as wise maintained that two regiments would suffice to march through the colonies.

The viceroy ordered troops from Puebla, Orizaba, and Toluca, to the capital; and at the same time, to conciliate the Mexicans, conferred important military commands on many creoles. In this way he corrupted one from whom much was expected, the Conde de Cadena, who forgot his country and died afterwards in defence of the Spanish authority. Calleja was ordered to march with his troops, a brigade, from San Luis de Potosi, against Hidalgo, who was excommunicated by his supeperior, the bishop of Valladolid. As people naturally asked what offence he had committed to bring on him the ecclesiastical censure, the archbishop Lizana and the inquisition, against the authority of whom he was a bold man who would appeal, were induced to ratify this sentence, and pronounce an excommunication against any who should doubt its validity. The assistance derived from this spiritual power was more than neutralized by the conferring of offices on all the Spaniards who participated in the deposition of the viceroy Iturrigaray, whom the Mexicans considered to be a sufferer in their cause. This most injudicious course renewed all the feelings of disaffection which had been excited by the deposition of the viceroy, and was turned to the best advantage by the friends of liberty.

When Hidalgo reached Valladolid he was at the head of fifty thousand men, and in addition to the numbers who joined him there, he was reinforced by the militia of the province and the dragoons of Michoacan, both of which were well equipped and in good discipline. The most valuable addition he received, however, was in the person of Don Jose Maria Morelos, also a priest, cura of the town of Nucapetaro, an old friend whom he knew well, and on whom he conferred the command of the whole south-western coast. On Morelos, after the death of Hidalgo, rested the mantle of command; and some idea of his enthusiasm may be formed from the fact that he set out, on the receipt of his commission, accompanied with but five badly armed servants, with the promise that within a year he would take Acapulco, a feat which he absolutely achieved. On the 19th Hidalgo left Valladolid, and on the 28th reached Toluca, which is but twelve leagues from the city of Mexico.

Vanegas had found means to collect about seven thousand men in and near the city of Mexico, under the command of Colonel Truxillo, and the afterwards celebrated Don Augustino Iturbide, then a subordinate officer in the royal artillery. This force was defeated by the insurgents commanded by Allende and Hidalgo in person, on the 30th of October, at *Las Cruces*, a mountain pass between Mexico and Toluca. Hidalgo's forces were supposed to have been in number not less than sixty thousand; those commanded by Truxillo did not exceed seven thousand. In the first action, as might have been reasonably anticipated, the royal troops were worsted; the native regulars, however, behaved with gallantry and determination, and it was easy to see that the undisciplined and badly armed mob of Indians, of which the curate's army consisted almost entirely, would be unable to resist the attack of a force much larger than that which had been repulsed.

In this action, it may be remarked, Truxillo committed an act which was ever considered by the patriots to justify all their subsequent outrages. An insurgent officer with a flag was decoyed within gunshot of the royal lines and basely assassinated.* This Truxillo boasted of in his despatch, and was justified and applauded subsequently by the viceroy Vanegas, who maintained that the ordinary rules of war were not to be observed towards Hidalgo's forces. Vanegas was, however, so much terrified at the near approach of the native army, that he, too, found it necessary to appeal to superstition; and having ordered the image of the Virgin of *Los Remedios* to be brought in great state from its famous chapel, besought her aid, and laid at its feet his *baton* of command. This may account for the often repeated story, that in a proclamation the Blessed Virgin had been appointed captain-general of the forces of the viceroy. The public accounts circulated in Mexico represented Truxillo as having gained a great victory, though *circumstances* compelled him to retreat, and recall to our minds some of the events of our own day. It is a matter of curiosity, that no Mexican general before or since the revolution ever could be induced to confess that he was defeated. Every preparation was made to defend the capital, against which Hidalgo advanced till he was in sight of the towers and domes, when he first halted and then began to recede. On this occasion his conduct has been gravely censured, and Allende, a true soldier, was, it is said, most indignant. His courage cannot be suspected; he had witnessed, without attempting to check them, too many excesses, for his conduct to be attributed to humanity and a desire to save Mexico from the horrors of a siege or an assault, necessary evils, which all who appeal to arms are aware can neither be vindicated or prevented. The true reason was, probably, that he could not conceive that the viceroy could collect such a force, and was aware that another victory like that of Las Cruces would be his ruin. His forces had committed all possible excesses, and had suffered from the batteries of Truxillo so fearfully, that he knew they could not again be brought to the charge. So ignorant were they of artillery, that they had attempted to muzzle the guns by cramming them with their straw hats, until hundreds had been thus slain. He was also nearly without ammunition; and we need not ask for more reasons.

He therefore commenced a retreat, but on the 7th of November fell in with the advance of the viceroy's army, commanded by Calleja. The viceroy's troops were chiefly creoles, who were wavering in their duty; and it is stated on the authority of officers who served there, that had Hidalgo delayed his attack, there is no doubt they would have sided with their countrymen. This was not done; the battle commenced, Calleja advancing in five separate columns, which broke the insurgent line and made all that followed a pursuit and a slaughter. The creole troops now had chosen their course, and for many years continued the chief support of Spain and the terror of the insurgents. They seem to have been ever led by their officers, Cadena, Iturbide, &c., and it was not until the dethronement of the latter, when the Spanish flag was furled for ever in Mexico, that they seem to have remembered they had a country. We cannot but admire the consummate skill which enabled the viceroy to make men fight against their own interests; and the history of this part of the Mexican revolution will more than once recall to us that part of the history of Italy made famous by the crimes and the talent of the Borgia and Sforza.

The number of Indians killed at Aculco is said to have exceeded ten thousand, but Hidalgo managed to collect a large army from the fugitives, and with most of the officers effected an escape to Valladolid. Allende retreated to Guanajuato, where he murdered in cold blood two hundred and forty-nine Europeans. Too much censure cannot be bestowed on this atrocity, which, however, will find a precedent in the history of most revolutions. At all events, it should not be complained of by the partisans of the viceroy, who had officially announced, that the customs of civilized war did not apply to the followers of the heretic and rebel, Hidalgo. There is much excuse to be made for all insurgents, who are ever treated as traitors until their success covers them with the glare of fame, if not the true gold of patriotism.

Hidalgo arrived at Valladolid on the 14th of November, whence he proceeded to Guadalajara, which his subordinates had occupied on the day of his defeat at Aculco. Here he was joined by the licenciate Ignacio Lopez Rayon, who afterwards became his recretary, and was to the establishment of a civil government in the provinces successively conquered by the insurgents, what Hidalgo and Morelos were in the military conduct of the revolution. Previous to the establishment of the junta of Zitácuaro, Rayon's first service, the insurgent was a man recognising no authority but arms, and their army but a band of men without any colorable authority.

On the 24th of November Hidalgo made a triumphal entry into Guadalajara, where, though still under excommunication, he participated in the *Te Deum*, in honor of his successes. It is here worthy of remark, that the native clergy generally sustained him in his course, and paid no attention to the ecclesiastical decree against him.

Allende here joined him, and the two proceeded to provide artillery to replace the guns they had lost at Aculco. This was effected by bringing from San Blas, the great dock-yard on the Pacific, of the Spanish government, of which Morelos had possessed himself, a great number of guns, some of which were of heavy calibre, transported by Indians over the western Cordillera, thought then impassable, and over which no road has as yet been constructed, except at a few widely distant spots. Here he committed one of those actions which must forever stain his character. Upwards of seven hundred Europeans who had remained quiet at home, were imprisoned and brought out by twenties and thirties at night, taken to quiet places, and murdered. This system he had commenced at Valladolid, where during three days seventy persons were beheaded in the public square, *because they were Spaniards.*

There is reason to believe he intended to act on this principle throughout the war; for, on his trial, an authentic letter was produced, written by him to one of his subordinates, in which he orders him to continue to arrest as many Spaniards as possible, and "if you find any among them entertaining dangerous opinions, bury them in oblivion by putting them to death in some secret place, where their fate may be for ever unknown." If this be from an authentic letter, we can but be thankful that Hidalgo's career was soon terminated. He had, however, lived long enough to accomplish his mission, to arouse his people, and to take the steps which cast his country in that sea of strife from which it could only emerge with the boon of independence.

This atrocity so disgusted Allende, who was by no means mawkishly sentimental, that he was only prevented from leaving him by the approach of Calleja.

The cannon obtained from San Blas were so numerous that Hidalgo determined, though he had but twelve hundred muskets, to risk a battle. Allende foresaw the consequences of the total want of discipline, and sought to dissuade him. A council of war was called, and as these bodies *generally* decide incorrectly, he was outvoted; and the bridge of Calderon, sixteen leagues from Guadalajara, was selected as the place of resistance and fortified. Calleja, after a delay of six weeks in Guanjauato, came in sight on the 16th of January, 1811, when a general battle took place, which realized all of Allende's predictions. The Mexicans were partially successful in the beginning, repulsing two or three attacks, in one of which the Conde de Cadena was killed. They were finally thrown into confusion by the explosion of an ammunition wagon, and compelled to retreat, which they did in an orderly manner, commanded by Allende and Hidalgo, towards the *provincias internas.* Rayon returned to Guadalajara to secure the military chest, which contained three hundred thousand dollars. So delighted was Calleja at his success, that he did not attempt to pursue the insurgents, or to enter Guadalajora until four days after the battle. For this he was made Conde de Calderon, a title under which he reappears in the history of Mexico after the lapse of ten years. The insurgent generals retreated to Saltillo, at the head of four thousand troops, and there it was determined to leave them under the command of Rayon, while Hidalgo, Allende, Aldama, and Abasolo, who had ever been the souls of the revolution, were to set out for the United States to purchase arms and procure the assistance of experienced officers.

On the road, however, they were surprised by a former partisan, Don Ignacio Elizondo, who could not resist the temptation of so valuable a capture. They were taken to Chihuahua on the 21st of March, 1811; where, from anxiety to extort a knowledge of their schemes, the trial was prolonged till July, when Hidalgo, who had previously been degraded from the priesthood, was shot, his comrades sharing his fate. With the cowardice and pusillanimity peculiar to weak governments, an attempt was made to produce an impression that they repented; but persons are now living in Chihuahua who testify that they died bravely and boldly as they had fought, and Hidalgo persisted in his conviction that the knell of the Spanish rule had been sounded; that though the viceroy might resist, the end would come. He was buried in Chihuahua; and a few years since, before the breaking out of the present war, the place of his execution was pointed out to a party of American travellers almost as a holy spot, sanctified by the blood of the fighting Cura of Dolores. None can deny his valor and patriotism, and his excesses were perhaps to be attributed as much to the character of the enemies against whom he contended as to himself. Had it been his lot to contend against a humaner foe, it is not improbable that he would have been merciful. The cause he fought in was holy, and it is therefore the more to be regretted that he suffered it to be sullied with unnecessary bloodshed. In the long roll of Mexican leaders we shall have occasion to refer to, one thing is sure: few, indeed, are less bloodstained than Don MIGUEL HIDALGO Y COSTILLA.

CHAPTER III.

THE REVOLUTION SUBSEQUENT TO THE DEATH OF HIDALGO.

Guerilla warfare—National junta—Manifesto of the revolutionists—Morelos—Evacuation of Cuautla—Expedition against Oaxaca—Valladolid—Morelos defeated—Expedition to Tehuacan—Morelos taken prisoner—Executed.

AFTER the death of Hidalgo, the character of the contest changed its phase materially. Rayon maintained the command of the remnant of the army which escaped from the bridge of Calderon; the Baxio was laid under contribution by Muniz and Naverrete, another priest of the country; Puebla was taken possession of by Serraño and Osorno, and far in the valley of Mexico partisans were so numerous that there was no communication between the capital and the provinces above it; even the sentinels at the gates of the city were not unfrequently lassoed. Notwithstanding this, the creoles were unable to keep the field in any body, and the royalists controlled most of the cities. It is impossible to follow the separate chiefs through all the mazes of a guerilla war, when every day some partial action occurred, without any other result than a slaughter of prisoners, quarter being never claimed or given. Rayon, we have already said, appears to have been the first who saw the necessity of union, the only thing which could enable the partisans to oppose an enemy then conquering them in detail. He conceived the idea of a national *junta*, to be created by some popular election, and to be acknowledged by all the insurgent chiefs. As the seat of this body, he selected the town of Ziticuaro, in Valladolid, public opinion decidedly sustaining the insurgents in that province. With this view he occupied that town towards the end of May, 1811, and was lucky enough to repulse an attack made on it by General Emperan, with two thousand men. He was enabled on the 10th of September, following, to instal a junta or provisional government of five persons, elected by as many landholders as could be collected for the occasion, in conjunction with the authorities and people of the town.

The principles propounded by the junta were nearly those afterwards made famous as the plan of Iguala, acknowledging Ferdinand VII., on condition that he would reside in Mexico, and professing a wish for an intimate union with Spain. This, however, was probably mere profession, as Morelos, who had pronounced in favor of the junta, had refused to acknowledge a king *on any terms;* and Rayon defended the proposition, only on the terms of expediency, the lower orders not having as yet shaken off all respect for the royal name, though they were in flagrant rebellion against his authority. The establishment of this government was hailed with great enthusiasm by the creoles throughout New Spain, which was never fully realized. The junta was no doubt honest, but its authority at first was not generally recognised; and when Morelos acceded to it, Calleja contrived to disperse its members. It was, however, the nucleus around which was formed the congress of Chilpanzingo, which gave consistency to the action of the insurgent chiefs. The manifesto it published is characterized with great moderation, and contained one proposition which placed the insurgents in the best position before the tribunal of the world. It offered to conduct the war on the principles of civilized nations, and to prevent, the wanton sacrifice of prisoners. This document, which has been attributed to Doctor Cos, father of the present general, pointed out to Vanegas the certainty of the final triumph of the patriot cause, boldly challenging the right of any junta in Spain to control Mexico during the imprisonment of the king; and finally proposed, if the Spaniards would lay down their offices, and permit a general congress to be called, not only their property should be respected, but their salaries paid. If they did this, the Mexicans would admit them to all privileges, recognise the king, and assist Spain in her struggle with their men and treasure. Had this offer been accepted, how vastly differently situated would Spain now have been? She need never have placed herself at the beck of England to shake off the weight of France, or perhaps now have been forced to cast her queen at the feet of Louis Philippe, to disenthral herself from the influence of England. Mexico might now have been a crown-property of Spain, as devotedly attached to her as Cuba and Porto Rico—the only colonies she retains in America, because they were the only ones the central junta did not interfere with. Vanegas had the proposals burned by the executioner of Mexico, and thereby the destiny of two nations was decided. It now becomes necessary to refer to one repeatedly mentioned already, the history of whose life is that of the Mexican revolution from the death of Hidalgo to his own.

Don Jose Maria Morelos.

MORELOS.

When Hidalgo was in Valladolid in October, 1810, previous to the battle of Las Cruces, he was joined by Don Jose Maria Morelos, cura of Nucupetaro, a town of that province, on whom he conferred a commission to act as captain-general of the provinces on the south-western coast, for which he set out with no other escort than a few servants armed with old muskets and lances. The first reinforcement he received was by a numerous party of slaves, who were eager to win their freedom; and his exigencies were so great that the discovery of twenty muskets at Petatan was thought an especial matter of congratulation. He was afterwards joined by Don Jose and Don Antonio Galeaño; and in November, 1810, was at the head of one thousand men, and marched against Acapulco. This, as is well known, was the great depot of the Manilla trade, probably the busiest town in Mexico, with a population as industrious as any people with Spanish blood and education can reasonably be expected to be. The possession of this city might in that quarter be expected to put an end to the strife. The commandant of the district, Don Francisco Paris, marched against him at the head of a numerous body of troops, and Acapulco was evidently to be no bloodless conquest.

Though commanding an inferior force, Morelos did not hesitate to attack him, and under the cover of night, surprised and signally defeated the royalist force, January 25th, 1811. The result of this battle was the possession of eight hundred muskets, five pieces of artillery, a large quantity of ammunition, and Paris's chest, in which was a large sum of money. At the same time seven hundred prisoners were taken, and, it is pleasant to say, treated with humanity. This was the first of Morelos's triumphs, and the base of the superstructure of fame he raised for himself. His success was not unnoticed; and having baffled the parties commanded by Llano and Fuentes subsequently, he became at once the idol of his countrymen and the terror of the Spaniards. Men of talent flocked to his army, among whom were Ermengildo Galeaño, the three Bravos, two of whom were executed by Calleja afterwards, and the other subsequently was placed with Victoria at the head of government in 1828. The whole of 1811 was, as we have said, consumed in a series of petty engagements, and by the great and successful efforts of Morelos to discipline his army, the mass of whom were negroes. With such an army, he deserves credit for the humane manner in which he generally was able to conduct the war.

After a series of successful actions, in January, 1812 Morelos pushed forward his advanced guard, under Bravo, to Calco, with outposts reaching to San Augustino de las Cuevas. Calleja had just defeated Hidalgo, and was summoned to oppose him with his his army, which Morelos was determined to fight at Cuautla Amilpas, about twenty-two leagues from Mexico.

Calleja immediately set out to obey the order of Vanegas, to oppose Morelos; but it is now necessary to describe the events which occurred on his march. The junta established by Rayon at Ziticuaro, was considered by the Spaniards as their most formidable enemy, and Calleja was ordered positively to disperse it. On the 1st of January, after a march of great hardship, he reached this place, and on the 2d carried it.

The junta escaped to Sultepec, and Calleja immediately rased the walls of the town, after having passed a fortnight there in the examination of Rayon's papers. This was not all; the people were decimated, and every house, except the churches, burned. From Ziticuaro he proceeded to Mexico, into which he made a procession, and a *Te Deum* in honor of his victories was sung in the cathedral.

On the 14th Calleja left the capital to oppose Morelos, who, as we have said, was at Cuautla Amilpas. On the 18th of February the two forces first came in contact; on which occasion Morelos, who had gone out to reconnoitre, was near being taken, and owed his safety entirely to Ermengildo Galeaño. On this occasion Jose Maria Fernandez, afterwards known as General Victoria, first appeared on the stage. His father was a land-owner in the neighborhood of San Luis de Potosi, and when the cura Hidalgo first pronounced against the government, Fernandez, just twenty-two, had concluded his studies for the law. He immediately determined to adopt the popular cause, but did not declare himself until he saw a man appear, whom he thought capable of ruling the storm. As soon as Morelos became known he at once recognised him as the man he sought, and left Mexico to place himself under his orders. In this skirmish he received a severe wound and saved Galeaño's life. On this occasion Morelos had the satisfaction to see his negro levies meet the Spanish veterans with a firmness which realized all he had hoped, but dared not anticipate. On the 19th, Calleja assaulted the town in four columns, with great fierceness. The Mexicans suffered him to approach till within one hundred yards, when they opened on them a fire which could not be withstood. The Spaniards fled precipitately, and Galeaño having discovered a Spanish colonel seeking to rally his men, sallied out, and in a hand to hand contest killed him. The consequence was, that all four columns were repulsed, after an action which lasted from seven A. M. till three P. M., and Calleja was forced to retreat, having lost five hundred men. So completely was he discouraged, that he wrote for a siege train to the viceroy, who immediately complied with his request, and sent him reinforcements under Llano, who had previously served against Morelos. The courier, however, who conveyed to Llano his orders, fell into the hands of the insurgents, and Morelos was informed of the approach of this body. He, however, was aware that all Mexico looked anxiously at Cuautla. He determined, therefore, to defend himself, and did so with the gallantry which was his characteristic. Llano was, when he received the viceroy's orders, about to attack Izucar, defended by Guerrero. During the revolution this general has received forty wounds, and undergone perils, his escape from which seem miraculous. In one instance a shell exploded in a house in which he was asleep and killed every individual but himself. Llano immediately deserted this formidable opponent, and on the first of March joined Calleja. On the 4th both attacked the place with their batteries. The cannonade continued for a long time, but Cuautla held out manfully. The Bravos and Lorios attempted to attack Calleja's rear, but failed. Calleja attempted to cut off the small stream which supplied Cuautla with water, but Galeaño, in his turn, contrived to thwart this plan.

After various other attempts, which were sometimes made by one and then by the other party, Morelos determined to evacuate the town, which he did successfully in the presence of a superior force, by a manœuvre so peculiar, that it deserves especial mention. On the 2d of May, in the middle of the night, the troops were formed, the main body under command of Morelos, the van of Galeaño, and the rear of the Bravos. They reached the Spanish lines and passed two of the batteries unobserved; nor was it until they reached a deep baranca or ravine, that they were noticed. Over this they were obliged to construct a bridge, which was done with hurdles borne by the Indians, so that a sentinel gave the alarm before Galeaño was able to cut him down. Immediately on crossing the baranca, the column was attacked both by Llano and Calleja. This had been foreseen, and orders given, should it occur, for a general dispersion and to rendezvous at Izucar. So well was it effected, that like the children of the mist, the patriots became invisible; and the royal troops, completely amazed, began to fire on each other. Izucar was in possession of Don Miguel Bravo, and on his arrival there Morelos had the satisfaction to find but seventeen were missing; among whom, however, was Don Leonardo Bravo, who was made prisoner. Calleja was for a long time afraid to enter Cuautla; when he did so it was to commit outrages which must ever stain his reputation. On the 16th the army returned to the capital, and an attempt was made to magnify its achievements into a triumph. Rumor had, however, preceded the army; and every one knew the *victor* had first been defeated and then outwitted, so that Calleja was ridiculed. Morelos had received a slight injury at Cuautla, which detained him some time at Izucar. On his recovery he again took the field at the head of his troops, whom one of his lieutenants, the Padre Matamoras, had brought to a high state of dicipline. He successively defeated three Spanish divisions, and made a triumphal entry into Tehuacan, a city of La Puebla, on the 16th of September, 1812. He carried the city of Orizaba by a *coup de main*, captnring nine pieces of artillery and an immense booty in money and tobacco. On being driven by a superior force from that place, he undertook his famous expedition against Oaxaca, the most beautiful spot perhaps of all Mexico.

At that time there were no roads in Mexico except those connecting the great cities, and the army suffered much hardship on the march. The city was commanded by the Brigadier Regules, who sought to defend it. The artillery of the insurgents, commanded by Don Miguel Mier y Teran, having silenced that of Regules, he made a last stand on the edge of the moat which surrounded the city, over which there was but one drawbridge, which was elevated, and the approach to it defended by the royalist infantry. The insurgents having paused at this obstacle, Guadalupe Victoria swam the moat, sword in hand, and cut the ropes of the bridge unresisted; the battle was thus won, and the capital of the vale of Oaxaca taken possession of by Morelos. He then released all political offenders (and many were confined in the prisons), and set about the conquest of the rest of the province, which he completed on the 30th of August, 1813, when Acapulco surrendered, having been besieged from the 15th of February by his army, now equal to any in discipline and effectiveness.

The Spanish flag having been hauled down for ever at Acapulco, Morelos returned to Oaxaca, where Matamoros had prepared all for the meeting of the national congress, which was composed of the junta of Ziticuaro, deputies elected by Oaxaca and selected from all those provinces in which the people dared not meet. This body convened September 13th, 1813, at the town of Chilpanzingo, and declared the independence of Mexico the 13th of November of that year. Had this event taken place earlier, it might have resulted in good; but Morelos soon after had an enemy to oppose him, so numerous, that he was unable fully to protect it. We have mentioned that, at Cuautla, one of the Bravos was taken prisoner, and refer to it again to mention an act of forbearance which would do honor to any country. Several engagements having taken place, the patriots were in possession of more than three hundred Spaniards, whom Morelos placed at the disposal of Nicolas Bravo, to enable him to effect an exchange for his father Leonardo, the captive, then under sentence of death in Mexico. The whole of these prisoners were offered to Vanegas for Leonardo, whom the viceroy immediately ordered to be executed. The son, instead of making reprisals, liberated the whole body, and assigned as his reason for doing so, that he feared he might not be able to resist the constant temptation to revenge, their presence exposed him to. On the 18th of November, 1813, at Palmar, Matamoros defeated the Spaniards after a severe fight, which lasted eight hours; cutting off the regiment of Asturias, which had been at Baylen, and won there the cognomen of invincible. This is not the only instance in which reputations won in the peninsular campaigns, were lost in America. The capture of this regiment, composed altogether of Europeans, was considered to have finally destroyed the prestige of Spanish superiority, which had long trembled before the fierceness of the attacks of Hidalgo and Morelos.

An expedition against Valladolid was agreed on, which would have placed Morelos in connexion with the insurgents of the *provincias internas*, to effect which he collected seven thousand men. At Valladolid, where he arrived on the 23d of December, he found Llano and Iturbide at the head of a formidable body of men, whom he immediately attacked, and by whom he was repulsed. On the next morning Iturbide made a sally which would have failed, the insurgents having after a short check been rallied. Unfortunately, a body of reinforcements for them, which arrived just then, were mistaken for enemies and fired upon. They immediately charged the force of Morelos. Of this scene of confusion Iturbide took advantage, and routed the whole army, which fled to Puruaran.

There they were again attacked, and Matamoros made prisoner. The patriot forces being signally defeated, January 6th, 1814, Morelos sought in vain to exchange for Matamoros a number of the prisoners taken at Palmar, when the regiment of Asturias was cut to pieces. Calleja, however, was now viceroy, and was inexorable, ordering Matamoros to be shot. We cannot censure the fearful retribution taken by the patriots, who immediately, in retaliation for him and Don Valentino Bravo, ordered all their prisoners to be put to death.

Morelos sent Don Manuel Mier y Teran to take command in La Puebla, and Victoria to the district of Vera Cruz. This was a dark period to the patriots; and after suffering several defeats, losing Miguel Bravo, who was executed, Galeaño, who died in battle, and being unable to protect the Congress, which was driven from Chilpanzingo to the woods of Aputzingan, where, however, it continued its labors and put forth the constitution of 1814; Morelos was induced to undertake the expedition to Tehuacan, in Puebla, where Teran had collected a body of five hundred men. On this expedition Morelos had but five hundred men, and had to march sixty leagues across a country in possession of the loyalists. Couriers he had sent to Guerrero and Teran were intercepted, so that these generals could not learn his position; and the royalists having ascertained how feeble he was, attacked him on the morning of the 15th, in a mountainous road. An admirable writer thus describes what follows of his history:

"He immediately ordered Don Nicolas Bravo to continue his march with the main body, as an escort to the congress, while he himself with a few men endeavored to check the advance of the Spaniards.

"'My life,' he said, 'is of little consequence, provided the congress be saved. My race was run from the moment that I saw an independent government established.'

"His orders were obeyed, and Morelos remained with about fifty men, most of whom abandoned him when the firing became hot. He succeeded, however, in gaining time, which was his great object, nor did the royalists venture to advance upon him, until only one man was left by his side. He was then taken prisoner, though he had sought death in vain during the action. There can be little doubt that his late reverses had inspired him with a disgust for life, and that he wished to end his days by a proof of devotion to his country worthy the most brilliant part of his former career.

"Morelos was treated with the greatest brutality by the Spanish soldiers into whose hands he first fell. They stripped him, and conducted him, loaded with chains, to Tesmalaca. But Concha (to his honor be it said), on his prisoner being presented to him, received him with the respect due to a fallen enemy, and treated him with unwonted humanity and attention. He was transferred, with as little delay as possible, to the capital, and the whole population of Mexico flocked out to San Agustin de las Cuevas, to see (and some to insult) the man, whose name had so long been their terror. But Morelos, both on his way to prison, and while in confinement, is said to have shown a coolness which he preserved to the last. Indeed, the only thing that seemed to affect him at all was his degradation ; a ceremony humiliating in itself, but rendered doubly so, in his case, by the publicity which was given to it. His examination was conducted by the Oidor Bataller (whose insolent assertion of the natural superiority of the Spaniards to the creoles, is said to have roused Morelos into action), and was not of long duration. On the 22d of December, 1815, Concha was charged to remove him from the prisons of the Inquisition to the hospital of San Christoval, behind which, the sentence pronounced against him was to be carried into execution. On arriving there, he dined in company with Concha, whom he afterwards embraced, and thanked for his kindness. He then confessed himself, and walked, with the most perfect serenity, to the place of execution. The short prayer which he pronounced there, deserves to be recorded for its affecting simplicity. 'Lord, if I have done well, thou knowest it ; if ill, to thy infinite mercy I commend my soul!'

"After this appeal to the Supreme Judge, he fastened with his own hands a handkerchief about his eyes, gave the signal to the soldiers to fire, and met death with as much composure as he had ever shown when facing it on the field of battle."

CHAPTER IV.

REVOLUTION—FROM THE DEATH OF MORELOS, DECEMBER 22D, 1815, TO 1820.

Dissolution of the Mexican congress—New Spanish constitution—Battles in Texas—Teran—Rayon—Nicolas Bravo—Guadalupe Victoria—Mina—Gloomy aspect of the revolutionary cause.

THE heroic days of the revolution thus terminated, and with Morelos apparently died all union, no one else seeming to have the power to induce the insurgent chiefs to act in concert. Each province considered itself independent; and in consequence of this fatal disunion, though supported in many parts of the country by great military ability, the cause of liberty decidedly lost ground. Morelos always intended the congress to be a source of union, to which his lieutenants might look, as to himself, in case of accident; but few of his officers recognised its authority as fully as he had done. On the 22d of October, 1814, the congress was driven by Iturbide from Apatzingan to Michoacan, whence Bravo escorted it to Tehuacan; there some difficulties having arisen between the military and civil authorities, Teran, on the 15th of December, 1815, forcibly dissolved it. This act has been severely reprobated, but has been perhaps misunderstood. There is no doubt but that the congress was valuable as a point of union, but it is also true that the demands of this body would have ruined the district he commanded. Among other things, the congress appropriated eight thousand dollars a year for each of its members, and took the management of the funds from the military commandant to yield it to one of its own officers; which made Teran, whose services had been great, a mere dependant. The remoter chiefs having refused to contribute to this body, Teran was in self-defence forced to dissolve it. The effects of the dissolution of this only central government Mexico had yet had were most disastrous, and resulted in the crushing, in succession, of Victoria, Rayon, Bravo, Guerrero, and Teran, each of whom was unable to call on the other for aid. A multitude of minor chiefs shared the same fate; and the arrival of fresh troops from the peninsula enabled the viceroy to keep open a communication through the whole country, and almost to restore Spanish authority. To effecting this consummation, not the least important adjunct was the publication of the *indulto* or pardon to all who would lay down their arms, which the viceroy Apodaca (Villeja having gone to Spain) was authorized to make, and which reduced to an inconsiderable number the insurgents who yet kept the field.

These reverses were, however, fully compensated for by the effect produced by the introduction into Mexico of the Spanish constitution sanctioned by the cortes of Cadiz, in which sat representatives from America to the number of fifty, while from all the rest of the empire there were but one hundred and thirty-two members, on the 29th of March, 1812. Some account of this constitution is necessary to the correct intelligence of the subsequent history of the Mexican war of independence.

By its provisions the Spanish nation was declared to consist of all Spaniards in either hemisphere. Spaniards were all free men, born and residing in the Spanish dominions, and others to whom the same privileges might be granted. Spanish citizens, who alone could vote, be elected, or be appointed to civil trusts and offices, were all Spaniards except those who were, by either parent, of African descent; the latter might, however, be admitted to those privileges under certain circumstances. The government was to be an hereditary monarchy, Ferdinand VII. being recognised as the king; the powers of the state, however, were divided into three branches—the legislative, the executive, and the judicial—the attributes of each of which were distinctly defined. The *legislative* power was to be exercised by a single body of deputies, chosen indirectly for two years, by the citizens, the king possessing only a limited right of veto upon its enactments; the *executive* duties were committed to the king, who was aided by a council of state, and acted through nine responsible ministers; to the *audiencias* or *courts* alone belonged the application of the laws in civil and criminal cases. The territories of the empire were to be divided into provinces, all of which were to be governed in the same manner by a chief, whom the king would appoint, and a provincial deputation composed of members chosen biennially by the citizens; the basis of the national representation was to be the same in every part of the dominions, the number of deputies sent by each province being proportioned to the number of Spanish citizens inhabiting it. The council of the Indies, which had disappeared in the course of the great political tempest, was replaced by a *minister of the kingdom beyond sea;* the press was freed from all restrictions, and from all responsibility, except such as might be imposed on it by the laws. In fine, throughout the whole Spanish empire, the same forms of administration were established, and the same civil rights were recognised, no privilege or disability being founded on birth-place or descent, except with regard to persons of African origin. The central government was empowered to delay the extension of the privileges in those parts of the dominions to which it should not be considered judicious to apply them immediately.

The constitution was made known in some parts of America before, and in others after, the arrival of the forces sent from Spain to reduce them to submission. Neither the arrow nor the olive branch proved effectual for that purpose; resistance was opposed to the former wherever it was practicable; the latter was generally rejected with scorn, and when accepted was only used as a means of offence against those who offered it. Long experience of the falsehood and injustice of the Spanish government had rendered the Americans suspicious with regard to its concessions; no confidence was placed in the sincerity of the cortes, in holding out these liberal terms, or in the power of that body to maintain the new institutions. Distrust was felt, if not expressed, by every thinking individual, and the patriots absolutely disregarded it in America. It had been published there under the viceroyalty of Vanegas, who soon saw he could not maintain his authority in the face of this constitution, and therefore, after two months, began to suspend provision after provision, till but its inanimate skeleton remained. It was, however, a concession which could not be revoked, and made the after revolution more popular and universal. The people had been determined to make use of their new privileges, and made this virtual revocation necessary.

We have previously neglected to mention that from time to time, in the northern provinces of Mexico, several attempts were made by persons coming from the United

States, either to co-operate with the insurgents, or to establish a new republic. During the year 1812 and 1813, several bloody battles were fought between the invaders and the royal forces in the province of Texas; the latter were ultimately successful, but the islands in the vicinity of the coasts became places of refuge and rendezvous for pirates, professing to act against Spain under commissions from various independent governments in America.

It is impossible to follow in detail the events of this period, but it will be necessary to give some sketch of the military events, and of the leaders who intervene between this period and the rise of Iturbide.

Teran, the first who presents himself to us after the dissolution of the congress on the 22d of December, 1815, was engaged for some months in an adventurous strife, in which he was generally successful, though his efforts were cramped for want of arms; to obtain which, he made an expedition to the mouth of the river Guasacoalco, where he was to be met by a vessel from the United States. To accomplish this, he had an escort of but three hundred men, having left the rest of his troops at a powder manufactory he had established at Cerro Colorado. Being overtaken by the rainy season, he made in ten days a road across the marsh leading to Amistar, which yet exists, and is acknowledged to be a most wonderful work. Thence he proceeded to Plaza Vicente, the *depot* of the Vera Cruz traders, and defeated a force of eleven hundred royalists, commanded by Topete, which attacked him on the 10th of September. His plan for seizing Guasacoalco having been discovered, he returned to Tehuacan, where he was forced to surrender, January 21st, 1817, to four thousand troops, detached by the viceroy against him, and commanded by Col. Bracho, who besieged him at Colorado. He then lived in obscurity until the revolution of 1821 at La Puebla, his life having been secured by the terms of his capitulation. He has been minister of war and plenipotentiary to England in 1825. He had the reputation always of being a good officer, and commanded probably the best brigade in the patriot service. He has never recovered from the prejudice excited against him for his suppression of the congress, and therefore has not held office as often as his high talents would have entitled him to. He was but a short time since alive, and if now living, can be but little over fifty.

Rayon had a far shorter career, and probably of all the men in the service was the most accomplished. He has been pointed out by those who knew him as an example of Cervantes' proverb, that the lance never dulled the pen or the pen the lance. He was one of Morelos's lieutenants, and exercised an independent command in the mountains of Valladolid, where he took advantage of the natural difficulties of the country and of the devotion of the natives to him. His principal strong hold was the Cerro de Corporo, in which he was besieged by Llano and Iturbide in January 1815, whom he beat off on the 4th of March. Corporo was afterwards besieged by Aguierre in Rayon's absence, and was surrendered January 2d, 1817. Don Ignacio Rayon was subsequently deserted by his followers and fell into the hands of Armijo, and was imprisoned in the capital till 1821. He was in 1828 a general, and occupied a high position in the esteem of the people. Amid the turmoils of the later revolutions he has disappeared from history.

Nicolas Bravo was one of a family of patriots with whom the reader is now familiar. After the dissolution of the congress, he wandered at the head of his command over Mexico, without being able to make head against any of his pursuers. When Mina landed (of whom more anon), he sought to fortify Corporo, but was driven from it by a royalist force, and afterwards taken by Armijo, in December, 1817, and confined in the capital till 1821. After aiding Iturbide to establish independence, he declared against him when he dissolved the congress, and contributed greatly to his deposition. He ultimately became the first vice-president of the republic, when Guadalupe Victoria was placed at the head of the nation.

No one of the insurgent chiefs were pursued with such inveteracy, by the royal troops, as this general, whose position, in the province of Vera Cruz, was a constant source of uneasiness to the viceroy. From the moment that he was deputed by Morelos to take the eastern line of coast, (1814,) he succeeded in cutting off almost all communication between the capital and the only port through which intercourse with Europe was, at that time, carried on. This he effected at the head of a force which seldom exceeded two thousand men; but a perfect acquaintance with the country, (which is extremely mountainous and intricate), and an unlimited influence over the minds of his followers, made up for all deficiencies in point of numbers, and rendered Victoria, very shortly, the terror of the Spanish forces.

It was his practice to keep but a small body of men about his person, and only to collect his force upon great occasions: a mode of warfare well suited to the wild habits of the natives, and, at the same time, calculated to baffle pursuit. The instant a blow was struck, a general dispersion followed: in the event of a failure, a rendezvous was fixed for some distant point; and thus losses were often repaired, before it was known in the capital that they had been sustained at all.

Nor were Victoria's exploits confined to this desul tory warfare: in 1815 he detained a convoy of six thousand mules, escorted by two thousand men, under the command of Colonel Aguila, at Puente del Rey, (a pass, the natural strength of which the insurgents had increased by placing artillery upon the heights, by which it is commanded), nor did it reach Vera Cruz for upward of six months. The necessity of keeping the channel of communication with Europe open, induced Calleja, in December 1815, to intrust the chief command, both civil and military, of the province of Vera Cruz, to Don Fernando Miyares, (an officer of high rank and distinguished attainments, recently arrived from Spain), for the special purpose of establishing a chain of fortified posts, on the whole ascent to the table-land, sufficiently strong to curb Victoria's incursions. The execution of this plan was preceded, and accompanied, by a series of actions between the insurgents and royalists, in the course of which Miyares gradually drove Victoria from his strong-holds at Puente del Rey and Puente de San Juan, (September 1815); and although the latter maintained the unequal struggle for upwards of two years, he never was able to obtain any decisive advantage over the reinforcements, which the government was continually sending to the seat of war. Two thousand European troops landed with Miyares, and one thousand more with Apodaca, (in 1816); and notwithstanding the desperate efforts of Victoria's men, their courage was of no avail against the superior discipline and arms of their adversaries. In the course of the year 1816, most of his old soldiers fell: those by whom he replaced them

National Bridge.—Puente Nacional, formerly called Puente del Rey.

had neither the same enthusiasm, nor the same attachment to his person. The zeal with which the inhabitants had engaged in the cause of the revolution, was worn out: with each reverse their discouragement increased, and, as the disastrous accounts from the interior left them but little hope of bringing the contest to a favorable issue, the villages refused to furnish any farther supplies; the last remnant of Victoria's followers deserted him, and he was left absolutely alone. Still his courage was unsubdued, and his resolution not to yield, on any terms, to the Spaniards, unshaken. He refused the rank and rewards which Apodaca proffered as the price of his submission, and determined to seek an asylum in the solitudes of the forests, rather than accept the *indulto*, on the faith of which so many of the insurgents yielded up their arms. This extraordinary project was carried into execution with a decision highly characteristic of the man. Unaccompanied by a single attendant, and provided only with a little linen, and a sword, Victoria threw himself into the mountainous district which occupies so large a portion of the province of Vera Cruz, and disappeared to the eyes of his countrymen. His after-history is so extremely wild, that I should hardly venture to relate it here, did not the unanimous evidence of his countrymen confirm the story of his sufferings, many of them heard it from his own mouth.

During the first few weeks, Victoria was supplied with provisions by the Indians, who all knew and respected his name; but Apodaca was so apprehensive that he would again emerge from his retreat, that a thousand men were ordered out, in small detachments, literally to hunt him down. Wherever it was discovered that a village had either received him, or relieved his wants, it was burnt without mercy; and this rigor struck the Indians with such terror, that they either fled at the sight of Victoria, or were the first to denounce the approach of a man, whose presence might prove so fatal to them. For upwards of six months, he was followed like a wild beast by his pursuers, who were often so near him, that he could hear their imprecations against himself, and Apodaca too, for having condemned them to so fruitless a search. On one occasion he escaped a detachment, which he fell in with unexpectedly, by swimming a river, which they were unable to cross; and on several others, he concealed himself, when in the immediate vicinity of the royal troops, beneath the thick shrubs and creepers with which the woods of Vera Cruz abound. At last a story was made up, to satisfy the viceroy, of a body having been found, which had been recognised as that of Victoria. A minute description was given of his person, which was inserted officially in the Gazette of Mexico, and the troops were recalled to more pressing labors in the interior.

But Victoria's trials did not cease with the pursuit: harassed and worn out by the fatigues which he had undergone, his clothes torn to pieces, and his body lacerated by the thorny underwood of the tropics, he was indeed allowed a little tranquillity, but his sufferings were still almost incredible: during the summer he managed to subsist upon the fruits of which nature is so lavish in those climates; but in winter he was attenuated by hunger, and he has been repeatedly heard to affirm, that no repast has afforded him so much pleasure since, as he experienced, after being long deprived of food, in gnawing the bones of horses, or other animals, that he happened to find dead in the woods. By degrees he accustomed himself to such abstinence, that he could remain four, and even five days, without taking any thing but water, without experiencing any serious inconvenience; but whenever he was deprived of sustenance for a longer period, his sufferings were very acute. For thirty months he never tasted bread, nor saw a human being, nor thought, at times, ever to see one again. His clothes were reduced to a single wrapper of cotton, which he found one day, when driven by hunger he had approached nearer than usual to some Indian huts, and this he regarded as an inestimable treasure.

The mode in which Victoria, cut off, as he was, from all communication with the world, received intelligence of the revolution of 1821, is hardly less extraordinary than the fact of his having been able to support existence amidst so many hardships, during the intervening period.

When, in 1818, he was abandoned by all the rest of his men, he was asked by two Indians, who lingered with him to the last, and on whose fidelity he knew that he could rely, if any change took place, where he wished them to look for him? He pointed, in reply, to a mountain at some distance, and told them that, on that mountain, perhaps, they might find his bones. His only reason for selecting it, was its being particularly rugged, and inaccessible, and surrounded by forests of a vast extent.

The Indians treasured up this hint, and as soon as the first news of Iturbide's declaration reached them, they set out in quest of Victoria. They separated on arriving at the foot of the mountain, and employed six whole weeks in examining the woods with which it was covered; during this time, they lived principally by the chase; but finding their stock of maize exhausted, and all their efforts unavailing, they were about to give up the attempt, when one of them discovered, in crossing a ravine, which Victoria occasionally frequented, the print of a foot, which he immediately recognised to be that of a European. By European, is meant of European descent, and consequently accustomed to wear shoes, which always give a difference of shape to the foot, very perceptible to the eye of a native. The Indian waited two days upon the spot; but seeing nothing of Victoria, and finding his supply of provisions quite at an end, he suspended upon a tree, near the place, four tortillas, or little maize cakes, which were all he had left, and set out for his village, in order to replenish his wallets, hoping that if Victoria should pass in the mean time, the tortillas would attract his attention, and convince him that some friend was in search of him.

His little plan succeeded completely: Victoria, on crossing the ravine, two days afterwards, perceived the maize cakes, which the birds had fortunately not devoured. He had then been four whole days without eating, and upwards of two years without tasting bread; and, he says himself, that he devoured the tortillas before the cravings of his appetite would allow him to reflect upon the singularity of finding them on this solitary spot, where he had never before seen any trace of a human being. He was at a loss to determine whether they had been left there by friend or foe; but feeling sure that whoever left them intended to return, he concealed himself near the place, in order to observe his motions, and to take his own measures accordingly.

Within a short time the Indian returned, and Victoria, who recognised him, abruptly started from his concealment, to welcome his faithful follower; but the man, terrified at seeing a phantom covered with hair, emaciated, and clothed only with on old cotton wrapher, advancing upon him with a sword in his hand, from amongst the bushes, took to flight; and it was only on hearing himself repeatedly called by his name, that he recovered his composure sufficiently to recognise his old general. He was affected beyond measure at the state in which he found him, and conducted him instantly to the village, where Victoria was received with the greatest enthusiasm. The report of his reappearance spread, like lightning, through the province, where it was not credited at first, so firmly was every one convinced of his death; but as soon as it was known that Guadalupe Victoria was indeed in existence, all the old insurgents rallied around him. In an incredibly short time, he induced the whole province, with the exception of the fortified towns, to declare for independence, and then set out to join Iturbide, who was, at that time, preparing for the siege of Mexico. He was received with great apparent cordiality; but his independent spirit was too little in unison with Iturbide's projects, for this good understanding to continue long. Victoria had fought for a liberal form of government, and not merely for a change of masters; and Iturbide, unable to gain him over, drove him again into the woods during his short-lived reign, from whence he only returned to give the signal for a general rising against the too ambitious emperor.

The history of the revolution now becomes identified with the life of Xavier Mina, who, while all in Spain thought the royal cause prospering, nearly ruined it. Among those who had been obliged to fly from Spain after the overthrow of the constitution by Ferdinand, in 1814, was Xavier Mina, a relation of the well known general of the same name. Burning with indignation and a desire of revenge, not only against the monarch who had, as he conceived, acted thus unworthily, but also, in fact, against the nation, which had so joyfully seconded the shameful deed, this young man came to the United States, where he succeeded in obtaining the means of fitting out a small expedition. With this force he sailed from the Chesapeake on the 1st of September, 1816; and, after various delays at Port au Prince, Galveston, and other places, where he made small additions to his troops and equipments, he landed on the 15th of April following, with three hundred men of all nations, near Soto la Marina, a small place on the western shore of the Mexican Gulf, at the mouth of the river Santander, and about eighty miles south of the entrance of the Rio del Norte. At this time, the fortunes of the independents in Mexico were in the ebb. The congress had published a republican constitution on the 22d of October, 1814; but all the advantages which were anticipated from this act, as a means of promoting union and subordination among the partisans of the cause, were lost before the end of the following year, by the seizure and subsequent execution of Morelos. While this devoted and energetic leader was in command, obedience was paid by all the insurgents to the orders of the congress; after his capture, however, this body was regarded rather as an incumbrance than otherwise, and was at length forcibly dissolved, or rather dispersed, by Don Manuel de Mier y Teran, a young chief to whose charge its defence had been committed. The insurgent leaders then partitioned the country among themselves, and each from his fort or fastness kept the surrounding district in awe and trouble. Guerrero betook himself to the Pacific coast near Acapulco; Rayon ruled in the mountains of Valladolid, and Guadalupe Victoria in those of Vera Cruz; Teran established himself on the borders of Oaxaca and Puebla; the barbarian, Padre Torres, with his band ravaged the beautiful region called the

Baxio of Guanaxuato, while Nicolas, the sole survivor of the gallant Bravo family, wandered about with his followers. The arrival of troops from Spain, after the restoration of Ferdinand, enabled Calleja, however, to keep up his chains of posts throughout the country, by means of which the insurgents were becoming daily more straitened, and their communications with each other were rendered more difficult.

In 1816 Calleja returned to Spain, having been replaced as viceroy of Mexico by Don Ruiz de Apodaca, a man of a comparatively mild disposition, who was charged to offer more favorable terms to the insurgents. As his character was well known, those terms were readily accepted, and ere he had been in power a year, many, not only of the subordinates, but also of the chiefs of the independents, accepted the *indulto*, or act of indemnity proclaimed by him, and returned to the occupations of peaceful life. Among the chiefs who thus submitted, were Nicolas Bravo, Osourno, and Rayon, all of whom remained in obscurity until 1821; Victoria about the same time disappeared, and was believed to be dead, and the only leader of consequence among the insurgents who, in 1817, remained in command, was the priest Jose Torres.

The viceroy had received notice from Havana, of the approach of Mina's expedition, to intercept which, he had sent out several ships of war; as he, however, could not learn where the invaders intended to land, his other preparations for defence were necessarily of a general character. From these circumstances, Mina found little or no opposition at Soto la Marina, and having built a temporary fort near that place, in which some men were left as a garrison, he commenced his march into the interior on the 24th of May, and the first action with the royalist forces took place on the 12th of June, at Peotillos, about forty miles from the city of San Luis Potosi; in this Mina was successful, and before the end of the month he effected a juncture with the redoubtable Father Torres, in the Baxio of Guanaxuato.

We cannot particularize the events of the short but brilliant career of Mina in Mexico; brilliant it was, from the constant display of boldness, energy and courage, under difficulties which, as he could not but have seen within a short time after his landing in Mexico, were insuperable. The number of his followers increased but little; the natives who joined him being scarcely more than sufficient to supply the place of those who fell in battle or from fatigue; while on the other hand, they fought with the incumbrances of women and children; to crown all, Mina soon found that he was himself the object of jealousy and hatred, on the part of Father Torres. Concert of action was thus impossible; the foreigners were viewed with mistrust and dislike by the people; and except when their protection was wanted, were soon left to provide for and to defend themselves as they might. Meanwhile the viceroy was unremitting in his exertions to destroy them; troops were gathering around them from every direction; escape was impossible, and they had only to sell their lives as dearly as they could.

The fort at Soto la Marina fell first; garrisoned by only a hundred and thirteen men, under Major Sarda, an Italian, it was attacked by General Arredondo, the commander of the eastern provinces, with no less than two thousand regular soldiers. The garrison held out for some days, until at length, its numbers having been reduced to thirty-seven, the fort was surrendered by capitulation, on the 15th of June. The terms of the capitulation were of course disregarded; and the unfortunate foreigners expiated their rashness and folly by imprisonment for the remainder of their lives in loathsome dungeons at Ulua, Ceuta, Cadiz, and other places.

The Sombrero, a fort in Guanaxuato, occupied by a body of Mina's men, under Colonel Young, an American, was also invested by a considerable force of royalists, commanded by General Liñan. On the night of the 19th of August, the able-bodied soldiers of the garrison, with the women and children, evacuated the place, leaving the sick and the wounded to the tender mercies of the Spaniards. Liñan, however, having learned their intention, set upon them during their retreat, and killed the greater part; he then butchered the wounded whom he found in the fort, and sent the prisoners, some to execution, others to join their comrades in their dungeons.

Mina had in the interval so far gained upon the feelings of the Mexicans, that he had assembled nearly a thousand men under his command. With these he at first established himself in another fort in Baxio, called Remedios, when he was joined by the remnants of the garrison of Sombrero; and removing thence, he, in a short space of time, reduced several of the strongholds of the royalists. At length, on the 23d day of October, he ventured to attack the city of Guanaxuato; having no artillery, his attempt proved vain, he was obliged to retreat and immediately found himself almost deserted. On the 27th, while reposing in a farm-house called the Venadito, he was betrayed, surrounded, and made prisoner.

The news of Mina's seizure was celebrated by public rejoicings and religious thanksgivings throughout Mexico. He was of course ordered to be instantly executed, and was accordingly shot on the 11th of November, at Tepeaca, in sight of the fort of Remedios, which was then besieged by the Spaniards. That fort soon after fell, and before the year 1817, not more than twenty of those who had landed with Mina at Soto la Marina in April, were alive and not in dungeons. In reward for the success of his efforts in effecting the overthrow of Mina, Apodaca was made Count of Venadito.

After the death of Morelos, the dismissal of the Mexican congress by Teran, and the complete destruction of Mina and his followers, the hopes of the partisans of independence rapidly sunk. The system of energy on the one hand, and of conciliation on the other, pursued by the viceroy, Apodaca, daily overthrew or disarmed the enemies of the Spanish authority. There was no longer among the insurgents any directing power, to which the various chiefs would bow; each was absolute over his own followers, and would brook no interference on the part of another leader; and combination of movements among them was rendered impossible by mutual jealousies and mistrusts. Under these circumstances, the war gradually became merely a series of contests between the legal authorities and hordes of banditti, and the wealthy and intelligent part of the population began to look to the standard of Spain as the symbol of order, and there was every prospect that quiet would be gradually restored. The pride of the people had also been flattered by the employment of natives in offices of trust, profit, and honor; in this way the elevation of Don Antonio Perez, a Mexican priest, of great talent, learning, and character, to the high ecclesiastical dignity of Bishop of Puebla, had great effect in reconciling the inferior clergy, hitherto the most determined opponents of European domination. The Spanish troops in

Mexico at this time did not exceed five thousand; there was, however, a large force of native soldiers, who were all well disciplined, and to secure whose fidelity every means consistent with prudence was employed by the government. The most prominent among the officers of this latter force, was Augustin Iturbide, a native of Michoacan, who had elevated himself to the rank of colonel, by his courage, his activity, and his ferocity towards the insurgents; soon after the arrival of Apodaca, however, he had for some reasons retired from the service, and devoted himself to the performance of religious acts, in which his scrupulous perseverance had caused him to be as much esteemed by the people, for the supposed sanctity of his character, as he had been before dreaded on account of its manifest ruthlessness. This was the man, whom the viceroy selected to carry into effect his scheme for maintaining the absolute authority of the king in Mexico.

CHAPTER V.

DON AUGUSTINO ITURBIDE.

Rise of Iturbide—His services in the Spanish cause—Plan of Iguala—O'Donoju—Treaty of Cordova—Iturbide proclaimed emperor—Abdicates—His "Statement"—Returns to Mexico —Arrested and executed—Republican constitution framed.

THIS person was, at the period we have reached, the leading character of his country. When the revolution broke out, he was a lieutenant in the militia of Valladolid, of which province he was a native. He was very handsome, of elegant address, and with polished manners, as well as bold and daring. He was one of the first to look into the nature of the quarrel between Mexico and the mother country, and to adopt the cause of his native land. How this connexion terminated is now a mystery, two stories having been told, the one by Iturbide, that he w disgusted with their projects and refused to participate in them, in spite of the great offers they made him; and the other by the insurgents, that he demanded more than they thought his services worth, so young and so little known as he was. One thing is, however, sure, the insurgents committed a great oversight, as Iturbide would have been an invaluable acquisition at any price. Be this as it may, all negotiations were broken off, and Iturbide joined the troops assembled by the viceroy Vanegas for the defence of Mexico in 1810, and distinguished himself under the orders of Truxillo at Las Cruces. From that moment his rise was rapid, and his knowledge of the country and people rendered his

Don Augustino Iturbide.

services invaluable in every expedition. As a guerilla chieftain his services were important, and he inflicted on the insurgents two of the most important blows they sustained, at Valladolid and Puruaran (where Morelos's army was defeated and Matamoros captured). He never failed but once, which was in the attack on Corporo in 1815 ; when he was foiled, as will be remembered, by one of the ablest men Mexico has yet produced. He was appointed afterwards to a separate command in the Baxio, a rare honor for a creole. In this command he sullied his high reputation by wanton cruelty; writing to the viceroy after a battle he had won at Salvatierra, he says: "In honor of the day (Good Friday) I have just ordered three hundred *excommunicados* to be shot!" Iturbide's friends deny the authenticity of this letter, but the original is said to be in the archives of Mexico. He, however, shared this reproach with almost all who were engaged in that war. He was afterwards recalled for rapacity and extortion, to Mexico, where he remained from 1816 to 1820, when Apodaca again employed him as the fittest agent to overthrow the remnant of the constitution, and sent him to the western coast, at the head of a body of men, with the assistance of whom he was to proclaim the restoration of the king's absolute authority. During his retirement, Iturbide had devoted himself to religious exercises, and extended his intercourse among the clergy, by whom he was highly esteemed, and through whose influence he regained much of the popularity he had destroyed by his cruelty.

In the month of February, 1821, Iturbide left the city of Mexico to take the command of a large native force, ostensibly with a view to act against the insurgents in the south, who, under Guerrero, were again becoming formidable; it is, however, supposed that he was really charged to keep in check the Spanish troops, who were principally collected in that quarter, whilst the viceroy should declare the re-establishment of the authority of the absolute sovereign at the capital.

Thus far, we have stated what appear to have been the facts; the remainder of Iturbide's proceedings are well known. On the 24th of February, 1821, he assembled the chief officers of his army at Iguala, and presented them a set of propositions for the institution of a national government in Mexico, which are termed in the history of that country, *The Plan of Iguala.* The amount of these propositions was:

1. That Mexico should form an independent empire, the crown of which should be offered to the king of Spain, and, in the event of his refusal, to the other princes of his family in succession, on condition that the person accepting should reside in the country, and should swear to observe a constitution to be fixed by a congress;

2. That the Roman Catholic religion should be supported, and the rights, immunities, and property of its clergy should be preserved and secured;

3. That all the actual inhabitants of Mexico, whatever might be their birth-place or descent, should enjoy the same civil rights.

These three propositions were termed *The three Guarantees*, and an army was to be raised for their establishment and defence. This plan is generally supposed to have been drawn up by the heads of the religious congregation of the *Profesa* in Mexico, under the direction of the bishop of Puebla, who was one of the most attached friends of Iturbide; the latter, however, always insisted that he himself had been the sole deviser of it, although he admits that it was shown to and approved by the other persons mentioned.

The proposed arrangements having been agreed to by the officers, were, on the 2d of March following, submitted to the troops, who received them with enthusiasm, and immediately assumed the name and colors of *the Army of the three Guarantees*. Guerrero, soon after, added his forces to those of Iturbide, and they also received an important accession in the person of Guadalupe Victoria, who had for the three years previous wandered in the forests of Vera Cruz without seeing or being seen by a human being. The news of the revolution spread rapidly throughout Mexico. At San Luis Potosi, Colonel Anastasio Bustamente, (afterwards president of the Mexican republic), with his whole regiment, declared in favor of the plan of Iguala; the province of Vera Cruz was in insurrection, and the city was besieged by Don Antonio Lopez de Santa Anna, then a young officer; Puebla, Guanaxuato, Queretaro, Durango, Valladolid, and all the principal places except the capital, were soon in quiet possession of the independents. The Mexicans, indeed, scrupled a little at first at the idea of receiving a Bourbon prince; but they soon became assured, that there was but little prospect of the execution of that part of the plan.

The viceroy, it is believed, was at first inclined to accede to the plan of Iguala; certain it is, that he took no very decided measures to oppose it, and he was on account of his apathy or apparent acquiescence deposed on the 6th of July, by the Spanish troops at the capital, who then placed General Novella at the head of the government. Ere the opposing parties could be brought in presence of each other, General O'Donoju, an old and highly respected officer, arrived at Vera Cruz from

Spain, with the commission of captain-general of Mexico; and seeing at once that all efforts to arrest the revolution by means of the Spanish forces in Mexico would be unavailing, he proposed to treat with Iturbide. This proposition was accepted, and the two generals met at Cordova, about sixty miles from Vera Cruz, on the 24th of August. The result of their conference was a treaty signed on the day of their meeting, by which the captain general recognised the independence of the Mexican empire upon the basis contained in the plan of Iguala: and it was agreed, that two commissioners should instantly be sent to Spain, to communicate it to the government of that country, and to offer the crown of Mexico as therein arranged. It was also agreed, that a junta should instantly be appointed, which should select persons to form a regency for the administration of the affairs of the empire, until the arrival of the sovereign, and that a cortes should be convened for the purpose of forming a constitution; moreover, that the army of the three guarantees should occupy the capital and strong places, and that the Spanish troops should, as soon as possible, be sent out of the country.

The independence of Mexico may be considered as commencing on the 24th of August, 1821, when this treaty of Cordova was signed by the highest legitimate Spanish authority in the country on the one hand, and on the other, by the person actually possessing the supreme power over it, by the will of the great majority of its inhabitants. Agreeably to its terms, the commissioners were immediately sent to Spain, the Spanish troops were withdrawn to places assigned for their reception, and the army of the three guarantees entered the capital on the 27th of September. On that same day, the junta was formed, its members being all chosen by the general-in-chief; this board immediately elected the bishop of Puebla as its president, drew up a manifesto to the nation which was issued on the 13th of October, summoned a cortes of the empire to meet in February following, and appointed a regency, the presidency of which was, of course, conferred upon Iturbide. This daring man was, at the same time, made generalissimo of all the forces, and invested with almost regal powers and dignities, for the support of which he was to receive one hundred and twenty thousand dollars per annum. O'Donoju could not survive the mortification of being obliged to countenance these proceedings, by which his country was robbed of its most valuable possessions, and on the 8th of October he died in the city of Mexico.

Iturbide now employed himself diligently, in preparing the Mexicans for receiving him as the chief of the nation. With this view, he did all in his power to ingratiate himself with the aristocracy, the clergy, and the army, sedulously separating himself from those by whom the war of independence had been maintained. His plans for the organization of the congress, were however, not accepted by the junta; instead of two houses, but one was allowed, composed of deputies elected by the people; it was, however, arranged, that those provinces which sent more than four members, should choose one ecclesiastic, one military man, and one lawyer.

The Mexican cortes or congress, thus constituted, met at the capital on the 24th of February, 1822; and ere they began their operations, an oath was taken by each member, separately, to support the provisions of the plan of Iguala. Notwithstanding this oath, however, they were soon divided into three parties; *the Republicans*, anxious to adopt a system similar to that of the

United States; the *Bourbonists*, in favor of the exact execution of the plan of Iguala; and the *Iturbidists*, who wished their idol to be elevated at once to the throne. The Republicans and the Bourbonists united against the third party, and the discussions became violent.

While these things were going on in Mexico, the Spanish cortes had, among other serious matters, been deliberating on the measures which should be adopted with regard to America, and various plans of pacification were proposed. At length arrived the news of the insurrectionary movement at Iguala, and afterwards, the commissioners who were empowered to offer the crown of the Mexican empire to the king and the other members of the royal family. How these propositions were likely to be received by the cortes, may be easily imagined; the convention of Cordova between Iturbide and O'Donoju was declared void, and orders were sent to the representatives of Spain, in other countries, to protest against any recognition of the independence of Mexico. It was also resolved, that efforts should be made for the preservation or recovery of the American possessions, by reinforcing the Spanish troops in those countries; this resolution could, however, only be regarded as an energetic expression of opinion on the part of the cortes, as not a man nor a dollar could then have been spared from the kingdom, torn by internal disturbances, and threatened by foreign enemies.

These determinations of the cortes, taken on the 12th of February, 1822, were made known in Mexico in April following, where they excited considerable sensation. In anticipation of such replies to the propositions made agreeably to the plan of Iguala, Iturbide had been employing every means in his power, to create a strong feeling in his favor among the people, as well as in the army. The congress, however, were in general opposed to him, and many of its members wished to retire, in order to avoid the scenes which they saw must follow. The crisis at length took place on the 18th of May, when the army and the people of the capital proclaimed Iturbide emperor of Mexico, and the remaining deputies of the congress sanctioned the choice by a decree. On the following day, the regency resigned its powers, the new emperor took the oath to support the independence, religion, and constitution of Mexico, and was installed in the ancient palace of the viceroys, under the title of Augustin the First.

It may be supposed, that this choice was not hailed with universal satisfaction, and that the old chiefs of the insurgents, who had for so many years been submitting to dangers and miseries, could scarcely by pleased to see one of their most bitter persecutors raised to supreme power over them in a moment. Accordingly, Guerrero, Bravo, and Guadalupe Victoria, soon prepared to betake themselves to their old haunts, and to reassemble their followers in opposition to the new sovereign; and even Santa Anna, the most ardent partisan of the imperial cause, showed signs of discontent. The congress, too, was loud in its complaints against the extravagance and the despotism of its master; who, having endeavored in vain to quiet this body, by imprisoning some of its members, at length, on the 30th of October, closed its doors, and replaced it by a constituent junta, composed of forty-five persons of his own selection.

The constituent junta, established by Iturbide, did nothing to satisfy the people; and an insurrection broke out in the northern provinces, headed by a man named Garza. This was soon put down by the forces of the government; Iturbide was not, however, equally successful with regard to the second attack made upon his authority. He had conceived suspicions of Santa Anna's fidelity, which induced him to withdraw that officer from his command, and he ordered him to appear at the capital. Santa Anna learned the news of his removal at Jalapa, a city on the road between Mexico and Vera Cruz; and without losing a moment, he set off for the latter place, which he reached before the arrival of the emperor's orders. Assembling the garrison, he harangued them upon the subject of the injustice and despotism of the existing government, and called upon them to aid him in overthrowing it; they received his proposition with joy, and immediately joined him in proclaiming a republic. Santa Anna having then reduced to submission the neighboring towns, marched against Jalapa; from this place, however, he was repulsed by Echavarri, the captain-general of the province, and forced to take refuge for a time in a mountain, overlooking the celebrated royal bridge, thirty miles from Vera Cruz. Here he was joined by Guadalupe Victoria, on whose appearance many flocked to the standard of the insurgents; their success nevertheless remained a matter of doubt, until Echavarri took part with them, and a new *plan* was formed on the 2d of February, 1823, called the *Act of Casas Matas*, by which that of Iguala was entirely superseded.

The Act of Casas Matas, guarantying a republican form of government, was universally adopted, and Iturbide, finding himself deserted by all parties, abdicated the throne on the 19th of March, just ten months after he had first ascended it. He was escorted to the coast near Vera Cruz, and on the 11th of May embarked with his family for Leghorn. No one can suspect Iturbide of cowardice, and what prompted him to abdicate is a mystery which, perhaps, can best be solved by his own statement:

The epoch in which I have lived has been a critical one; equally critical is the moment at which I am about to submit to the world a sketch of my political career. The public are not uninformed of my name, or of my actions; but they have known both through a medium greatly discolored by the interests of those persons who have transmitted them to distant countries. There is one great nation particularly, in which several individuals have disapproved of my conduct, and have misrepresented my character. It becomes my duty, therefore, to relate my own history. I shall tell with the frankness of a soldier, both what I have been and what I am. My actions and their motives may thus be fairly judged by every impartial person of the present age, still more by posterity. I know no other passion or interest save that of transmitting to my children a name which they need not be ashamed to bear.

It would be an idle waste of time to set about refuting the various attacks which have been circulated against me; they are framed in terms calculated only to reflect dishonor upon their authors.

It was my good fortune to break the chains which enthralled my country: I proclaimed her independence: I yielded to the voice of a grateful and a generous people, and allowed myself to be seated on a throne which I had created, and had destined for others; I repressed the spirit of intrigue and disorder. These are my crimes; notwithstanding which I now appear, and shall continue to appear, with as sincere a countenance before the Spaniards and their king, as I have worn before the Mexicans and their new rulers. To both countries I have rendered important services, though neither knew how to profit by the advantages which I acquired for them.

In the year 1810, I was simply a subaltern officer; a lieutenant in the provincial regiment of Valladolid, my native city. It is well known, that the individuals who serve in those troops receive no pay. The military profession was not the principal object of my pursuit. I possessed an independence, and attended to the improvement of my property, without disturbing my mind with the desire of obtaining public employments. I did not stand in need of them, either for the purpose of affording me a subsistence, or of adding distinction to my name, as it pleased Providence to give me an honorable origin, which my forefathers have never stained, and which down to my time all my kinsmen have supported by their conduct.

When the revolution, set on foot by Don Miguel Hidalgo, curate of Dolores, broke out, he offered me the rank of lieutenant-general. The offer was one that might have tempted any young man without experience, and at an age when his ambition might be excited. I declined it, however, because I was satisfied that the plans of the curate were ill contrived, and that they would produce only disorder, massacre, and devastation, without accomplishing the object which he had in view. The result demonstrated the truth of my predictions. Hidalgo, and those who followed his example, desolated the country, destroyed private property, deepened the hatred between the Americans and Europeans, sacrificed thousands of victims, obstructed the fountains of public wealth, disorganized the army, annihilated industry, rendered the condition of the Americans worse than it was before, by exciting the Spaniards to a sense of the dangers which threatened them; they moreover corrupted the manners of the people, and far from obtaining independence, increased the obstacles which were opposed to it.

If, therefore, I took up arms at that epoch, it was not to make war against the Americans, but against a lawless band who harassed the country. The Mexican congress, at a later period, proposed that statues should be erected to the leaders of that insurrection, and that funeral honors should be paid to the ashes of those who perished in it. I have warred with those chiefs, and I should war with them again under similar circumstances. The word insurrection in that instance did not mean independence and equal liberty; its object was, not to reclaim the rights of the nation, but to exterminate all the Europeans, to destroy their possessions, and to trample on the laws of war, humanity, and religion. The belligerent parties gave no quarter: disorder presided over the operations on both sides, though it must be acknowledged, that one party are censurable, not only for the evils which they caused, but also for having provoked the other party to retaliate the atrocities which were perpetrated by their enemies.

About the month of October, in the year 1810, I was offered a safe conduct for my father and family, together with assurances that his property and mine should be exempted from conflagration and plunder, and that the people attached to them should not be subject to assassination (which was at that time a matter of ordinary occurrence), on the sole condition that I should quit the standard of the king and remain neutral. These propositions were made to me by the leaders of that disastrous insurrection, and are well known to the Mexicans. I was then at San Felipe del Obraje, commanding a small detachment of infantry, and at a distance of four leagues from me was Hidalgo with a considerable force. I gave the same answers to these overtures, as to the propositions already mentioned. I always looked upon that man as criminal, who, in a season of political convulsions, sheltering himself in cowardly indolence, remained a cold spectator of the evils which oppressed his country, and made no effort to mitigate, at least, if he could not remove, the sufferings of his fellow-citizens. I therefore kept the field, with a view equally to serve the king, the Spaniards, and the Mexicans.

I was in consequence engaged in several expeditions, and had the good fortune to see victory never desert the troops under my command, except on one inconsiderable occasion (in 1815), when I made an attack on Coporo, a military point which was well fortified, and inaccessible from the nature of the ground. I then served under the orders of Llanos, a Spanish general. He commanded me to attack the place; delicacy forbade me to offer any opposition to his mandate, though I was fully convinced that the result could not be favorable. As soon as I was on the march, I communicated my opinion to the general by despatch: I retreated, as I had foreseen I should do, but I had the good fortune to preserve four-fifths of my force, in an action in which I apprehended that I should have lost the whole.

I engaged with the enemy as often as he offered battle, or as I came near him, frequently with inferior numbers on my part. I led the sieges of several fortified places, from which I dislodged the enemy, and I rendered them incapable of serving afterwards as asylums for the discontented. I had no other opponents than those of the cause which I defended, nor any other rivals than those who were envious of my success.

In 1816 the provinces of Guanajuato and Valladolid, and the army of the north were under my command; but I resigned my office through a sense of delicacy, and retired to pursue my natural disposition, in the cultivation of my estates. The reason of my resignation was this: two inhabitants of Queretaro, who were subsequently assisted by four or five families in Guanajuato, three of which consisted of the families of three brothers, and ought therefore to be considered as one, sent a memorial against me to the viceroy. Many were the crimes of which they accused me; they could not, however, find one witness to support their charges, though I had resigned for the purpose of removing every obstacle to their coming forward, by taking away the motives of hope on the one side, or of fear on the other. The families of the countess dowager of Rul, and of Alaman, gave proof, by abandoning the accusation, that they had been taken by surprise, and that they had been deceived. The viceroys, Calleja and Apodaca, took cognizance of the matter, and after hearing the reports of the Ayuntamientos, the curates, the political chiefs, the commandants and military chiefs, and of all the most respectable persons in the two provinces, and the army (who not only made my cause their own, but gave me tokens of their unqualified approbation), they affirmed the dictamen of their auditor, and of the two civil ministers, declaring that the accusation was false and calumnious in all its parts, that I had permission to institute an action of damages against the slanderers, and that I might return to discharge the functions of the office which I had resigned. I did not choose to resume the command, nor to exercise my right of action, and I gave up the pay which I enjoyed.

The ingratitude which I experienced from men had

wounded my feelings deeply; their insincerity, to call it by no severer name, made me shun every opportunity of again becoming the object of their attacks. Besides, the anger of the contending parties having expended itself, and the country having returned to a state of comparative tranquillity, I was relieved from that sense of obligation which six years before had compelled me to have recourse to arms. My country no longer stood in need of my services, and without betraying my duty, I thought that I might now rest from the toils of the camp.

In 1820 the constitution was re-established in Spain The new order of things, the ferment in which the Peninsula was placed, the machinations of the discontented, the want of moderation amongst the supporters of the new system, the vacillation of the authorities, and the conduct of the government and cortes at Madrid (who, from the decrees which they issued, and the speeches which some of the deputies pronounced, appeared to have determined on alienating the colonies), filled the heart of every good patriot with the desire of independence, and excited amongst the Spaniards established in the country, the apprehension that all the horrors of the former insurrection were about to be repeated. Those who exercised the chief authority, and had the forces at their command, took such precautions as fear naturally dictated; and those persons who at the former epoch had lived by disorder, made preparations for again turning it to advantage. In such a state of things the richest and most beautiful part of America was about to become again the prey of contending factions. In every quarter clandestine meetings took place, for the purpose of discussing the form of government which ought to be adopted.

Among the Europeans, and their adherents, some wished for the establishment of the Spanish constitution. They succeeded in realizing their views to a certain extent, but the system was badly understood, and the loose manner in which it was obeyed, indicated the shortness of its duration. There were some who conceived that it ought to undergo modifications, inasmuch as the constitution framed by the cortes at Cadiz was inapplicable to "New Spain." Others there were who sighed after the old absolute government, as the best support of their lucrative employments, which they exercised in a despotic manner, and by which they had gained a monopoly. The privileged and powerful classes fomented these different parties, attaching themselves to the one or the other, according to the extent of their political information, or the projects of aggrandizement which their imaginations presented. The Americans wished for independence, but they were not agreed as to the mode of effecting it, still less as to the form of government which they should prefer. With respect to the former object, many were of opinion that in the first place, all the Europeans should be exterminated, and their property given up to confiscation. The less sanguinary would have been contented with banishing them from the country, thus reducing thousands of families to a state of orphanage. The moderate party suggested only that they should be excluded from all public offices, and degraded to the condition in which they had kept the natives of the country for three centuries. As to the form of government, one party proposed a monarchy, tempered by the Spanish, or some other constitution; a second party wished for a federative republic; a third for a central republic; and the partisans of each system, full of enthusiasm, were impatient for the accomplishment of their different objects.

I had friends in the principal towns, many of whom had been long connected with my family; others I had known in my expeditions, and during the period when I held my command. The army, I had reason to believe, was strongly attached to me. All those who knew me did their utmost to supply me with information. I had visited the best provinces, obtained accurate information as to the nature of the country and the character of the inhabitants, the points capable of being fortified, and the resources upon which dependence might be placed. I saw new revolutions on the eve of breaking out; my country was about to be drenched in blood; I was led to believe that I had the power to save her, and I did not hesitate to undertake so sacred a duty.

I formed my plan, known under the title of "the plan of Iguala." A pamphlet, which I have seen, has asserted that that project was the work of a club of serviles, who held their meeting at the *profesa*, a building belonging to the congregation of St. Philip, in Mexico. Any person who reads the document must be convinced, from its contents alone, that it could not have been dictated by servilism; I put out of the question the opinions of those persons to whom it is attributed, and shall only say that they are matters upon which the multitude is very commonly mistaken. For me, I look upon those persons as men eminently respectable for their virtues and their knowledge. After the plan had been drawn out, I consulted upon it with distinguished individuals of different parties; not one of them disapproved of it; it was not modified in any manner; nothing was added or erased.

In tracing out this project, my aim was to give independence to my country, because such was the general desire of the Americans; a desire founded on natural feelings, and on principles of justice. It was, besides, the only means by which the interests of the two nations could be secured. The Spaniards would not allow themselves to be convinced that their decline began with their acquisition of the colonies, while the colonists were fully persuaded that the time of their emancipation had arrived.

The plan of Iguala guarantied the religion which we inherited from our ancestors. To the reigning family of Spain, it held out the only prospect which survived for preserving those extensive and fertile provinces. To the Mexicans, it granted the right of enacting their own laws, and of having their government established within their own territory. To the Spaniards, it offered an asylum, which, if they had possessed any foresight, they would not have despised. It secured the rights of equality, of property, and of liberty, the knowledge of which is within the reach of every one, and the possession of which, when once acquired, every man would exert all his power to preserve. The plan of Iguala extinguished the odious distinction of castes, offered to every stranger safety, convenience, and hospitality; it left the road to advancement open to merit; conciliated the good opinion of every reasonable man; and opposed an impenetrable barrier to the machinations of the discontented.

The operation of putting the plan into execution was crowned with the happy result which I had anticipated. Six months were sufficient to untwist the entangled knot which had bound the two worlds. Without bloodshed, without fire, robbery, devastation, without a tear, my country was free, and transformed from a colony into an empire. In order to render the work conformable to received customs, only one additional circumstance was required—a treaty, which the diplomatists would add to the long catalogue of those which they already possess, and which commonly turn out to be only so many proofs of the bad faith of men, as they are not seldom violated when it is the interest of one of the parties, and he happens to be the strongest. Nevertheless, it is right to follow the laws of custom. On the 24th of August, I had an interview with that most worthy Spanish general, Don Juan de O Donoju; and on the same day was concluded between us a treaty, which bears the name of the place where it was signed, and was sent off to his majesty, Ferdinand VII., by an officer of O Donoju's suit.

The treaty of Cordova opened to me the gates of the capital, which otherwise I could have forced. But it is always delightful to me to be spared the necessity of exposing my men, and of shedding the blood of those who had been my companions in arms.

There were persons who raised questions on the treaty of Cordova, by doubting my authority, as well as that of O Donoju, to enter into a compact upon a matter of so much delicacy. It would be easy to answer them, by saying that in me was deposited the will of the Mexican people at that period; in the first place, because that which I signed in their name was conformable to what they must have desired; and secondly, because they had already given proofs of their sentiments; such as were able to bear arms, by joining me, and others by assisting me in every way which lay in their power. In every place through which I passed, I was received in the most enthusiastic manner. Seeing that no one was forced to exhibit these demonstrations, it is to be inferred that they approved of my intentions, and that their ideas accorded with mine. With respect to General O Donoju, he was the principal authority furnished with credentials from his government, and even though he might not have received specific instructions for that particular case, the circumstances authorized him to do the best he could for his country.

Had this general commanded an army superior to mine, and possessed resources sufficient to enable him to carry on war against me, he might have properly refused to sign the treaty of Cordova, without first communicating with his government, and receiving its answer. But attended as he was with scarcely a dozen officers, the whole country being in my power, his mission being adverse to the sentiments of the people, unable to procure intelligence of the state of things, without any knowledge of the localities, shut up in a weak fortress, which was exposed to our fire, with an army in front of him, and the few troops of the king who had remained in Mexico, commanded by an intrusive chief; under such circumstances, let those persons who disapprove of the conduct of O Donoju say what they would have done if they had been in his place, or what they imagine he ought to have done? He must have signed the treaty of Cordova, or have become my prisoner, or have returned to Spain! he had no other alternative. If he had chosen either of the latter, all his countrymen would have been compromised, and the government of Spain would have lost every hope of those advantages which it then obtained; advantages which it never would have acquired, if I had not been in the command, and if O Donoju had not been an able politician as well as a faithful Spaniard.

I entered Mexico on the 27th of September, 1821;

on the same day was installed the junta of government which is spoken of in the plan of Iguala, and the treaty Cordova. It was nominated by me, but not according to my arbitrary choice; for I wished to assemble together such men of every party, as enjoyed the highest reputation amongst their friends. This was the only means which could be resorted to in such extraordinary circumstances for consulting the public opinion.

Up to this point my measures gained general approbation, and in no instance were my hopes deceived. But as soon as the junta began to exercise its functions, it perverted the powers which had been granted to it; and within a few days after its installation, I saw what was likely to be the issue. From that moment I shuddered for the fate that awaited my fellow-citizens. It was in my power to resume the whole authority, and I asked myself, ought I not to resume it, if such a step be essential to the safety of my country? I considered, however, that it would have been rash in me to resolve on undertaking such an enterprise, relying solely on my own judgment. If I were to consult with others, my design might transpire, and intentions, which had sprung solely from my love for my country, and from a desire to promote its happiness, might be attributed to ambitious views, and construed into a violation of my promise. Besides, even if I were to accomplish everything which I proposed, I could not have done it without infringing on the plan of Iguala, which it was my great object to maintain, because I looked upon it as the ægis of the public welfare. These were the true reasons which, together with others of less importance, restrained me from taking any decisive measures. They would have brought me into collision with the favorite feelings of the cultivated nations of the world, and have rendered me, for some time, an object of hatred to a set of men, who were infatuated by chimerical ideas, and who had never learned, or had soon forgotten, that the republic which was most jealous of its liberty, possessed also its dictators. I may add, that I have always endeavored to be consistent in my principles; and as I had proposed to form a junta, I fulfilled my promise, and was reluctant to undo the work of my own hands.

There were at this time some deputies in Mexico who set little value on the public happiness, when it is opposed to their private interest, and who had acquired reputation by some actions that appeared generous to those who were benefited by them without knowing the secret views by which they had been prompted. They were well acquainted with the mysteries of intrigue, ever ready to stoop to servility when they found it expedient, and to assume insolence when their star was in the ascendant. These men disliked me because I had hitherto been successful in my career, and they began to foment those parties which were afterwards known under the titles of Republicans and Bourbonists, and which, however they differed on other points, were united in their opposition to me.

The republicans were hostile to me, because they well knew they could never bring me to contribute to the establishment of a government, which, whatever might be its attractions, did not suit the Mexicans. Nature produces nothing by sudden leaps; she operates by intermediate degrees. The moral world follows the laws of the physical. To think that we could emerge all at once from a state of debasement, such as that of slavery, and from a state of ignorance, such as had been inflicted upon us for three hundred years, during which we had neither books nor instructors, and the possession of knowledge had been thought a sufficient cause for persecution; to think that we could gain information and refinement in a moment, as if by enchantment; that we could acquire every virtue, forget prejudices, and give up false pretensions, was a vain expectation, and could only have entered into the visions of an enthusiast.

The Bourbonists, on the other hand, wished for my fall, because as soon as the decision of the government of Madrid was made known, through its decree of the 13th of February, which was subsequently transmitted by the minister for the colonies, and in which the conduct of O Donoju was formally disapproved, the treaty of Cordova became null and void, as to that part of it which invited the Bourbons to the crown of Mexico, and effective with respect to the nation's entering into the full enjoyment of its right to elect as sovereign the individual whom it would deem most worthy of that high office. The Bourbonists, therefore, no longer expecting that a Bourbon would reign in Mexico, thought only of our returning to our former state of dependence; a retrogression which was impossible, considering the impotence of the Spaniards, and the determination of the Americans.

Hence I became the object of attack to both these parties, because as I had the public force at my command, and was the centre of general opinion, it was necessary to the preponderance of either party that I should cease to exist.

The leaders of the factions spared no pains to gain proselytes; and certainly they found many to adhere to them. Some who were the least experienced, suffered themselves to be easily led away; because they saw nothing more in the projects on foot than what was represented to them, and there is no design of which different views may not be given; some hoped that by the subversion of the government they might advance their own fortunes; and others, the natural enemies of established order, in whatever system it prevails, were anxious only for a change. Among the latter, one might be named who values himself on his literary accomplishments, and has made himself conspicuous in the revolution.*

The first duty of the junta after its installation, was to frame the Convocatoria, or proclamation for the assemblage of a congress, which was to give a constitution to the monarchy. The junta took more time to perform this duty than the urgency of the case permitted, and committed several errors in framing the convocatoria. It was extremely defective, but with all its imperfections it was accepted; I could do no more than perceive the evil, and lament it. The census of the provinces was not consulted; hence, for instance, one deputy was appointed for a province containing a hundred thousand inhabitants, and four for a province scarcely peopled by half that number. Nor did it at all enter into the calculations of the junta, that the representatives ought to be in proportion to the civilization of the represented. Three or four individuals might be easily selected from among a hundred well-educated citizens, who might possess the qualifications necessary to constitute good deputies; whilst among a thousand, who are without education, and are ignorant of the first rudiments, scarcely one man can be met with of sufficient ability to know what is conducive to the public walfare—whose mind is sufficiently enlarged to take

* The individual here referred to is probably Don Lucas Alaman.

accurate views of public affairs, or at least to save him from extravagant errors respecting them; who has sufficient firmness of character to vote according to what he thinks best, and not to deviate from his opinion when once convinced of its truth; and whose experience enables him to perceive the grievances which afflict his province, as well as the remedy which they require. For, although that remedy might not always be within his reach, such experience would enable him, on hearing others proposed, to form a sound judgment upon them.

These defects were quite sufficient to extinguish every hope, that any benefits would be derived from the convocatoria of the junta. It had many other faults which I have not mentioned, as I do not mean to comment upon them. But there is one which I cannot pass over in silence, that of having the deputies nominated at the will, not of a district (*partido*), for that would be of a majority of the citizens, but of the Ayuntamientos of the principal towns. See the injury thus done to the country people at large! In the elections a vote was given by the junta, to the electors, chosen by the country people; and a voice was also given to the individuals who composed the Ayuntamiento of the principal town of each department. But in electing the Ayuntamientos, it was possible to get into them by a little management, as was in fact frequently done; because the wish of aspiring to the functions of these bodies, was not so general as the ambition of obtaining a seat in congress. The Ayuntamientos were, therefore, filled up at their own pleasure, and were consequently vitiated; and as all the members possessed a vote in the elections for deputies, the Ayuntamientos became almost the only electors. This is evident to any one who knows how thinly the population is distributed over that country, and how great a disproportion exists between the number of inhabitants in a town, and in its dependencies.

To render this clearer, let it be supposed that a principal town of a province contains four, eight, or ten thousand inhabitants, leaving out of the question the city of Mexico, the population of which exceeds one hundred and seventy thousand souls, and other cities densely inhabited. The Ayuntamiento of such a town consists, perhaps, of fifty or sixty members; the departments which have to send electors to the principal town, name no more than eight or ten. This small number, therefore, acting in conjunction with all the members of the Ayuntamiento, is reduced to a cipher, and the election terminates according to the pleasure of that body. Thus the people were deceived by being told, that in *them* resided the sovereignty, which they were to delegate to the deputies whom they were about to name; when in fact there was no such nomination, except on the part of the Ayuntamiento, or rather, indeed, of the directors of the junta, who, after the dissolution of that body, passed into the congress, in order to continue their manœuvres.

To this system, so framed, was added intrigue in the elections; the most worthy men were not sought for, nor even those who were decided for any particular party. It was quite sufficient if the candidate were my enemy, or so ignorant that he might easily be persuaded to become so. If he possessed either of these requisites, he was deemed competent to discharge the sacred functions which were to be intrusted to him.

If the archives of state have not been spoliated, remonstrances may be found amongst them from almost all the provinces, pointing out the nullity of the powers conferred on the deputies. Several individuals were elected who had been accused of conduct notoriously scandalous; some had been prosecuted as criminals: others were men of broken fortunes, tumultuous demagogues, officers who had capitulated, and who, violating the laws of war and their paroles, had again taken up arms against the cause of liberty, and after suffering defeat had surrendered a second time. Some of the new deputies were obstinate anti-independents, and one was an apostate monk, although by law no member of the religious orders could have a seat in congress. The authors of the remonstrances offered also to prove, that the rules for the conduct of the elections, as they were laid down in the convocatoria, had been infringed; and that the persons returned were not those whom the majority approved, but those who were the most skilful in intrigue. These documents were all sent to my department, when I was generalissimo and admiral-in-chief; when I became emperor, I directed them to be transmitted to the department of the interior, for the purpose of being deposited in the archives. I did not wish to lay them before the congress, because even if justice were done, which could hardly be expected, I saw that they would be productive only of odium, and of legal prosecutions. I considered that time would be lost in new elections, as it would be necessary to have the most of them renewed, and I felt that our most important care was first to organize the government. Besides, I thought that the errors into which this congress might fall, might be corrected by that which should succeed it. This mode of reasoning, which would have been questionable perhaps under any other circumstances, was suitable to those which then existed, because the object was to avoid greater evils.

The result of the elections, therefore, was the formation of a congress, perfectly comfortable to the wishes of the party who influenced its nomination. A few men of undoubted virtue and wisdom, and of the purest patriotism, whose fair reputation was so widely extended that no machinations could prevent them from having a majority of suffrages, found themselves confounded with a multitude of intriguers, of assuming manners and sinister intentions. I do not desire to be credited on my mere assertions; examine the acts of the congress during the eight months that elapsed from its installation until its suspension. The principal object of its assembling was to draw up a constitution for the empire: not a single line of it was written. In a country, naturally the richest in the world, the treasury was exhausted; there were no funds to pay the army or the public functionaries; there was no revenue, not even a system of finance established, as that which had existed in the time of the Spanish rule had been abolished, without any other system having been substituted for it. The congress would not occupy itself in matters of such essential importance, notwithstanding the repeated and urgent solicitations which I made to it in person, and through the secretaries of state. The administration of justice was wholly neglected; in the changes which had taken place some of the officers had left the empire, some died, others had embraced new avocations, and the offices and tribunals were nearly deserted. Upon this subject also the congress declined to take any steps: in short, although the empire was in the weakness of infancy, and wanted their assistance at every point, they did nothing. The speeches which were pronounced, turned on matters of the most trifling description, and if any of them happened to touch on topics deserving of consideration, they were, to say the least of them, foreign to the exigencies of the moment. What honors should be paid to the chiefs of the insurrection who had fallen? What should be the form for the oath of an archbishop? Who ought to nominate the supreme tribunal of justice? Such, together with a demand for an apostate friar who was a prisoner in the castle of San Juan de Ulua, and other similar subjects, formed the grave occupations of a body so august in its institution! Add to this, that not a single regulation was made for the government of the interior. The result was, that the congress became the opprobrium of the people, and fell into a state of abject contempt. The public prints exposed its defects, and even one of the deputies stated his opinion that it stood in need of reformation.

It soon became manifest that the object of those who gave all its movements to that machine, was only to gain time, and to deceive each other until they found an opportunity, for the arrival of which they secretly labored, in order to throw off the mask. Notwithstanding the cunning which they used, and the dissimulation with which they endeavored to carry out their designs, the people and the army saw through their real views. Neither the army nor the people desired slavery on one hand, or republicanism on the other; nor did they wish to see me deposed, or even in any manner offended, and from these feelings arose that distrust with which the whole nation received all the resolutions that originated in so vitiated a body.

About the month of April, 1822, a state of agitation was observable, which threatened to end in anarchy. A public measure, effected in a scandalous manner, discovered the hypocrisy of its authors. The congress deposed three of the regents, leaving in office with me only one, who was well known to be my enemy, for the purpose of reducing my vote in the executive to a nullity. They did not attempt to depose me, from an apprehension that they would be resisted by the army and the people, of my influence with whom they were well aware. This resolution was passed in the most precipitate and singular manner. The question was proposed, discussed, agreed to, and carried into execution in one sitting, whereas it had been previously settled by decree that every proposition which was submitted to the congress, should be read three times, at three distinct sittings, before it should be discussed. After this step they proposed another; a commission, appointed for that purpose, presented a regulation concerning the regency, in which the command of the army was declared incompatible with the functions of the executive power. They were jealous of my having the soldiery at my disposal: to such men fear was very natural. This regulation, although it did not receive the sanction of the legislature on account of the want of time, left no doubt of the designs which were entertained against me, and was the immediate cause which accelerated the event of the 18th of May. At ten o'clock on that memorable night the people and garrison of Mexico proclaimed me emperor. "Live Agustin the First!" was the universal cry. Instantly, as if all were actuated by the same sentiment, that extensive capital was illuminated; the balconies were decorated, and filled with the most respectable inhabitants, who joyously echoed back the acclamations of the immense crowds of people which thronged all the streets, especially those near the house where I resided. Not one citizen expressed any disapprobation, a decided proof of the weakness of my enemies, and of the universality of the public opinion in my favor. No accident or disorder of any kind occurred. The first impulse of my mind was to go forth and declare my determination not to yield to the wishes of the people. If I restrained myself from appearing before them for that purpose, it was solely in compliance with the counsel of a friend who happened at the moment to be with me. "They will consider it an insult," he had scarcely time to say to me, "and the people know no restraint when they are irritated. You must make this fresh sacrifice to the public good; the country is in danger; remain a moment longer undecided, and you will hear their acclamations turned into death-shouts." I felt it necessary to resign myself to circumstances; and I spent the whole of that night in allaying the general enthusiasm, and persuading the troops to give time for my decision, and in the meanwhile to render oedience to the congress. I went out repeatedly to harangue them, and wrote a short proclamation, which was circulated the following morning, and in which I expressed the same sentiments as those I addressed to the people. I convened the regency, assembled the generals and superior officers, communicated what had occurred by despatch to the president of the congress, and requested him to summon immediately an extraordinary sitting. The regency was of opinion that I ought to yield to public opinion; the superior officers of the army added that such also was their unanimous opinion, that it was expedient I should do so, and that I was not at liberty to act according to my own desires, as I had dedicated myself entirely to my country; that their privations and sufferings would be useless if I persisted in my objections; and that having compromised themselves through me, and having yielded me unqualified obedience, they had a claim to my compliance. They subsequently drew up a memorial which they presented to the congress, requesting it to take this important matter into its consideration. This paper was signed also by the individual who subsequently officiated as president of the act of Casa-Mata, and by one of the present members of the executive body.

The congress met on the following morning; the people crowded to the galleries and the entrance to the chamber: their applauses were incessant; a joyous agitation was observable in every face; the speeches of the deputies were interrupted by the impatience of the multitude. It is difficult to obtain order in moments like these; but such an important discussion required it, and in order to attain that object, the congress required that I should be present at the sitting. A deputation was appointed, who communicated the invitation to me. I declined it, because as they were about to treat of me personally, my presence might be considered as a restraint on the freedom of debate, and an impediment to the clear and frank expression of each individual's opinion. The deputation and several general officers, however, prevailed on me to accept the invitation, and I immediately went out in order to proceed to the place where the congress was assembled. The streets were scarcely passable, so crowded were they with the inhabitants of the capital; they took the horses from my carriage, and I was drawn by the people, and amidst their enthusiastic acclamations, to the palace of the congress. On entering the hall where the deputies were assembled, the *vivas* were still more enthusiastic, and resounded from every quarter.

The question of the nomination was discussed, and there was not a single deputy who opposed my accession to the throne. The only hesitation expressed by a few, arose from a consideration that their powers were not extensive enough to authorize them to decide on the question. It appeared to them that it would be necessary to notify the subject to provinces, and to require from them an enlargement of powers already granted, or new powers specifically applicable to this case alone. I supported this opinion, as it afforded me an opportunity of finding out some means for evading the acceptance of a situation which I was most anxious to decline. But the majority were of a contrary opinion, and I was elected by seventy-seven voices against fifteen. These latter did not deny me their suffrages; they confined themselves simply to the expression of their belief, that the provinces ought to be consulted, since they did not think their powers ample enough, but at the same time they said that they were persuaded that their constituents would agreed with the majority, and think that what was done was in every respect conducive to the public welfare. Mexico never witnessed a day of more unmixed satisfaction; every order of the inhabitants testified it. I returned home as I had proceeded to the congress, my carriage drawn by the people, who crowded around to congratulate me, expressing the pleasure which they felt on seeing their wishes fulfilled.

The intelligence of these events was transmitted to the provinces by express, and the answers which successively came from each of them, not only expressed approbation of what had been done, without the dissent of a single town, but added that it was precisely what they desired, and that they would have expressed their wishes long before, if they had not considered themselves precluded from doing so by the plan of Iguala and the treaty of Cordova, to which they had sworn. I received also the congratulations of an individual who commanded a regiment, and exercised great influence over a considerable part of the country. He told me that his satisfaction was so much the greater, as he was anxious to avoid making himself remarkable; but, at the same time, that he had made arrangements for proclaiming me, in case it had not been done in Mexico.

The authors of the libels which have been written against me, have not passed over the occurrences of the 18th and 19th of May, amidst which they represent me as acting the part of an ambitious tyrant, attributing the proceedings which took place to secret management on my part, and the intrigues of my friends. I feel assured that they never can prove the truth of these assertions, and that they will receive no credit from those who know, that on my entry into Mexico, on the 27th of September, as well as on my swearing to our independence, on the 27th of October, it was likewise generally wished that I should be proclaimed emperor. If I was not so proclaimed at that time, it was because I did not wish it, and it was with no small difficulty that I prevailed on those who were then raising the shout, to desist from their purpose.

If, as has been imputed to me, I at that time conceived any intention of assuming the crown, I should not have declared the very reverse in the plan of Iguala, adding this difficulty to those with which the enterprise was already attended. Nay, if that plan had been framed for the purpose of deluding the country, as some persons have been pleased to assert, what reason was there for repeating the same clause in the treaty of Cordova, when I was under no necessity of dissembling?

If even up to that period I wished for some particular cause to conceal my design, what occasion could I have found more favorable to its accomplishment than the 27th of September and the 27th of October, in that year? The whole empire was then actually ruled by my voice; there were no troops except those which were under my command; I was generalissimo of the army; the soldiers were all attached to me, and the people called me their liberator; no enemy threatened me on any side, and there were no longer any Spanish troops in the country. The cabinet of Madrid had not an individual throughout all New Spain, to whom it could address its decrees; the exertions of that court did not alarm me, as I was not ignorant of the extent to which they could reach. If I did not grasp the sceptre at a time when I not only could have been emperor, but had to vanquish a thousand difficulties in order to prevent being so, how can it be said that I obtained it afterwards only by intrigue and cabal?

It has been asserted also, that there was not sufficient freedom in the congress for my election, inasmuch as I was present while it was carried on. It has been already seen that I attended because the congress itself invited me. That the galleries did not allow the deputies to deliver their sentiments is untrue; each member, who chose to rise, expressed his opinion without more than some few interruptions, which always happens where matter of such importance is under deliberation, without the decrees so discussed, being therefore considered less binding than those which are passed at a secret sitting. It has been further alleged that some superior officers accompanied me on that occasion. The office which I then held, and the object for which I had been invited to attend, required that I should have around me those to whom I could communicate my orders in case of necessity. However vehemently they may assert that my retinue imposed restraint on the congress, the very persons who state this are convinced that it is not true. Four aides-de-camp and the commanding officer of my escort accompanied my suite; besides these I saw six or eight captains and subalterns, who were first mingled with the crowd that thronged the entrance of the hall; these did not go in with me, and were, therefore, no more than so many spectators, wishing to gratify their curiosity; but neither the latter nor the former, neither the soldiers nor the people, said or did anything which could be construed to menace, or in any manner restrain the congress, even if it had been composed of the most timid characters, and had been electing the weakest of mankind. It is equally false that the hall had been filled with the people, and that the deputies were confounded amongst them. Unfortunately this has been affirmed by the congress itself; thus proving that it was composed of men as changeable as they were weak, who were not ashamed to declare in the face of the world, that they voted under the influence of fear against their conscientious opinions, on a question of the gravest importance which could be presented for their deliberation. What confidence can the provinces repose in them? What duties can be confided to their care with the hope of an auspicious result? What laws can be dictated by a legislature devoid of probity? And what opinion can be formed of a body which has no firmness, and blushes not to proclaim its servility? I should have considered as a libeller, any man who said that the congress had not acted from its own free will; but as it has itself declared the same thing, and as I am not in a situation to give judgment on the matter, those who have heard both sides will decide according to what appears to them, and posterity, I doubt not, will form an opinion of that assembly little honorable to its reputation.

It has been further alleged that the number of deputies present was not sufficient to give validity to the election. Ninety-four attended, one hundred and sixty-two was the total number for that portion of the empire which was previously called the viceroyalty of Mexico; from the kingdom of Guatemala which was subsequently added to it, deputies could not be received, because in some of the districts the elections were carried on conformably to the Spanish constitution, and in others according to a particular convocatoria which they framed. An exception must also be made as to the deputies who were to have come for the provinces of San Salvador, who are included in the calculation of my adversaries, but who ought not to be enumerated, because that country had declared a government independent of Mexico. However, taking even the twenty-four deputies for Guatemala into account, the total number would be one hundred and eighty-two, the half of which is ninety-one. The sitting was attended by ninety-four deputies, although only ninety-two voted; whence it follows that allowing all the restrictions which are demanded, there were still the half and one more present, according to the rule of the Spanish constitution, which, it was agreed, should be observed upon this point; although many decrees had the force of law, at the passing of which no more than seventy or eighty deputies had been present. And what will the supporters of the nullification say to the fact, that on the 22d of June, 1822, without any desire on the part of the government, without any extraordinary assemblage of the people which might overawe the deputies, without being pressed for time in their deliberations, without my presence serving as an obstacle, without any agitation in the capital, and the whole garrison being in profound tranquillity, the congress of its own accord resolved, with the entire unanimity of one hundred and nine deputies who were present, that the crown should be hereditary in my family in lineal succession, giving the title of Prince of the Empire to my eldest son, whom they designated as the heir apparent, of Mexican Princes to the rest of my sons, Prince of the Union to my father, and Princess de Iturbide to my sister? They also prescribed the regulations for my inauguration, and all this they did without its having been preceded, or attended, by any of those causes which compelled them, as they alleged, to join in the first acclamation. I mention this, not for the purpose of establishing rights, which I have renounced with the most perfect good will, but to answer the cavils which have been thrown out against me, and to show the bad faith with which I have been treated.

In order to avoid murmurs, I did not, after my election, bestow those favors which are usually lavished on such occasions. It is not true that I distributed money, or that I gave away any appointments, except that of a captain to a sergeant, not for his having contributed to my elevation, but because he bore the best character in his regiment, and I wished to give the soldiers a proof of my attachment for them, by promoting an individual whom they considered worthy of a superior rank.

I have already frequently said, and I cannot too often repeat it, that I accepted the crown only with the view to serve my country, and to save it from anarchy. I was well persuaded that my personal situation was anything but improved; that I should be persecuted by envy; that the measures which I could not avoid adopting, would dissatisfy many; that it was impossible to please all; that I was about to clash with a body which was full of ambition and pride, and which, at the very moment it was declaiming against despotism, labored to concentrate within its own circle all the power of the state, leaving the monarch reduced to a mere phantom and assuming to itself not only the enactment, but the administration and execution of the laws; a tyranny which is always more intolerable when in the hands of a numerous body, than when deposited in those of a single individual. The Mexicans would have been less free than the inhabitants of Algiers, if the congress had carried all its designs into effect. At one time or other they will be undeceived; may it not be so late as that the difficulties which surround them shall be found insuperable! I was well aware that I was about to become the slave of business; that the duties which I undertook would not be looked upon with a favorable eye by all parties; and that by a fate which some would consider fortunate, but which I would have always avoided if it were possible, I was about to abandon everything which I had inherited and acquired, and with which my children would have been enabled to live independently, wherever they chose.

Upon my accession to the throne, it appeared as if all dissensions had subsided into repose. But the fire, though latent, continued to burn; the different parties, though they dissembled for a short time, still carried on their machinations; and the conduct of the congress became the scandal of the people. I repeatedly received information of clandestine meetings, which were held by several deputies, for the purpose of devising the subversion of the government—a government, be it remembered, that was sworn to by the whole nation, which solemn act was performed in different provinces solely upon the intelligence being transmitted through private letters, without waiting for official advices. The conspirators were fully aware that they were proceeding in direct contradiction to the general will; and, in order to have a pretext for their treasons, they found it necessary to propagate a report that I was desirous of becoming an absolute monarch. Not a single reason did they ever allege in proof of such an accusation. Indeed, how could they bring any proof against one who twice refused to accept the crown that was offered him; who, at a time when he knew no rival in the opinion of the people or army, not only did not seek to preserve the unlimited power which he had obtained, but dismembered and parted with it? When I entered Mexico, my will was law; I commanded the public forces; the tribunals possessed no attributes, save those which emanated from my authority. Could I be more absolute? And who compelled me to divide my power? I, and I alone; because I considered it just. *Then*, at least, I did not wish to be absolute; could I have desired it afterwards? How can they reconcile my adoption of such opposite extremes?

The true cause of the conduct pursued by the congress is that this machine was set in motion by the impulse received from its directors; and these persons saw with secret aversion, that I achieved the independence of the country, without the assistance of any one of them; whereas they desired that everything should be ascribed to themselves. Although they had not the resolution to act in the season of peril, they sought to render themselves conspicuous by deluding the multitude with schoolboy disputations, and by setting themselves up as sages to whom the ignorant were to look up with reverential respect!

In the meantime, so many denunciations, complaints, and remonstrances, reached my hands, that I could not avoid attending to them, both because the public tranquillity and safety were exposed to danger, and because documents of the same description were sent to me by the different departments of government; and if any misfortune occurred (and misfortunes of the most formidable kind were on the eve of happening), I should have been responsible to the nation and the world.

I resolved, therefore, on proceeding against those who were implicated, as I was authorized to do by the attributes which I possessed; if any person dispute their extent, he may see them defined in the 170th article of the Spanish constitution, which so far was in force. On the 26th of August, I ordered the apprehension of the deputies who were comprised in the denunciations, and charged with being conspirators. In order to see if that charge were founded on circumstances sufficient, in point of law, to sustain it, and whether I had reason to urge me to take a step which has been called violent and despotic, reference must be made to the report of the fiscal of the *sumaria*, which was approved in all its parts by the council of state.

The congress demanded, in an imperious manner, that the deputies should be given up to them, and required to be informed of the causes of their detention, in order that they might be tried by the tribunal of cortes. I resisted giving them up until the sumaria was concluded, and until it was decided by what tribunal they were to be tried. I could not agree that they should be sent before the tribunal just mentioned, which was composed of individuals of the congress, who were suspected of being connected with the conspiracy. They were, besides, partial members of an assembly, the majority of which was in bad repute; and which, amongst other proofs of its bad faith, had treated with indifference the disclosures which I had made to it on the 3d of April, respecting the secret manœuvres of some of their own body.

The interval, until the 30th of October, was spent in mutual contention. At that period the discontent of the people increased, and they threatened to put an immediate end to their sufferings which had been so much abused; the public writers repeated their invectives against the congress with more vehemence than ever, and the provinces refused to contribute to the stipends of delegates, who did not discharge the duties intrusted to them. The national representation had already brought itself into contempt, by its apathy in all that related to the public welfare, by its activity in creating evils, by its insufferable insolence, and by its permitting some of its members to maintain in public sittings, that no respect was due to the plan of Iguala, or the treaty of Cordova, although they had sworn to observe both upon their admission into the sanctuary of the laws, and although those documents formed the basis given them by their constituents for the guidance of their conduct.

They endeavored at that time merely to depreciate the plan of Iguala, because they could do no more, while I supported it as the expression of the will of the people. But since my abdication, they have not been content with speaking against it; relying on a mere sophism they have annulled one of its fundamental principles, and under the pretence of doing away with the invitation given to the Bourbons, they have abolished the limited monarchy altogether. What connexion was there between one and the other? On the 8th of April, 1823, the congress passed a decree, in which they declared that the plan of Iguala, and the treaties of Cordova, ceased to have force, as to those parts which referred to the form of government, and the calling in of the Bourbons, and that the nation was fully at liberty to constitute itself. In fact, those documents had already ceased to have force as to that portion which the congress annulled, relating to the invitation given to the Bourbons; but they lost their effect thus far, not because such was the will of the people, when conferring their powers on the deputies, but because the government of Madrid did not choose to ratify the treaty signed by O Donoju, nor to accept the invitation which the Mexicans freely offered to that family. It was not competent to the congress to say that at no time did there exist any right to bind the Mexican nation by any law or treaty, except through the nation itself, or its representatives. For although the proposition, taken by itself, is true, it is false if it be taken with reference to the plan of Iguala and the treaty of Cordova; first, because both were the expression of the general will of the Mexicans, as I have already said, and secondly, because the powers which were conferred on the deputies as well as their oath, were founded on the principles, and supported on the bases, of both these documents. They were instructed by their constituents to organize the government of the empire, as to its fundamental bases, conformably to the plan of Iguala, and the treaty of Cordova. If, therefore, these bases were not conformable to what the public right of every free nation requires, whence did the deputies derive their authority to create a congress, and whence could such a body have received its attributes of legislation? Numerous are the decrees of that assembly, which evince a similar absence of discernment. They might have very properly said that the invitation given to the Bourbons was null, because those princes declined to accept it. But to assert that, therefore, the plan of Iguala and the treaty of Cordova were null, in every part, is the extreme of absurdity. And it is the extreme of ignorance or of malice to add, that the legislative body could not be bound to adhere to the basis of that form of government, which was considered most expedient by those who gave to the congress its existence as a congress. If that assembly had known its duty, and had proceeded with honor and good faith, it would have respected the plan of Iguala as the source of its own authority, and the foundation of the edifice of the state. But it took an opposite course.

For such an abuse of their authority as this, no palliation was sufficient, and no remedy could be found. Such a congress neither could nor ought to continue. This was not only my opinion, but that of every one whom I consulted on the subject, particularly of a meeting which I held publicly in my palace, and to which I summoned such persons as were most distinguished by the respectability of their character, the ministers, the council of state, the generals and other superior officers, and seventy-two deputies.

On the 30th of October, I transmitted a despatch to the president of the congress through a superior officer, informing him that that body had ceased to exist, and without any other formality, without violence or further occurrence of any sort, the congress was closed at noon on that day. No person sympathized with them in their fall; on the contrary, I received congratulations from all quarters, and in consequence of this proceeding I was again called the "Liberator of Anahuac," and "the father of the people."

In order that a body so respectable by its institution should not be entirely wanting to its duty, and lest it should be supposed that I arrogated to myself the power of making the laws, I formed the same day, an assembly which I called the "Instituent Junta," consisting of members of the congress, and selected from all the provinces. They amounted to forty-five in number, exclusive of eight supplemental deputies.

All of these had been elected by their respective provinces, and for all the provinces there were representatives. Their duty was confined to the formation of a new convocatoria, and they exercised the functions of the legislative power only in cases of urgent necessity. They understood that with respect to the convocatoria, they were to avoid those defects which the first junta of government had interwoven in it, and particularly to attend to the rights of the people to whom they were to leave the full measure of their liberty, and whom they were, at the same time, to protect as much as possible from the intrigues and cabals of those who would not hesitate to abuse their simplicity.

Happily so far my measures were attended with general approbation, and I also received congratulations on the installation of the "Instituent Junta."

At this period the empire was tranquil, the government was actively engaged in consolidating the public prosperity, and our interior grievances were removed. It only remained for us to get possession of the castle of San Juan de Ulua, the sole point which was in the possession of the Spaniards, and which commanded Vera Cruz; its garrisons were relieved by troops from the Havana, and on account of its proximity to the island of Cuba, it offered every possible advantage to an internal enemy.

The Brigadier Santa Anna commanded the fortress of Vera Cruz, and was commandant-general of the province, under Echavarri, who was its captain-general. Both of these had instructions relative to the capture of the castle; some jealousies arose between them concerning their respective authority, which they carried to such an extreme, that the former attempted to have the latter assassinated during a sortie made by the Spaniards; for which purpose he had so well concerted his measures, that Echavarri, according to his own account, owed his life to the bravery of a dozen soldiers, and to a panic which seized those who attacked him. In consequence of this circumstance, added to the repeated complaints against Santa Anna, which I received from the former captain-general, from the provincial deputation, from the consulate, from a number of the inhabitants, from the lieutenant-colonel of the corps which he commanded, and from several officers, who expressed themselves strongly against his arbitrary and insolent conduct as a governor, I was under the necessity of divesting him of his command. I had conferred it upon him, because I thought he possessed valor; a virtue which I esteem in a soldier, and I hoped that the rank in which I had placed him, would correct his defects, with which I was not unacquainted. I also hoped that experience, and an anxiety not to displease me, would have brought him to reason. I confirmed to him the rank of lieutenant-colonel which the last viceroy had given him by mistake, I bestowed on him the cross of the order of Guadalupe, I gave him the command of one of the best regiments in the army, the government of a fortress of the greatest importance at that period, the appointment of brigadier (*con letras*), and made him the second chief of the province. I had always distinguished him, nor did I on this occasion wish that he should be disgraced. I intimated to the minister that the order of recall should be framed in complimentary terms, and accompanied by another summoning him to court, where his services were required for the execution of a mission which he might consider as a promotion.

All this, however, was not sufficient to restrain his volcanic passions; he felt bitterly offended, and determined to revenge himself on the individual who had heaped benefits upon him. He flew to excite an explosion at Vera Cruz, where the intelligence of his having lost his command had not yet arrived, and where a great part of the inhabitants are Spaniards, who exercise great influence on account of their wealth, and are averse to the independence of the country, because it put an end to that exclusive commerce which was the inexhaustible source of their riches, to the prejudice of other nations, including that of Mexico itself, from which they demanded and obtained such prices as they pleased. There it was that Santa Anna proclaimed a republic. He flattered the officers with promotions, he deluded the garrison with promises, he took the respectable portion of the inhabitants by surprise, and intimidated the neighboring towns of Alvarado and Antigua, as well as the people of color in the adjacent hamlets. He attempted also to surprise the town of Jalapa, and was defeated with the loss of all his infantry and artillery, and the total rout of his cavalry, who saved themselves only by the fleetness of their horses. Whilst Santa Anna was attacking Jalapa, the towns of Alvarado and Antigua placed themselves again under the protection of the government.

This was the proper moment for putting an end to the rebellion, and punishing the traitor. General Echavarri and Brigadier Cortazar, who commanded strong divisions, and had been directed to pursue him, might have taken the fortress of Vera Cruz without any resistance; and by placing themselves between it and Santa Anna, might have captured the whole of the remains of the cavalry that could have rallied; but nothing was done.

The affair of Jalapa undeceived those who had afforded any credit to the delusive promises of Santa Anna; he was now shut up within the fortress of Vera Cruz and the imperial bridge, a position truly military; which was defended by two hundred mulattoes, under the command of Don Guadalupe Victoria. Being thus confined to the fortress, he shipped his baggage and made arrangements for his own escape by sea, as well as for that of such of his companions as were committed in his cause, who were all prepared to fly the moment they should be attacked.

Although the apathy of Echavarri should have been perhaps, a sufficient cause for exciting distrust as to his fidelity, it was not so with me, because I had formed the highest opinion of him. Echavarri had experienced from me the greatest proofs of friendship; I treated him like a brother; I had raised him from insignificance in the political career to the high rank which he enjoyed; I was as unreserved with him as if he were my son; and it pains me now to be compelled to speak of him, because his actions do him no honor.

I gave orders for the siege of the fortress, I authorized the general to act according to his own discretion, on such occasions as he deemed necessary, without waiting for instructions from the government. Troops, artillery, provisions, ammunition, and money, were supplied him in abundance, the garrison was dismayed; the officers were determined to fly; the walls, low and feeble, offered every facility for an assault, if he did not wish to open a breach, which might have been effected in any direction in the course of an hour. Notwithstanding all these advantages, only a few skirmishes took place, and the siege lasted till the 2d of February, when the convention of Casa Mata was agreed to; in consequence of which, the besiegers and the besieged united together for the re-establishment of the congress, the only object which, as they then said, they had in view.

The fault which I think I committed in my government was, that I did not assume the command of the army the moment I had reason to suspect the defection of Echavarri. I deceived myself by reposing too much confidence in others. I now feel that to a statesman such a disposition is always injurious, because it is impossible to fathom the depth to which the perversity of the human heart descends.

It has been already seen, that it was not love for his country which actuated Santa Anna in raising his voice for a republic; let the world judge also, if it was the feeling of a patriot which guided the conduct of Echavarri, knowing, as he did, that at that period commissioners had arrived at San Juan de Ulua from the Spanish government, for the purpose of *pacifying* that part of America, which it considered to be in a state of rebellion. Echavarri entered into a correspondence with them, and with the governor of the castle; he suddenly forgot his natural resentment against Santa Anna, and joined with him in opinion; he forgot the friendship which I had shown him; he forgot the duty which he owed to the Mexicans; he forgot even his honor, in order to accept the system of a man who was not only his public, but his personal, enemy; and by entering into a capitulation with him, though at the time in command of superior numbers, he crowned his disgrace, and brought a stain upon his character, which no lapse of time can remove. Can it be, that Echavarri, remembering his native land, wished to render his countrymen such a service, as might expiate his former conduct? I shall pass no judgment upon him. Let those do it who cannot be charged with partiality.

After the convention of Casa Mata, the besiegers and the besieged united, and rushed like a torrent over the provinces of Vera Cruz and Puebla, without paying any regard to the government, or the least respect to me, although it was expressly stipulated that a copy of the convention should be sent to me by a commission. This commission was reduced to one officer, who arrived when the whole army was in motion, and when every point was taken possession of, which the time allowed, without waiting to know if I wholly or partly approved, or rejected that convention. It was also expressly provided in that act, that no attempt should be made against my person or authority.

The Marquis de Vivanco commanded the provinces of Puebla *ad interim*. He was also one of those who had experienced my favor. He never was, nor ever can be, a republican; he abhorred Santa Anna personally, and he was hated by the army as being an anti-independent, and on account of a certain want of frankness in his character. Notwithstanding all this, Vivanco joined the rebels, and Puebla refused to obey the government.

I went out to take a position between Mexico and the

rebels, for the purpose of reducing them without violence, by agreeing to everything which was not incompatible with the public good. I resolved to draw a veil over the past, and to put out of the question everything relating personally to myself. We agreed that a new congress should be convened, the convocatoria for which had been already settled on the 8th of December, by the instituent junta, and was printed and about to be issued. Limits were fixed to the troops on both sides, and it was stipulated that they should remain within their lines, until the national representation should meet and decide the question, all parties agreeing to submit to its determination. Such was the agreement entered into with the commissioners whom I had sent for that purpose; but those on the other side violated the stipulations into which they had entered, by despatching emissaries to the provinces, for the purpose of persuading them to abide by the Act of Casa Mata. Several of the provincial deputations did accede to it; but at the same moment that they did so, they expressed a resolution to respect my person, and to resist any attempt that might be made against me, notwithstanding the arts and menaces which were used in order to change the current of their feelings.

It has been said that I wished to assume absolute power; I have already demonstrated the falsehood of this charge. I have been accused, also, of enriching myself from the public treasury, although at this moment I have no other dependence than the property which has been assigned to me; and if there be any man who knows that I have funds in any foreign bank, I hereby cede them to him, that he may make such use of them as he thinks fit.

The best proof that I have not enriched myself, is

that I am not rich; I have by no means so much as I possessed when I undertook to establish the independence of my country. I not only did not misapply the public funds, but I have not even received from the treasury the sums which were granted to me. The first junta of provisional government made an order, that a million of dollars should be paid to me out of the property of the extinct inquisition, and also assigned to me twenty square leagues of territory in the inland provinces. I have not received from these resources a single real. The congress passed a decree that all my expenses should be supplied by the treasury to whatever extent I should require, and the instiutent junta granted me an annual income of a million and a half of dollars. I received no more than was barely necessary for my subsistence, and this was drawn in small sums by my steward, every four or six days, preferring always the exigencies of the state to my own and those of my family. I may mention another circumstance, which shows that self-interest is not my passion. When the instituent junta granted me the annuity of a million and a half of dollars, I appropriated the third part of that sum to the formation of a bank, which might contribute to the encouragement and assistance of the mining trade, a principal branch of industry in that country, but which had gone to ruin in consequence of the late convulsions. Regulations for the institution were drawn up by individuals experienced in the subject, and specially commissioned for the purpose.

As little did I enrich any of my relatives by giving them lucrative employments. I listened to no private influence; those who obtained official situations through me, obtained them as matter of justice in the scale of promotion, or through the consequences of the revolution, according to the rank in which they stood when the government was changed, without their situation being at all improved by my elevation to the throne.

It has been said that I acted arbitrarily by imprisoning some of the deputies of congress, and afterwards suspending it. To this charge I have already answered. It has been alleged, too, that I paid no respect to property, because I made use of the convoy of specie, amounting to one million two hundred thousand dollars, which left Mexico, bound for the Havana, in October, 1822. At that time the congress had been strongly pressed by the government to supply the means for meeting the exigencies of the state, and it gave me authority to appropriate to that purpose any existing fund. It informed me privately, through some of its members, that in adopting this measure, it had particularly in view the convoy in question; but that it had made no allusion to it in the decree, because the promulgation of that document would warn the proprietors to abstract their respective shares, before the necessary orders could be issued. There were no means for the support of the army; the public functionaries were without pay; all the public funds were exhausted; no loan could be obtained at home; and those resources which might be solicited from abroad, required more time than the urgency of the moment could allow. At that period a treaty was pending for a loan from England, and the negotiations had every appearance of a successful issue; but they could not be concluded within five or six months at the least, and the necessities of the state were too pressing to be postponed.

At the same time, impressed as I always have been with the deep sense of the sacredness of private property, I should never have acceded to the wishes of the congrees, if I had not had good reason to believe that specie was remitted in that convoy for the Spanish government under fictitious names, and that almost the whole of it was intended for the Peninsula, where it would indisputably contribute to support the party which was opposed to the Mexicans. I trust that this will sufficiently appear to have been my view of the transaction, from the circumstance that all foreigners who could prove any part of those funds to belong to them, immediately obtained an order from me for its restitution. But even supposing (which, however, I cannot concede), that it was wrong to seize the above-mentioned funds, to whom is the error to be attributed? Is it to be ascribed to me, who had no authority to levy contributions or loans, or to the congress, which, in a period of eight months, had arranged no system of revenue, nor formed any plan of finance? Is it to be imputed to me, who could not avoid executing a peremptory law, or to the congress which dictated it?

The act of Casa Mata fully justified my conduct in August and October, with respect to the congress. The last revolution has only been the result of the plans which were then formed by the conspirators. They have not adopted a single step that varies from the *sumaria*, which was taken at that time. The places where the cry of insurrection was first to be raised, the troops who were most deeply committed in the plot, the persons who were to direct the revolution, the manner in which I and my family were to be disposed of, the decrees to be passed by congress, the kind of government which was to be established, all are to be found enumerated in the declarations and results of the *sumaria*. Neither the imprisonment of the deputies, nor the reform of the congress, nor the seizure of the convoy, were the true causes of the late revolution.

I repeatedly solicited a private interview with the principal dissenting chiefs, without being able to obtain anything more than one answer in a private note from Echavarri. Their guilt prevented them from facing me; their ingratitude confounded them. They despaired of receiving indulgence from me (which was another proof of their weakness), although they were not ignorant that I was always ready to pardon my enemies, and that I never availed myself of my public authority to avenge personal wrongs.

The events which occurred at Casa Mata united the republican and the Bourbon parties, who never could agree but for the purpose of opposing me. It was as well, therefore, that they should take off the mask as soon as possible, and make themselves known, which could not have happened if I had not given up my power. I reassembled the congress, I abdicated the crown, and I requested permission, through the minister of relations, to exile myself from my native country.

I surrendered my power, because I was already free from the obligations which irresistibly compelled me to accept it. The country did not want my services against foreign enemies, because at that time it had none. As to her domestic foes, far from being useful in resisting them, my presence might have proved rather prejudicial to her than otherwise, because it might have been used as a pretext for saying that war was made against my ambition, and it might have furnished the parties with a motive for prolonging the concealment of their political hypocrisy. I did not abdicate from a sense of fear; I know all my enemies, and what they are able to do. With no more than eight hundred men

I undertook to overthrow the Spanish government in the northern part of the continent, at a moment when it possessed all the resources of a long-established government, the whole revenue of the country, eleven European expeditionary regiments, seven veteran regiments, and seventeen provincial regiments of natives, which were considered as equal to troops of the line, and seventy or eighty thousand royalists, who had firmly opposed the progress of Hidalgo's plot. Had I been actuated by fear, would I have exposed myself to the danger of assassination, as I did, by divesting myself of every means of defence?

Nor was I influenced in my resignation by an apprehension that I had lost anything in the good opinion of the people, or in the affection of the soldiers. I well knew that at my call the majority of them would join the brave men who were already with me, and the few who might waver would either imitate their example, after the first action, or be defeated. I had the greater reason to depend on the principal towns, because they had themselves consulted me with respect to the line of conduct which they ought to pursue under the circumstances of the moment, and had declared that they would do no more than obey my orders, which were that they should remain quiet, as tranquillity was most conducive to their interests as well as to my reputation. The memorials from the towns will be found in the ministry of state and the captaincy-general of Mexico, together with my answers, which were all in favor of peace and against bloodshed.

My love for my country led me first to Iguala, it induced me to ascend the throne and to descend again from so dangerous an elevation; and I have not yet repented either of resigning the sceptre or having proceeded as I have done. I have left the land of my birth after having obtained for it the greatest of blessings, in order to remove to a distant country, where I and a large family, delicately brought up, must exist as strangers, and without any other resources than those which I have already mentioned; together with a pension, upon which no man would place much dependence, who knows what revolutions are, and is acquainted with the state in which I left Mexico.

There will not be wanting persons who will charge me with a want of foresight, and with weakness in reinstating a congress, of whose defects I was aware, and the members of which will always continue to be my determined enemies. My reason for so acting was this, that I should leave in existence some acknowledged authority, because the convocation of another congress would have required time, and circumstances did not admit of any delay. Had I taken any other course, anarchy would inevitably have ensued, upon the different parties showing themselves, and the result would have been the dissolution of the state. It was my wish to make this last sacrifice for my country.

To this same congress I preferred a request that it would fix the place where it wished me to reside, and select such troops as it might think proper to form the escort that was to attend me to the place of embarkation. It fixed on a point in the bay of Mexico for my embarkation, and gave me for escort five hundred men, whom I wished to be taken from among those that had seceded from their allegiance to me, and to be commanded by the Brigadier Bravo, whom I also selected from my opponents, in order to convince them that he who now surrendered his arms, and placed himself in the hands of those persons whose treachery he had already experienced, had not avoided meeting them in the field through any personal fear.

On the day fixed for my departure from Mexico, the people prevented me from leaving it. When the army calling itself (for what reason it knew not) the liberating army, made its entry, there were none of those demonstrations which usually evince a favorable reception. The superior officers were obliged to post the troops through the capital, and to plant artillery at the principal approaches. In the towns through which I passed, (which were but a few, as it was so managed that I should be conducted with as much privacy as possible from one hacienda to another), I was received with ringing of bells, and notwithstanding the harshness with which they were treated by my escort, the inhabitants crowded anxiously to see me, and to bestow upon me the most sincere proofs of their attachment and respect.

After my departure from Mexico, the new government was obliged to resort to force in order to prevent the people from crying out my name; and when the Marquis of Vivanco, as general-in-chief, harangued the troops whom I left at Tacubaya, he had the dissatisfaction to hear them shout, "Live Agustin the First!" and to see that they listened to his address with contempt. These, and a thousand other incidents which might appear too trifling if they were particularized, fully demonstrate that it was not the general will which effected my separation from the supreme command.

I had already said that the moment I should discover that my continuance at the head of affairs tended to interrupt the public tranquillity, I should cheerfully descend from the throne; and that if the nation should choose a form of government which in my view might be prejudicial, I would not contribute to its establishment, because it is not consistent with my principles to act contrary to what I think conducive to the general welfare. But on the other hand, I added, that I would not oppose it, and that my only alternative would be to abandon my country. I said this in October, 1821, to the first junta of government; and I repeated it frequently to the congress, to the instituent junta, to the troops, and to several individuals, both in private and in public. The case for which I had provided arrived; I complied with my word, and I have only to thank my enemies for having afforded me an opportunity of unequivocally showing that my language was always in unison with my intentions.

The greatest sacrifice which I made, has been that of abandoning for ever a country so dear to my heart, which still retains an idolized father whose advanced age rendered it impossible to bring him with me, a sister whom I cannot think of without regret, and kinsmen, and many a friend who were the companions of my infancy and youth, and whose converse formed in better days the happiness of my life!

Mexicans! this production will reach your hands. Its principal object is to show you that your best friend has never deceived the affection and confidence which you prodigally bestowed upon him. My gratitude to you shall cease only with my latest breath. When you instruct your children in the history of our common country, tell them betimes to think with kindness of the first Chief of the army of the Three Guarantees; and if by any chance my children should stand in need of your protection, remember that their father spent the best season of his life in laboring for your welfare! Receive my last adieus, and may every happiness await you!

At my country-house in the vicinity of
LEGHORN, 27th of September, 1823.

POSTSCRIPT.

Not having been allowed, as I had intended, to print this work in Tuscany, the time that has elapsed since I finished it, has afforded me an opportunity to observe that the events which have taken place in Mexico, since my departure, fully confirm everything which I have said with respect to the congress. It has been seen endeavoring to prolong the term of its functions, in order to engross all the different branches of power, and to form a constitution according to its own pleasure; a proceeding inconsistent with the limited authority which has been delegated to it, and demonstrative of its contempt for the public voice, and for the decisive representations addressed to it from the provinces, desiring that it should confine itself to the formation of a new convocatoria. Hence, it has happened that the provinces, in order to force the congress to compliance, have taken such strong steps as even with force of arms to refuse to obey its ordinances, and those of the government which it has created. This fact is an unequivocal proof of the bad opinion which the people entertain of the majority of the deputies. A new congress necessarily requires time and expense; and, therefore, it may be inferred, that the people never would have adopted the idea of forming such a congress, if they looked upon the majority of the present deputies as wise, temperate, and virtuous legislators, or if the proceedings of those deputies, since their reinstatement in the sanctuary of the laws, had been conformable to the general welfare, instead of being subservient to their own ambitious and sinister designs.

LONDON, January, 1824.

The new congress passed an act annulling the coronation of Iturbide, the acts of his government, and several of the decrees of the former congress. It also settled upon him during life a pension of twenty-five thousand dollars per annum, provided that he should take up and continue his residence in some part of Italy, and upon his family, after his death, unconditionally, the sum of eighteen thousand dollars annually. This condition, unfortunately for him, he did not keep; his partisans encouraged him to return and head them; imitating Napoleon, he complied with the invitation, and leaving Europe secretly, he landed at Soto la Marina, on the 8th of July, 1824. Here he terminated his life, like Murat, having been immediately arrested by the authorities and shot.

On the 14th of November, 1824, Count Charles de Beneski, a Polish exile, who had long been attached to Iturbide, and who seems really to have borne towards him the same devotion Poniatowski entertained to Napoleon, published in New York an account of the last moments of the ex-emperor, and of the conduct of Garza, who betrayed him to his enemies, and also seemed to tantalize the unhappy man with alternate depressions and exaltations of hope in a manner altogether unworthy of a gentleman and a soldier. At one period of the march from Soto la Marina to the seat of the congress, the whole escort absolutely pronounced in favor of Iturbide, though but a few hours afterwards he was a close prisoner.

After his execution the body was followed to the grave by the congress, which had ordered him shot, and he was mourned by them as a public benefactor.

One of two things is undeniable, either Iturbide was a patriot, and his execution was altogether unjustifiable, or he was a traitor, and did not deserve better. In either case the congress was wrong.

It must not be forgotten that Iturbide landed without arms from a peaceful vessel, and that the decree by virtue of which he was executed, had been passed during his absence and never been imparted to him.

He died like a brave man, receiving two balls in his head, and two in that breast which he maintained had ever beat with hope and love for his country; and when we look over the long array of Mexican rulers, we cannot find one who had done so much good for his country and so little harm. The idea that Mexico is capable of self-government has long been exploded, and should it happen that God in his wrath send her a king (and such, in fact, are all her presidents and dictators), it cannot be doubted that it would be better for herself and her neighbors, that this monarch should be one of her own children, than a member of the exhausted Spanish Bourbon family.

Iturbide would have governed Mexico ably. He knew the wants of his country, her great men, her vices, and her virtues, and had he lived, history would probably have known no Santa Anna, no Alaman or Ampudia. The Mexican flag would now have been respectable, and not have been looked upon as the equal of the robber states of Barbary, to be restrained within the bounds of national law by fear alone.

He seems to have foreseen all that happened at Soto la Marina before he left Italy, and under that feeling to have written the following letter to his friend and solicitor:

"My dear Sir,—It is probable that as soon as my departure is known, different opinions may be expressed, and that some of them may be falsely colored. I wish, therefore, that you should know the truth in an authentic manner.

"By a misfortune that is much to be deplored, the principal provinces of Mexico are at this moment disunited; all those of Goatemala, New Galicia, Oajaca, Yacatecas, Queretaro, and others, sufficiently attest this fact.

"Such a state of things exposes the independence of the country to extreme peril. Should she lose it, she must live for ages to come in frightful slavery.

"My return has been solicited by different parts of the country, which consider me necessary to the establishment of unanimity there and to the consolidation of the government. I do not presume to form such an opinion of myself; but as I am assured that it is in my power to contribute in a great degree to the amalgamation of the separate interests of the provinces, and to tranquillize in part those angry passions which are sure to lead to the most disastrous anarchy, I go with such an object before me, uninfluenced by any other ambition than the glory of effecting the happiness of my countrymen, and of discharging those obligations which I owe to the land of my birth—obligations which have received additional force from the event of her independence. When I abdicated the crown of Mexico, I did so with pleasure, and my sentiments remain unchanged.

"If I succeed in realizing my plan to the extent which I desire, Mexico will soon present a government consolidated, and a people acting upon one opinion, and co-operating in the same object. They will all recognise those burdens, which, if the present government continued, would only fall upon a few; and the mining and commercial transactions of the country will assume an energy and a firmness of which they are now deprived. In anarchy nothing is secure.

"I have no doubt that the English nation, which knows how to think, will easily infer from this statement the probable political situation of Mexico.

"I conclude with again recommending to your attentions my children, in my separation from whom will be seen an additional proof of the real sentiments which animate the heart of your very sincere friend,

AGUSTIN DE YTURBIDE.

"MICHAEL JOSEPH QUIN, Esq., *Gray's Inn*."

Count de Beneski was tried afterwards for participating in the schemes which induced Iturbide to return, but was acquitted, and but lately resided in Mexico in high repute and esteem. If Iturbide deserved death, Beneski should have shared his fate. Mexico now honors the latter; why then was Iturbide executed?

The family of Iturbide have for some years resided in the cities of Washington and Philadelphia, and won popularity and universal esteem. One of his sons has, we believe, returned to Mexico, and is at this time a colonel of cavalry, and has the reputation of having inherited his father's courage as well as his name.

The Spanish troops had been removed during the reign of Iturbide from the republic, with the exception of a few who continued to hold out the strong castle of San Juan de Ulua, situated in the sea, within six hundred yards of Vera Cruz. Here they remained, obstinately refusing to depart or to surrender, until the 20th of December, 1825, when they evacuated the fortress, to the great relief of the citizens of the place, which lay under their guns.

After the abdication of Iturbide, the executive power

was confined to a commission of three, until a constitution could be provided by a competent assembly. After some time, this was effected, and, on the 4th of October, 1824, a constitution, framed almost entirely upon that of the basis of the United States, was solemnly proclaimed; the Catholic religion was, however, supported to the exclusion of all others, and there was no trial by jury. The territory was divided into nineteen states and four territories, corresponding nearly in names and limits with the *intendencies* under the Spanish regime; the general legislature was composed of two chambers, constituted nearly like those of the United States, and the chief executive power was committed to a president, chosen for four years by the entire majority of the states; during whose absence or inability, a vice-president was charged with the same duties. In the election of these chief officers, the candidate having the greatest number of votes after the president, became vice-president. In the first election, General Victoria was made president, and General Bravo vice-president. These appointments were in every respect unfortunate. Victoria and Bravo, though active and persevering as leaders of guerillas, were totally unfit to guide the concerns of a state; they were both men of moderate capacity, uneducated, and unacquainted with any other than the simplest relations between the governors and the governed. Moreover, they had long been rivals, and the mode of their election only served to excite jealousy and mistrust. Fears of such results were entertained at the time of their election, and were afterwards fully confirmed.

CHAPTER VI.

MEXICAN REPUBLIC.

Recognition by the United States of the independence of the revolted colonies of Spain—Congress of Panama—Mr. Poinsett plenipotentiary to Mexico—Treaty of alliance and commerce—Boundary question—Victoria president—Influence of Masonry on politics—Triumph of the Yorkino party.

WE have heretofore only incidentally noticed the connexion of the United States with the Mexican revolution, as it had had but little influence on the contest. While Ferdinand was a prisoner, there had been no communication between the Union and any of the rival authorities. An attempt to procure the recognition of Joseph Bonaparte failed before Congress in 1809, while on the other hand, Don Jose de Onis, the agent of the central junta, was never recognised *in that capacity.* The earthquake at Caraccas, and the offer of food by the nation, afforded an opportunity of indirect intercourse, and *eclaireurs* were sent to Chili, La Plata, Venezuela, &c., at different times.

In 1818, a proposition was officially made by the government of the United States to that of Great Britain, for a concerted and provisional acknowledgment of the independence of La Plata; it was declined, and is believed to have given offence to the sovereigns assembled in conference at Aix la Chapelle. Public opinion, however, grew stronger in the United States in favor of the patriots of Spanish America, being daily increased by the details of the horrible proceedings of Morillo and the other monsters in Colombia, and by the seizure of the vessels of the United States on the coast of that country in virtue of the pretended blockade. Many attempts were also made in Congress, particularly by Mr. Henry Clay, to procure a public recognition of the independence of those portions of the southern continent from which the Spaniards had been expelled. At length, on the 8th of March, 1822, President Monroe, in a message to the national legislature, declared his conviction, that the United States could not consistently, with justice or with policy, longer delay the commencement of relations with these countries, as they were *de facto* free from the authority of their former European rulers. On the day after this message had been sent, the Spanish minister at Washington remonstrated, officially, against the recommendation thus made, and he subsequently communicated to the president the decrees of the cortes, protesting against the admission, by any other government, of the claims of those countries to be considered as sovereign states. Nevertheless, both houses of congress adopted the views presented in the message, and on the 4th of May, appropriations to a large amount were made by the house of representatives, for the expenses of such missions as the president should think proper to send to the countries in question.

Propositions were also made for a general congress of all the governments of North and South America, to meet at Panama, and after a long debate the congress determined to send delegates, by a vote taken April 21st, 1826; and accordingly Mr. Richard Anderson, envoy to Colombia, and John Sergeant, of Philadelphia, were appointed. Mr. Anderson, however, died on his passage, and Mr. Sergeant having deferred his passage until too late, the United States were not represented.

The result of this congress of delegates from Peru,

Mexico, Central America, and Colombia, at which agents from Great Britain and Holland were present, was the production of treaties of offensive and defensive alliance, to which all the other powers of America might accede. It separated to meet again at Tacubaya in February, 1827. The treaties it concluded, however, were not ratified; no congress met at Tacubaya, and all its schemes ended in smoke.

In 1825, Mr. Poinsett arrived in the city of Mexico as plenipotentiary of the United States, after having previously filled high charges of a similar nature in other countries. About the same time Great Britain was represented by Mr. Ward, and to these two gentlemen the world is indebted for almost all the reliable information it possesses about Mexico. Mr. Ward immediately concluded a treaty of peace in behalf of England, which, however, was not ratified, and Mr. Poinsett sought to negotiate a similar one for his government. Mr. Poinsett also sought to obtain the assent of Mexico to a new line further to the west than the one then existing by virtue of the treaty with Spain, which had been settled February 22, 1819, when Florida became a part of the United States. The Mexican minister of foreign relations was however, a shrewd politician, and would, on this latter point, conclude no negotiations; probably seeing that this was an exhibition of a desire of aggregation, since certainly maintained by the United States. All Mr. Poinsett could do was to conclude a treaty of alliance and commerce, which he did on the 10th of July, 1826. This treaty was not, however, ratified by the United States, the senate of which declared that it would approve of no treaty unless the boundaries should be settled according to the terms of 1819. It may be said, as the United States had never refused to confirm that boundary, and Mexico had insisted upon an examination (which was never made) of the territory, in order to fix a new one, this resolution seems to have been at least unnecessary, and may perhaps be esteemed as frivolous. Possibly, it may have been intended to accelerate the movements of the Mexican executive upon the subject.

Mr. Poinsett was then instructed by his government, on the 15th of March, 1827, to propose to purchase the desired tract of territory from Mexico, so as to fix the western boundary of the United States on the river Colorado, or even on the Rio del Norte; but this proposal was rejected by the Mexicans, and years passed on without any determination either of the limits, or of the rules and principles by which the intercourse between the two republics was to be conducted, although this intercourse was daily increasing. Meanwhile, grants of land in Texas were daily made to individuals, natives of the United States, and of other countries, as well as Mexicans, and a population was rising in that region, essentially foreign to Mexico in language, habits, and religion. From Great Britain, Mexico received a vast amount of capital, which was expended in almost every instance fruitlessly, in attempts to work new silver mines, or to restore to use those which had been abandoned; the mining operations were, however, much improved, and the proportion of the precious metal obtained has been much greater since than before the separation from Spain.

During the administration of Guadalupe Victoria, little was done to bring Mexico to that state of quiet and security, so indispensable for the happiness and advancement of a country. The finances were badly administered, and peculation was openly practised in every direction. The president and vice-president, as before stated, were enemies; the latter headed the opposition, and actually, on one occasion, in January, 1828, appeared at the head of forces in insurrection against the constituted authorities. He was, however, on this occasion, defeated and made prisoner by Guerrero. Independently of the evils arising from the personal ambition of various individuals, there were strong parties, at war with each other upon material points of government. One party wished to maintain the privileges of the aristocracy and the clergy, and for that purpose was desirous of seeing established a central system of government; the other, a democratic party, wished to reduce these privileges, and to maintain the federal constitution. By the exertions of the latter, a law was passed in 1826, putting an end to all titles of nobility, and restricting parents with regard to the distribution of their property among their children. Another question, which strongly agitated the people, was, whether the Spaniards should be allowed to remain in the republic or not; by the influence of the same party, the expulsion of this class of the population was effected, in virtue of a decree passed on the 8th of March, 1828.

The affairs of the state also became involved with Masonry, which produced as much evil in Mexico as it appeared once to threaten in our own country. Those who are adepts in Masonry, know that there exists a schism in the masonic world on the subject of rites, ceremonies, and opinions; one party adhering to those of the *Scotch* Lodge, (*the word Lodge is here used collectively,*) the other submitting to the rules of *York;* the lodges in the United States are all constituted upon the York principles. Masonic societies, professing the Scotch rites, had existed in Mexico for some time previous to the extinction of the Spanish authority, and during the wars of the revolution they had afforded facilities for the propagation of plans of insurrection, and of other information among the people. On the establishment of the republic, these societies were filled chiefly with persons professing aristocratic principles of government; they were used as the means of combining operations for the maintenance of such principles, and were accordingly favored by the representatives of Great Britain, which was then by no means anxious for the extension of the republican system throughout America. The grand master of the Scotch masons was General Bravo, who was for some time their favorite candidate for the presidency; they had endeavored to raise him to that station at the first election, and are supposed to have been the advisers of his insurrection in 1828, which terminated so unfortunately for him. There were some York lodges in Mexico, the members of which were democratic in their principles, and opposed politically the *Escoceses*.

On his arrival, Mr. Poinsett was induced to obtain a charter for the establishment of a York lodge in the city of Mexico, which was granted by De Witt Clinton, of New York, at that time high in authority in the masonic order; and thenceforth the York lodges were generally diffused and extended, and the two terms, *Yorkino* and *Escocese*, became what whig and tory are in England. Mr. Poinsett, it may be presumed, never had any connexion with either branch of the order in Mexico. In 1828, the second election for president and vice-president of Mexico was to be held. The Escoceses failing in their plan to have their grand master Bravo elected, put forward the minister of war, General Gomez Pedraza, a man of strong character and capacity, much disliked, however, in the army, on account of his arbitrary principles. The candidate of the Yorkinos was General Vincent Guerrero, the persevering Indian chief, who had just defeated and taken Bravo, who had never bent to the threats or bribes of the Spaniards, and had never despaired of the independence of his country; bold, honest, and frank, but weak and illiterate, he was much better qualified for conducting a rapid march through a region occupied by enemies, than for counteracting intrigues, and devising measures for the recovery of the finances, and for the pacification of a troubled country. The election was held in September, and the result was that Pedraza was chosen by a small majority over Guerrero. The announcement created great satisfaction on the one hand, and a corresponding disappointment on the other. Scarcely was it made known ere an insurrection broke out.

General Santa Anna, on account of some disturbances, had been removed from his command at Vera Cruz, and taken up his residence at Jalapa. Here, considering the election of Pedraza as offering a good opportunity for an insurrection, he prevailed on the troops to join him, and, on the 10th of September, 1828, followed by a large body of men, he suddenly left Jalapa, and marched upon the fortress of Perote, situated thirty miles distant on the road to Mexico. Having obtained possession of this fortress, and of a large amount of public money, he declared himself commander of the liberating army, and proposed his *plan* for the reform of the government, which is known in Mexican history as the *Plan of Perote.* By the terms of this plan, the election of Pedraza was pronounced fraudulent, and the legislature was required to make a new choice.

President Victoria immediately declared Santa Anna

an outlaw, and sent forces against him under generals Calderon and Rincon, by whom he was at least kept at bay. In the capital, however, was a strong party in favor of this plan of Perote, headed by Lorenzo de Zavala, the governor of Mexico, a man of influence, talent, and honesty, and possessing sufficient firmness for his support, in the trying scenes to which he was exposed. The government which was in favor of Pedraza, suspecting Zavala to be engaged against him, ordered his arrest, but he escaped to the mountains, and joining other friends, they planned a scheme of resistance. It was carried into effect on the 30th of November, 1828, when a body of soldiery seized a large building, called the *Acordada*, opposite the *Alameda* or public gardens of the capital, and took possession of the arms stored there. The excuse for this movement, was to have the Spaniards expelled; but this was soon forgotten, in the general cry of *Long live Guerrero*. That chief appeared and headed the troops and people; nearly all the foreigners except the members of the American legation quitted the city, and for three days Mexico was the scene of combats and plunder. A party of the mob attacked the house of Mr. Poinsett, who was accused of protecting some Spaniards; he, however, advanced on the balcony and unfolded the star-spangled banner of his country, at the sight of which the crowd cheered and passed on.

The result of this movement was the triumph of the Yorkino party; a new election took place, in which Guerrero was chosen president, and Don Anastasio Bustamente vice-president, Pedraza being sent in exile to the United States. Victoria retired into private life, and the new chiefs of the state entered upon their respective duties on the 1st of April, 1829. Santa

Anna, after having been nearly forced to surrender to Calderon at Oaxaca, was himself placed at the head of the very army which had deposed him, and was restored to his government. Mr. Poinsett soon returned home, leaving Mr. Butler chargé of the legation of the United States.

It is now time to refer to the man of Mexico whose history, more than any other's, embodies that of the nation for twenty-six years, and to review the progress we have made towards completion of our task. We have thus far followed the successive transitions of the state of Mexico, during the present century. We have observed it under the viceroys, bowed down by an absolute despotism, its people so oppressed that they dared not even look upward. We have seen it in possession, in fact, of a wealth which equals the treasures of fairy history, yet pouring out all its resources at the feet of a monarch beyond the ocean, who cared not for its devotion, and valued its wealth only as a means of perpetuating its servitude and preserving his authority over other of his dominions. We have seen it so long governed by foreigners, that it looked on the rule of a native as impossible, and so constantly a prey to tyrannical power, cupidity, and avarice, that it looked on justice and humanity as superhuman virtues. We have seen the people superstitious, abject, and humiliated, looking on heretic and rebel as synonymous terms, thinking any one who dared exert the precious boon of reason as derelict in duty and loyalty. We have seen that people, animated by the Promethean fire of Liberty of Thought, burst the mental fetters which weighed on it, and rise to the dignity of thinking men. We have seen its children enact scenes which recall the brightest days of ancient Greece, and seen its martyrs march to the place of execution cheered by that consciousness, which the old English patriots were so awake to, that their blood would but increase the fertility of the soil of Freedom, and aware that "the good old cause must triumph."

We have seen the great men who had won the liberty of Mexico pass away, one by one hurried from view by war and disease. Guerrero, Victoria, all have passed from the scene as utterly as Hidalgo, Morelos, and Iturbide; and we now behold Bravo, Bustamente, and Farias occupying a position subordinate to Alaman and Santa Anna, the two powerful minds which would long ago have destroyed even the shadow of Mexican nationality, had it not been that they kept each other in equipoise, or, like two poisons, neutralized each other.

We have now to trace a sad descent. We are to see the people gradually become corrupt, until it appears almost to lose the faculty of distinguishing right and wrong. We are to watch the course of its principal men, see them become gradually more degraded, and cease at last even to pretend to virtue. We shall see the treasury looked upon as spoils and proclaimed as an inducement to win partisans.

We shall learn that a people may have no annals, and yet not be blessed, and see that it is not more unimportant to mankind, that the fate of every animal which falls in the great *plaza de toros* should be chronicled, than the defeat of the grasping and ignobly ambitious chieftains, who rise successively on the horizon and disappear from it, should be recorded. We shall see their threats derided, see their fortresses bombarded almost without resistance, and see them incompetent to profit by the teachings of experience, rush headlong into a contest whence there can be no honorable egress with safety, yet see them unable to resolve to fight like men in defence of their national existence.

We shall see evidence after evidence of this degradation rise before us, until we shall almost be inclined to doubt the truth of that holy maxim, that nowhere has any race or class been formed to be "hewers of wood and drawers of water" to another.

The person who probably has contributed more than any other to bring about this condition of affairs has been General Santa Anna. In the following pages, we shall always find him him watching his opportunity, and, remembering the maxim of *divide et impera*, seeking to array the other eminent men of Mexico against each other, and uniformly taking advantage of their collisions to strike out a new path for himself. Wily and astute, his hand has rarely been seen, though all have been convinced he only has pulled the wires in obedience to which the political puppets have moved, so that though all hold him accountable for most that has occurred, we can but confess it must be only on the grounds, that "whenever a series of crises occurs, and one man is uniformly found to take advantage of all of them, it is *probable* he has contributed to bring it about."

We shall witness the exhibition of great intellectual power, of a ready wit and cunning hand, which never has deceived him, and see him gather resources almost from his defeats. We shall see the hundred minor chieftains, ever anxious to ruin each other, bend submissively to him, and look on him with a devotion other men pay only to their country.

We shall watch him, while a prisoner in a hostile camp, exerting an influence in the capital of his country, and rushing from the torpor of long repose into action, to make political capital out of a repulse which would have ruined another.

From the contemplation of this period of Mexican history we shall rise with disgust, wondering for what inscrutable purpose God has given so fair a land in captivity to such a ruler, and hesitating if the old creed of Visigothic conquerors, that beautiful countries were confided to degraded races until a firmer and worthier stock were ready to occupy them, may not be true; or perhaps shrink back with terror from that climate and soil which has made of the children of two such rugged races as the Spaniard of the fifteenth century and the North American Indian, beings as degraded as are the present Mexicans. We shall be inclined to doubt if the country be not in worse hands than when it was ruled by Montezuma, and if the unfurling of the Spanish flag in America has not retarded the progress of human enlightenment. Finally, we shall wonder how long Mexico will be punished, and if any servitude will purify her from her many sins.

ARISTA. SANTA ANNA. LANCER.

A Guerilla Group.

CHAPTER VII.

SANTA ANNA.

Santa Anna—Mango de Clavo—Pronounces against Iturbide—President—Zacatecas—Texan War—Revolution—Exile—Proclamation, &c.

In regard to Don Antonio Lopez de Santa Anna, we have as little positive information, as about any other of the Mexican military chieftains. Of his early history, we know nothing certainly—one account representing him as the son of a Spanish officer, and the other, as born of obscure parentage. In the sketch of the life of Iturbide, it has been seen how important a part in his dethronement was sustained by Santa Anna, of which it may not, however, be improper to make a recapitulation here.

The road from Vera Cruz to Mexico, for some distance, is by the side of the sea, and then crosses a sandy desert, barren and sterile as can be imagined. It then passes close to a tranquil bay, the green ripples of the surface of which, after even so short an absence from the broad expanse of the gulf, seem grateful indeed, and then becomes lost amid the masses of a tropical forest, extending farther than the eye can reach. The traveller, even amid its natural arcades, hears the murmur of the ocean mingled with the whispering of the leaves, and, delighted, surrenders his ear to this harmony, which, if he travel in a *Mexican coach* (a litter or palanquin), lulls him to sleep; or, if on horseback, fills his mind with all the poetry with which the country around him is instinct. From time to time, he discovers through the thick undergrowth a herd of asses, or the brow of an untamed bull, which exhibits but for a moment his rugged form, and in an instant becomes lost in the impenetrable thicket. The traveller, who would be prompted by curiosity to ask to whom these herds belong, would be told they came from the hacienda of *Mango de Clavo*, and belong to General Santa Anna.

It is to this *hacienda*, a term which corresponds nearly with the English manor, that the man who, since 1821, has been the hero of all the revolutions of Mexico, has come, now conquered, now victorious, to seek repose from the misfortune of defeat or the turmoil of victory. There he has matured new plans, and changed his political antipathies into personal friendships; has meditated on schemes to overthrow those whom he has fostered, and to protect persons whom he had previously bitterly opposed. There he has lived retired, sometimes forgotten almost, until the arrival of one of those crises when men of genius make all things their own, and when his war-cry has been heard from one end of Mexico to another. To understand what will follow in this story of Santa Anna's life, it is necessary that the reader should remember that Mexico is now in the same condition in which England was under the Tudors, and that it cannot be estimated by the rules which we apply to the present history of the civilized world. Each Mexican general occupies the position of a feudal baron, and each department and command is, as it were, an apanage. Facts alone can describe the versatile character of Santa Anna; the aspirations of a man who, Richelieu-like, knows no such word as *fail*, who has found ruin in his victories and success in his defeats, who sports with his own life and fortune heedlessly as he does with that of others; who sheds blood in torrents, yet is not, except in the United States, thought cruel; and who understands the rash and impulsive nature of his compatriots well enough to dare all things without incurring the accusation of temerity.

Santa Anna must be about forty-five or forty-six years old; his stature is tall, and age has made no impression on him as yet. He is pale, has black eyes and raven hair, which curls over a brow lofty and expressive of daring. He has the air and manners of a gentleman, and a ready elocution, which fascinates all who can understand him in his native tongue, which he speaks with a purity rare in Mexico. He possesses an intuitive perception of character, and knows what springs of the human soul to touch to effect the wonderful combinations for which he is so famous.

He appears for the first time in the history of Mexico, in 1821. At this time, though very young, he commanded a body of insurgents, at the head of whom he took possession of Vera Cruz. After having been favored by the emperor Iturbide, whom he supported with all his power, he was summoned to appear before him to give an account of some act of grave insubordination. He was deprived of his command, a punishment which he richly deserved, yet by no means expected. He returned to Vera Cruz, placed himself at the head of the garrison, which was attached to him; and after a brief harangue, declared against the imperial authority and proclaimed Mexico an independent republic. General Echavarri was sent to oppose him, but, contrary to all expectation, joined him. The cities of Oaxaca, Guadalajara, Guanajuato, Queretaro, San Luis de Potosi, and

Puebla, followed his example, and within one year after Santa Anna's dismission, Iturbide was dethroned. A few months after the installation of the new republic, the first champion of which he had been, Santa Anna revolted against the authority of congress.

In 1828 Santa Anna was again governor of Vera Cruz, and a revolt was discovered in Mexico, in which he was thought to be an accomplice, and was therefore recalled to the capital. One who had disobeyed the brave and gallant Iturbide, was by no means likely to yield to the headless congress. Far from surrendering his command, which extended only over the city of Vera Cruz, Santa Anna usurped authority over the whole province, appealed to the faithful Vera Cruzanos, defeated the troops which were sent against him, and took possession of the castle of Perote. The congress declared Santa Anna an outlaw, and other troops were sent against him.

Santa Anna did not, in his turn, declare the congress outlaws, but commenced against it one of those wars of skirmishes in which he has almost always been successful. In this campaign his constant attendant and companion was Arista.

The soldiers of Santa Anna were all from the tierra caliente; men whose bodies, of the color of bronze, seem to suffer from exposure no more than that metal does. The *vomito* had no effect on them, while the forces of the government, from the tierra templada, died by hundreds; they were able to support hunger, fatigue, the hot air, and the broiling sun, with no sustenance frequently after a day's march, other than the fruits of the country and the excitement of a cigar. At the head of such men, Santa Anna laughed at pursuit by enemies who died by the wayside from fatigue. After a long campaign, he was, however, forced to leave Perote and retire towards Tehuacan and Camino de Oaxaca, in which city he fortified himself.

Followed up by a superior force, he was forced to retreat from house to house, from street to street, and finally to shut himself up with his party in the vast convent of *Santo Domingo*, which, like most other ecclesiastical buildings in Mexico, was protected by high walls with loop-holes, defended by a massive gate, and more than all, by the sanctity attached to it. He was under no apprehension of a storm, for no man in Mexico would lift a hand against a consecrated building, and famine alone could force him to submit to his assailants.

Santa Anna knew with whom he had to deal, and therefore, without paying any attention to his enemies, quietly laid himself down for his *siesta* (an indispensable in war or peace to a Mexican), in the coolest part of the convent. The leaguerers were less composed, but were also ready enough to take their chocolate and rest. On the next day the firing began, for though it would have been impious to injure the walls of the church, there was no objection to slaying the men who were behind them. The party of Santa Anna, protected by the walls, suffered little, while his enemies were mowed down by his deadly musketry. A day and night passed as the first twenty-four hours had done, except that the skilful Santa Anna had under the shelter of the night managed to drive into the court-yard of the convent, a large number of oxen, by the side of which, with their horses saddled, stood a large party of the hardy *rancheros* from the tierra caliente. A signal was silently given, each sprang on his steed, and the besieged, who it was fancied were satisfied with their success, threw wide the gates as was the custom in solemn processions. Instead, however, of the banners of the church, of chasubles and priests, the besiegers saw lancers with their red flags and dragoons with their yellow jackets. The towers, instead of displaying waving flags and ringing with peals of joy, were filled with soldiers, who fired into the ranks of the besiegers, who were on their part almost too much astonished to notice a detachment of the garrison of Santo Domingo dashing at full speed towards a neighboring convent, of which it immediately took possession. The commander of the government troops saw at once how grievous a fault he had committed by failing to take charge of this convent, from the towers of which he could have incommoded so much the besieged. He was forced at once to change his position, for he was between two fires, since Santa Anna's last manœuvre. After a lapse of many days, during which Santa Anna, as was his wont, bided his time, and the government officer sought by all means to get the better of his wily antagonist, the latter cast his eyes on the belfry of the building last occupied, and then turning to his adjutant, said: "Unless I am mistaken, Don Cayetano, instead of those agile soldiers so busy in shooting us for three days past, I see monks in the towers. The long-beards cannot have joined Santa Anna!"

"Señor, they must have done so, otherwise they could not have afforded to make such a detachment."

Soon after the hoods and frocks of the friars were distinguished every where on the *azotea*, or roof of the convent, and the bells began to sound as if they rang for the deliverance of their house, or to make up for lost time.

One monk especially seemed to excel his comrades

in zeal and activity, and in his enthusiasm suffered his hood to fall off and discover for a moment a bright red moustache. The elevation of the tower prevented this from being observed. The general of the congress had observed what was going on, and immediately ordered the convent to be occupied. A regiment at once obeyed, and advanced with shouldered arms. Suddenly the monks let fall their gowns, and brilliant uniforms appeared in their place. A shower of balls fell on the advancing regiment, from both convents, the effects of which cross-fire decimated them before they could recover from their surprise.

The position of Santa Anna, however, had become critical, for his finances were exhausted. Arista, who was the person with the red moustache, had contrived to join him, after an expedition to the neighboring mines of Oaxaca.

"Tell me, Arista," he is represented to have said on this occasion, "how much money do you bring me?" "Not a *peso!*" replied he; "but I have brought the *administrador*, who protests he has not one *rial!*" Santa Anna bade him tell his *muchachos* (his boys) that he had no money; but promised them an increase of one-third of their pay, whenever he could get it.

But chance just then came to the aid of Santa Anna. There was a report that Mexico had been the scene of another revolution. Besieged and besiegers rushed together, and called each other friends and brothers. The monks were restored to their convent, the *administrador* to his mines, and the soldiers of Santa Anna to the tierra caliente. He, too, returned to Manga de Clavo. This part only was sustained by him in the revolution which deposed Pedraza. He reaped much advantage from it, however, the command of the state of

Vera Cruz being conferred on him immediately, and subsequently a seat in Pedraza's cabinet as minister of war, at that time a promotion which no one could have anticipated, or he have hoped. What followed in the next few years we have already referred to, and will therefore omit all that ensued until the arrival of that part of Santa Anna's career which established him as the man of the nation.

The Mexican people had been so long free from the Spanish rule that they looked on a return of their old masters as impossible, until, in the summer of 1829, General Barradas landed at Tampico in command of an army of four thousand Spanish veterans. Santa Anna was not then at Vera Cruz, but in Mexico in charge of his bureau; he was no sooner informed of the landing of Barradas, than with seven hundred men in open boats he crossed the Bahia and landed at Tuspan, avoiding the Spanish vessels most dexterously in his hazardous voyage of seventy miles across the gulf. From Tuspan in canoes or perogues he crossed the lagoon of Jamaihua, and landed within three leagues of Tampico, which was then occupied by Barradas's forces, the general having gone on an expedition into the interior with three thousand men, and left one thousand to garrison the city. Santa Anna resolved on an immediate attack at daylight the next morning, August 1st, 1829, and after a contest of four hours the town capitulated. Scarcely had this occurred than General Barradas reappeared. Santa Anna was impeded from retreat by the river which intervened between him and the city, and it was evident nothing could save him but one of those stratagems which have so often decided the fate of armies, and which the mind of Santa Anna seems so peculiarly qualified for conceiving. By means of his agents he contrived to persuade Barradas that he was at the head of an overwhelming force; and the Spaniard, instead of an attack, entered into negotiations, with the understanding that while they were progressing, Santa Anna should retire into his own quarters. Santa Anna of course consented, and, with drums beating and banners waving, crossed the river and returned in safety. When Barradas learned how he had been duped, his mortification was extreme, but the mistake could not be remedied. The effect of this ruse was such that the Mexican army was not attacked until Santa Anna had been reinforced, and the Spaniard saw it would then be vain. Every night the Spaniard was attacked by his persevering foe; and on the 11th of September a vigorous assault was made on the fort at the bar, which forced the Spanish general into a capitulation, by which he laid down his arms and soon after sailed with the remnant of his force, twenty-two hundred men, to Havana. This was the last effort of Spain against Mexico, a convulsive effort which was near success in consequence of the wildness which had animated it, and against which it was impossible to provide.

As Mr. Thompson, the envoy of the United States, says, this defence of Santa Anna recalls to us the history of General Jackson's famous defence of New Orleans; the strong point of which was not, as has generally been supposed, the defence of the city behind the cotton bags, but the night attack on the British immediately after their landing amid the wind and the rain, which enabled the officers of engineers to throw up the breastworks which such men as it was the privilege of the American general to command, could defend against any force. One thing, however, is sure, the strategy of Santa Anna on that occasion was second to no feat of arms which has occurred on this continent, except the defence of New Orleans. The result of this affair was the promotion of Santa Anna.

Guerrero was then president, a gallant man and soldier, but altogether incompetent for the administration of a civil government, and the people were generally dissatisfied with him. It would undeniably be treason of the blackest kind in the United States to raise the standard of disobedience to the constituted authorities of the country; but it may be doubted if in Mexico, just emerged from a civil war, where all was yet confused, circumstances did not at least excuse, if not justify the deposition of any one manifestly unable to administer the affairs of the nation. Though the opposition to Guerrero was general, Yucatan first threw down the gauntlet on the 4th of December, by seceding from the republic. General Bustamente soon after raised the standard of revolt, Santa Anna remaining apparently undecided at Vera Cruz, where he was suffered to command. The result was, that by the plan of Jalapa, Guerrero was deposed, and Bustamente assumed the presidency, apparently with the full consent of all. For three years the republic was devastated by wars; and after remaining quiet for a short time, Guerrero took arms, but was defeated by Bravo at Chilpanzingo, on the 2d of January, 1831, and became a refugee. Thus situated, he went to Acapulco and embarked for Europe in a Genoese vessel, but was delivered by the captain, Picaluga, to the authorities of a neighboring port, Guatulco. He was thence removed to Oaxaca, tried by a military commission, and shot at Cuilapa, a town in the neighborhood. He is said to have been betrayed at the instance of Alaman, Bustamente's secretary of state, who paid the rascally Italian (a protegé of Guerrero in his prosperity), in consideration of this treason, the sum of fifty thousand dollars.

The government of Bustamente was not, however, peaceful. General Alvarez and other chiefs maintained themselves in opposition during all 1831, and in 1832 another revolution was effected with greater bloodshed than those which had exalted Guerrero and Bustamente.

On the 3d of January, supported by the garrisons of Vera Cruz and San Juan de Ulloa, Santa Anna declared against the existing government, an example soon followed by the commander of Tampico, General Moctezuma. To repress these demonstrations, General Calderon was sent by Bustamente with a large body of troops; and Santa Anna, on the 3d of March, was defeated at Talome, about six leagues from Vera Cruz, and afterwards besieged in the latter place. Before the summer, however, had passed away, Santa Anna was reinforced, and obliged Calderon to fall back, in consequence of which and the increasing demonstrations against the president, the latter was forced to come to terms and to consent to quit the country, and Pedraza declared to have been duly elected in 1828. Pedraza's presidency expired on the 31st of March, 1833, previous to which Santa Anna was chosen to succeed him, with Gomez Farias as his vice-president. In consequence of some difference between the congress and president, relative to the passage of laws abridging the power of the aristocracy and clergy, the former declared freedom of discussion was violated, (which in fact was really the case, Santa Anna having plainly intimated to it, that if it did not comply with his wishes, he would use force), and suspended its sessions, May 14th, 1834. Immediately on this, Santa Anna appealed to the people in a proclamation, to sustain peace and order, which he represented as threatened by the congress, and effected the pronunciamento of *Cuernavaca*, on the 25th of May, the object of which was the repeal of certain laws against the church, the banishment of certain individuals, and the reorganization of the government; until which was effected, Santa Anna was endowed almost with the powers of a dictator.

A new congress met in 1835, nearly all its members coming with instructions from the people or the legislatures of the states, consenting that the form of the governments might be altered according to the will of the majority; and congress accordingly determined it had a right to alter the government in any point not affecting the maintenance of a republican system, the Roman Catholic church, the independence of the country, and the freedom of the press. The legislatures of a great many of the states had declared in favor of an alteration of the constitution. Yucatan, which had remained separate since 1829, became united, and declared itself ready to submit to the action of the congress. The state of Texas and Coahuila remained opposed to a change, but General Cos, the military commandant, summarily dispersed the legislature; and Zacatecas having declared against a change, Santa Anna marched against it in person, and by a bloody battle, on the 11th of May, reduced it to submission. There was elsewhere no opposition, except on the part of old Bravo, who had fought too long for the liberty of the country thus to see it frittered away. He long continued in arms in the south.

Notwithstanding this opposition, congress proceeded with its labors, and a constitution was formed annihilating the state governments, dissolving their legislatures, and uniting all the states into *one government, whole and indivisible.* Thus was formed the constitution of Mexico, which has produced all its later troubles, and is the present government of Mexico, pronounced by all, from its unwieldy character, probably the worst that ever existed. Its features are these: A president, selected for eight years; a house of deputies and a senate; the latter selected in the most complicated manner by electors thrice removed from the people; and a supreme court. It also embraces what is termed the supreme conservative power, with a *veto* on everything, composed of five members, and, in the words of the organic law, "*responsible to God and public opinion alone.*"

While the legislature was thus remodelling the constitution, occurred the Texas revolution. The country west of the Sabine had long since attracted the attention of the frontier population of the United States, masses of which were strewn in various parts of the country, having received grants of land, and been permitted to settle on certain conditions which the adoption of the new constitution violated. In December of 1835, a congress of nine persons assembled at Goliad, and declared themselves independent, which was followed by a more formal declaration in March, 1836, at Washington, Texas. A provisionary government was organized, and General Samuel Houston was appointed commander-in-chief. Hostilities had commenced immediately after the first declaration, between the Mexican garrisons and the settlers, and Santa Anna despatched General Cos to Monclova, the seat of government of Coahuila and Texas, with orders to humble that department, and immediately afterwards repaired to the city of Mexico.

When General Cos had reached the seat of government he acted as if he expected no difficulty, and required the surrender to the president of the governor of the state and many eminent citizens, both of American and Spanish extraction, among whom was Lorenzo de Zavala, who had previously been governor of Mexico, and had been compelled to expatriate himself at the time of the plan of Jalapa. It may not be improper here to state, that Zavala identified his fortunes with those of Texas, the vice-president of which he became, and received the compliment of having one of the cruisers of the new republic called after him. He was a man of rare energy and great decision of character, and an ornament to his native province, Yucatan.

Of course the requisition was not complied with. The legislature was dispersed, and the governor forced to escape. The rights of the state were thereby finally destroyed; and, to put the last finish to the military despotism, the arms of the American settlers were ordered to be surrendered. The people of Texas, however, were no hybrid men, but true Americans in feeling, and they determined to resist the invaders, and make good by the bow and spear the titles to the settlements they had made by virtue of the invitation and grants of the Mexican nation, which had yielded to them rights and assumed duties not to be revoked or laid aside at the will of either party to the contract.

Cos had already crossed the boundary of the state with an army of fifteen hundred men, and had entrenched himself at San Antonio de Bexar, a strong town on the river San Antonio, near where the twenty-second parallel of latitude crosses it. He sent forward a party under Colonel Castonedo to Gonzales, on the Guadalupe, which empties into the San Antonio, with an order for the people to surrender their heavy ordnance. They not only refused to do this, but collected a party of about one hundred men to attack him. They did attack Castonedo, and with such good will, that though he had twice as strong a force as they, he was defeated and compelled to fall back in the greatest haste on San Antonio de Bexar, or Bexar, as the Texans usually call it. The war now began, and the Texans determined not to be whipped without at least a show of resistance. A national convention was called, which gave its adhesion to the constitution of 1824, declared null by Santa Anna, and appealed to the people of the other departments of the republic to stand by them in defence of constitutional liberty. As when the American congress appealed to the people of Ireland, Scotland, and England, this address was disregarded, and it became evident that arms alone could decide the controversy. A Texan general, named Burleson, was then before the walls of the Alamo, a fortress of Bexar, with six hundred Americans, awaiting the developments of time, when Milam, who had long been a prisoner in Mexico, made his appearance. Milam had effected his escape, and had gone through great difficulties in reaching them, so that when he joined the force of Burleson, and was told of the destruction of even the shadow of liberty, in the republic, he had no difficulty in obtaining volunteers to the number of two hundred and sixteen men. With these he immediately marched from the Alamo to attack the principal defences, in which, as has been stated, was Cos, with fifteen hundred men. The scene subsequently enacted on a large scale in the streets of Monterey, then occurred in San Antonio de Bexar. The deadly western rifle and knife in the hands of such men, induced after five days of incessant strife a surrender of the garrison, which had lost more men than the besiegers numbered, with four hundred stand of arms, &c. The Texans' loss was small, but important, for Milam had been killed. Ill news flies apace. Santa Anna soon heard of the defeat of Cos, and in the winter of 1836, crossed the Rio Grande with an army of ten thousand men, in the van of which was borne a red flag, a token that he intended to give no quarter. The advance proceeded to lay siege to the Alamo, in which was a Texan officer named Travis, with one hundred and forty-five men. Messengers were immediately despatched to the eastern part of Texas, to say that the fort was besieged, and appealing in these Spartan terms to his companions:

"The enemy have demanded me to surrender at discretion, otherwise the garrison is to be put to the sword. I have answered his summons with a cannon-shot. Our flag still floats proudly from the walls. We shall never surrender or retreat. Liberty or death!"

It is to be regretted that the Alamo was not evacuated, for any reinforcements which could have been sent would have been lost before Santa Anna's overwhelming force, and the place was by no means valuable as a military position.

Travis resisted for six days, repulsing every attack, but at last Santa Anna arrived and assumed the command in person. For four days longer they held out, until at last their fire was almost silenced. Two attempts to scale the walls were repulsed, the Texans using the buts of their guns with great effect. The third attempt succeeded, though not without immense loss. No quarter was asked for and none offered; and when Santa Anna, after the capture, mustered his army, fifteen hundred had been killed, ten times the number of the Texans engaged. The pages of history record no greater carnage, and from this time for ever, Texas was separated from the United States of Mexico. In the defence of the Alamo fell Travis, Crockett, and Bowie; the latter, while on his bed unable to move, having been bayoneted by order of Santa Anna. The bodies of all the defenders were collected into a heap and burned.

When Santa Anna declared himself dictator, Texas was not alone in her opposition to this usurpation, Coahuila and Zacatecas having united with her. The one, however, had been intimidated, and the other conquered, and the battle was evidently to be fought by Texas alone. When, therefore, Santa Anna, flushed by his success, was overrunning the whole country, there remained but one alternative; and, on the 2d of March, 1836, Texas declared itself independent.

How the campaign in Texas progressed is now well known, and more than a glance at some of its events is unnecessary. One event, however, deserves especial mention and reprobation. A number of volunteers commanded by Colonel Fanning surrendered to Urrea (whose notoriety is derived solely from his concern in this transaction, and his participation with Farias in a pronunciamento in 1840), with a written stipulation that they were to be treated as prisoners of war, and be permitted to embark at Coporo for the United States. By order of Santa Anna, this capitulation was violated, and the defenceless men were on their march made to halt and shot in cold blood.

Santa Anna subsequently when in the United States was taken to task for this assassination by General Jackson, and stated to the American minister at Mexico, Mr. Thompson, that he thus accounted for it. The campaign was undertaken in obedience to an act of the Mexican congress, which ordered no quarter to be given, and that the terms allowed by Urrea were a violation of this law. The terms of capitulation would, however, have been observed, but that on the route to Coporo the prisoners became mutinous, and the officer in command asked for instructions how he should proceed. In this emergency, Santa Anna sent a copy of the act, and consequently all were shot but two surgeons, who were retained to attend on the Mexican invalids. This explanation could not possibly have satisfied General Jackson, for it has obvious feeble points. Imprimis, if General Urrea exceeded his power, he was responsible for it, but the capitulation should have been not the less observed; in the second place, Santa Anna had ten thousand men in Texas, and could have furnished any guard needed. The world will ever continue to look on the transaction as a wholesale deliberate murder, for which he must account to history if not to the kinsmen of his victims.

General Samuel Houston about this time commanded twelve hundred men, and was gradually retreating towards the eastern shore of Texas, whence but few men as yet had come. He wished to induce Santa Anna to separate his forces in two portions, and was confident that with the five hundred men he expected from the country on the Red river and Sabine, he could defeat him in detail and drive him from Texas. With this view he left the Colorado and crossed again the Brazos, a circumstance which dispirited his men. It happened, however, as he had designed. Santa Anna divided his forces, and with fifteen hundred men marched in person towards San Felipé. Small parties were left behind him, and Houston continued to retreat. Santa Anna was deceived and pushed on, leaving his heavy artillery behind him, without a doubt but that he would drive Houston across the Sabine. The latter concealed his forces until the Mexicans had crossed the Brazos and marched towards Harrisburg. Then Houston turned, marched at once towards Buffalo Bayou, and on the 19th of April came up with the enemy. The next day was passed in skirmishing, without any decided advantage on either side.

The two armies became engaged on the 31st of April, where the Bayou discharges itself into the San Jacinto. How Santa Anna was beaten has always been a mystery; he had the advantage of position, and had his artillery, a portion of which had reached him, well posted. A person who served there, and who has had long experience in warfare, informed the author that he never saw a more unpromising yet a more resolute charge, than the one by the Texans headed by Houston on Santa Anna's forces. They rushed up the hill with their guns at a trail, until within about twenty-five yards of the enemy, when they halted and delivered four distinct volleys with a precision which was frightful. The enemy's artillery were not idle, but delivered more than one fire with great coolness, which the Texans avoided by throwing themselves on their faces at the flash, and rising at the report with fearful yells to renew their fire. At length one company dashing forward went pell-mell over the Mexican position and captured the guns. The order for a charge was given by Houston, and his men rushed like a tempest on the enemy. All opposition was over. The slaughter at the Alamo and the massacre of Fanning were fearfully avenged by the death of seven hundred and twenty Mexicans, and the capture of six hundred more, among whom, sad to tell, was the redoubtable Santa Anna.

How Santa Anna was taken has been often described, and all accounts of it should be received with great aLowance. Three persons have in the presence of the author avowed their participation in his capture, and each gave an entirely different location and detail to the event. Suffice it to say, he was taken; and, when brought before Houston, said, "Sir, yours is no common destiny; you have captured the Napoleon of the west," and immediately engagements were entered into which it was hoped would terminate the war.

Before deciding, however, Houston called a council. Under no other circumstances would the Texans have treated with him and done aught but order Santa Anna to be shot by the quarter-guard for his slaughter of Fanning's men, but the certainty that Filasola, an accomplished Italian in the Mexican service, was marching towards them at the head of a force more numerous than theirs induced deliberation. It was determined, consequently that the president and the captured army should be released and permitted to return to Mexico.

One clause of the then formed treaty stipulated, "that the president Santa Anna, in his official character as chief of the Mexican nation, and the Generals Don Vicente Filasola, Don Jose Urrea, Don Joaquin Ramires de Sesma, and Don Antonio Guano, as chiefs of armies, do solemnly acknowledge, sanction, and ratify the full, entire, and perfect independence of Texas, with such boundaries as are hereafter set forth and agreed upon for the same. And they do solemnly pledge themselves, with all their personal and official attributes, to procure, without delay, the final and complete ratification and confirmation of this agreement, and all the parts thereof, by the proper and legitimate government of Mexico—by the incorporation of the same into a solemn and perpetual treaty of amity and commerce, to be negotiated with that government at the city of Mexico, by ministers plenipotentiary, to be deputed by the government of Texas for this purpose."

Santa Anna was permitted to visit Washington city, and was sent home in a man-of-war at the expense of the people of the United States. It need not be said that Mexico violated every promise made to Houston, under the plea that Santa Anna was in duress, and therefore not competent to act.

It is a matter of surprise that the Texans did not shoot Santa Anna, and it cannot be denied they would have been justified in doing so. They acted, however, more humanely, and thus giving him his life.

There is a story told by an interesting French writer in relation to this circumstance, which is altogether too epigrammatic to be true. "While the council of war discussed the disposition to be made of the captive president, an old man rose and said: 'We are at war with Mexico, and it is our duty to do all we can to injure her. Santa Anna has for a number of years tyrannized over his country, and nearly ruined it. Let us release him, he will return thither and in a few years Mexico will be too feeble to give us any trouble.'"

It is probable that if Santa Anna had remained president after his return, this would have been the case.

The difficulty with Texas was preceded by one with Zacatecas, already briefly referred to. This state also was devoted to the federal system, and had at its capital five thousand persons determined to defend the constitution. Santa Anna marched against them in person. When he reached Zacatecas, it was arranged that General Andrade should pretend to be disaffected, and espouse the cause of the constitutionalists. The governor of the state being inexperienced in military affairs, willingly received him, and confided to him the command of the state troops. In a very short time Andrade marched his men outside the city and encamped in the plain, and at the same time detached his cavalry to some distance from the foot, whom he bade not to keep on the alert any longer, as he had no fear of an attack. The order was universally obeyed, except by the commander of the artillery, D'Harcourt, by birth a German, who still acted with all military precaution. Santa Anna, adroitly contrived to place himself between the forces of Zacatecas and the town, rendering their escape impossible, and commenced a fire on them. D'Harcourt fought manfully, and was near defeating him with his artillery. At last he was forced to give way, and the city was taken, when an indiscriminate massacre was ordered, in spite of the remonstrances of the Mexican officers. This beautiful city was thus nearly destroyed, and from it General Cos marched to Texas.

The constitution, it will be remembered, was completed during the absence of Santa Anna, who, while at the head of his army, was unable to assure those arrangements that would have secured him the control of the new government, which enured exclusively to the benefit of the last man whom he would have wished to benefit. After his expulsion in 1832, General Bustamente had been in Europe, it is not improbable in want, certainly in dependence. It is doubtful if Mexico possesses a purer man than him, against whom even his enemies have not been able to make one allegation of dishonesty or peculation. Though he had long been in office, his salary was small, and for several months undrawn; and he is said to have been so poor that he sold everything he possessed to pay his debts, including even his watch and cane, the latter of which was offered for sale to Mr. W. Thompson, during his mission to Mexico. This anecdote, as Mr. T. says, recalls to mind the stories of those days in ancient Rome, when her dictators were so poor as to require to be buried at the public expense. This is especially creditable to one who has been president of Mexico, where so little check is imposed either by law or reputation, on the desire and manner of becoming rich. Bustamente was at once aware that the government, as proposed to be administered, could not last; and had, in the early part of 1837, returned to Mexico. He was then elected president, and entered on his duties in May of that year.

During the administration of Bustamente, Mexico became involved in a serious difficulty with France, arising from outrages on the persons and property of French citizens, at different periods since the revolutions. In the spring of 1838, the French government, wearied with making ineffectual demands for reparation, proposed the following *ultimata*, which were placed in the hands of Admiral Baudin: The government of France required pecuniary reparation for all losses incurred by Frenchmen, the dismissal of certain obnoxious functionaries, a concession that henceforth Frenchmen should enjoy the privileges of the most favored nations, and the restoration of the right of carrying on the retail trade. After some months spent in negotiation, the French admiral, on the 27th November, 1838, made an attack on the Castle of St. John de Uloa.

In 1582, sixty-one years after they had set foot on Aztec soil, the Spaniards began this fortress, in order to confirm their power. The centre of the space which it occupies, is a small island, where the Spaniard, Juan de Grijalva, arrived one year before Cortes reached the Mexican continent. Having found the remains of two human victims there, they asked the natives why they sacrificed men to their idols, and receiving for answer, that it was by orders of the kings of *Acolhua*, the Spaniards gave the island the name of Ulua, by a natural corruption of that word.

It is pretended that the fortress cost four millions; and though this immense sum is no doubt an exaggeration, the expense must have been very great, when we consider that its foundations are below the water, and that for nearly three centuries it has resisted all the force of the stormy waves that continually beat against it. Many improvements and additions were gradually made to the castle; and, in the time of the viceroys, a first-rate engineer paid it an annual visit, to ascertain its condition and to consider its best mode of defence, in case of an attack. In 1603, however, Vera Cruz was sacked by the English corsair, Nicholas Agramont, incited by one Lorencillo, who had been condemned to death for murder in Vera Cruz, and had escaped to Jamaica. Seven millions of dollars were carried off, besides three hundred persons of both sexes, whom the pirates abandoned in the Island of Sacrificios, when they re-embarked.

In 1771, the viceroy, then the Marquis de la Croix, remitted a million and a half of dollars to the governor, in order that he might put the castle in a state of defence; and the strong bulwarks which still remain, attest the labor that has been bestowed upon it. The outer polygon, which looks towards Vera Cruz, is three hundred yards in extent; to the north it is defended by another of two hundred yards, whilst a low battery is situated as a rear guard in the bastion of Santiago; and on the opposite front is the battery of San Miguel. The whole fortress is composed of a stone which abounds in the neighboring island, a species of coral, excellent for building, *piedra mucara.*

In 1822, no stronghold of Spanish power remained but this castle, whose garrison was frequently reinforced by troops from Havana. Vera Cruz itself was then inhabited by wealthy and influential Spaniards. Santa Anna then commanded in the province, under the orders of Echavarri, the captain-general, and with instructions from Iturbide, relative to the taking of the castle. The commandant was the Spanish general Don José Davila. It was not, however, till the following year, when Lemaur succeeded Davila in the command of the citadel, that hostilities were begun by bombarding Vera Cruz.

Men, women and children, then abandoned the city. The merchants went to Alvarado, twelve leagues off, whilst those who were driven from their houses by a shower of balls, sought a miserable asylum amongst the burning plains and miserable huts in the environs. Some made their way to Jalapa, thirty leagues off; others to Cordova and Orizava, equally distant. With some interruptions, hostilities lasted two years, during which there was nearly a constant firing from the city to the castle, and from the castle to the city.

The object of General Barragan, now commander-in-chief, was to cut off all communication between the garrison of the castle and the coasts, and to reduce them to live solely upon salt provisions, fatal in this warm and unhealthy country. In 1824, the garrison, diminished to a mere handful, was replaced by five hundred men from the peninsula; and very soon these soldiers, shut up on the barren rocks, surrounded by water, and exposed to the dangers of the climate, without provisions and without assistance, were reduced to the most miserable condition. The next year, Don José Copinger succeeded Lemaur, and continued hostilities with fresh vigor.

This brave general, with his valiant troops, surrounded by the sick and the dying, provisions growing scarcer every day, and those that remained corrupt and unfit to eat, yet resolved to do his duty, and hold out to the last. No assistance arrived from Spain. A Mexican fleet was stationed off the Island of Sacrificios and other points, to attack any squadron that might come from thence; while the north winds blew with violence, keeping back all ships that might approach the coasts. "Gods and men," says a zealous republican (Zavala), "the Spaniards had to contend with; having against them, hunger, sickness, the fire and balls of the enemies, a furious sea covered with reefs, a burning atmosphere, and above all, being totally ignorant as to whether they should receive any assistance."

The minister of the treasury, Estevan, then came from Mexico, and proposed a capitulation; and the Spanish general agreed that should no assistance arrive within a certain time, he would give up the fortress; evacuating it with his whole garrison, and with the suitable honors. The Spanish succors arrived a few days before the term was expired, but the commander of the squadron, seeing the superiority in point of numbers of the Mexican fleet, judged it prudent to return to Havana to augment his forces. But it was too late. On the 15th of September, the brave General Copinger, with the few troops that remained to him, marched out of the fortress, terminating the final struggle against the progress of revolution, but upholding to the last the character for constancy and valor which distinguished the sons of ancient Spain.

Of its last assault by the French squadron in 1838,

there is no need to say anything. Every newspaper gave an account of the capitulation of what the French gazettes called San Juan de Ulua, the St. Jean d'Acre of the new world, which sailors of the gulf saluted as the Queen of the Seas and bulwark of Mexico.

For two years after his return from the United States, Santa Anna was apparently forgetful and forgotten at Mango de Clavo, during all that had been taking place, but was aroused by the echoes of the French artillery, then directed against the previously impregnable fortress of San Juan de Ulloa. He hurried to Vera Cruz, where he found an appointment of military commander, from the authorities at Mexico, already awaited him. He was unable to prevent the capture of the castle, which was, it has been stated, almost in a dismantled condition, but was far more successful on the main-land. The French admiral, Baudin, having possessed himself of the former, resolved to make a demonstration against Vera Cruz, and at five o'clock in the morning despatched an expedition, in which the Prince de Joinville participated, to the city. The day chanced to be foggy and damp, so that it was impossible for the boats from t e vessels to keep together, and also for the people of the town to discover them, two circumstances which compensated the one for the other. The French landed; but Santa Anna, who was in bed, soon rallied a force sufficient to beat back the invaders. During the retreat, however, hotly pursued as they were, a sailor discharged a cannon which chanced to point towards the Mexicans, by which Santa Anna was unfortunate enough to lose his leg. This attempt on the city was sufficient to satisfy the admiral, that if he had stumbled on success in his attack on the castle, his force was far too feeble to make any impression even on Vera Cruz.

Both parties, however, had now seen enough of the "horrors of war," to give great attention to the mediation proposed by Mr. Packenham, who most opportunely arrived with an English fleet; by whose influence or the persuasive effect of the British guns, France was induced to lower her demands nearly two hundred thousand dollars, and did not longer insist on the retail trade being allowed to her citizens. In the events of this war, a conspicuous part was borne by the Prince de Joinville, a younger son of Louis Phillippe, who was the *nominal* commander of one of the French vessels employed in the attack. On this part of the history, it is scarcely necessary to dwell, as the events are so recent as to be remembered by all. It is one of the evils attendant on the exercise of authority in countries like Mexico, that all the mischances of war are attributed to the mis-government of the chief authorities, and President Bustamente, was heavily visited for this attack dictated by the French king's cupidity and desire of pandering to the false ambition of his subjects.

Santa Anna subsequently remained at his estate, and Bustamente occupied the executive chair, without, however, being unaware that there were around him elements of contention, which, sooner or later, must break out. On the 15th of July, 1840, a revolution arose in the city of Mexico, which was forcibly taken possession of by the federalists. General Urrea, who had been imprisoned by the government, was released by his adherents, headed by Gomez Farias, who surprised the palace and imprisoned the president. After a fight of twelve days, in which three hundred men were killed and wounded in the streets of the capital, the insurgents were forced to yield to Governor Valencia, who arrived with a reinforcement of troops; and on the 27th of July, they capitulated, on condition, among other things, that Valencia would use his influence to bring about a reform in the constitution, and that all acts of the malcontents should be buried in oblivion. The outbreak was not attended with any unusual degree of excess, property having been on both sides respected. General Bustamente again resumed the direction of affairs, and Santa Anna, who had been recalled from Perote, quietly returned thither. While, however, at Mexico, he managed to arrange his various schemes, so that on the 31st of August another revolution broke out. Valencia, who but two months before had opposed the insurrection of Farias and Urrea, now pronounced against Bustamente, whom he had till then defended in the most positive manner. As all the subsequent history of Mexico hinges on this revolution, if that title can be applied to the substitution of one chieftain for another, it may not be improper to reproduce the various documents, which we take from the admirable letters generally attributed to Madame Calderon de la Barca, whose husband, then in the capital, was the first Spanish ambassador ever sent to Mexico, Spain having for a series of years most strenuously refused to acknowledge the independence of that tributary which had so long acknowledged the authority of her kings.

"Soldiers! The despotism of the Mexican government, the innumerable evils which the nation suffers, the unceasing remonstrances which have been made against these evils, and which have met with no attention, have forced us to take a step this evening, which is not one of rebellion, but is the energetic expression of our resolution to sacrifice everything to the common good and interest. The cause which we defend is that of all Mexicans; of the rich as of the poor; of the soldier as of the civilian. We want a country, a government, the felicity of our homes, and respect from without; and we shall obtain all; let us not doubt it. The nation will be moved by our example. The arms which our country has given us for her defence, we shall know how to employ in restoring her honor—an honor which the government has stained by not acknowledging the total absence of morality and energy in the actual authorities. The army which made her independent shall also render her powerful and free. The illustrious General Santa Anna to-day marches to Puebla, at the head of our heroic companions of Vera Cruz, while upon Queretaro, already united to the valiant General Paredes, the brave General Cortazar now begins his operations.

"In a few days we shall see the other forces of the republic in motion, all co-operating to the same end. The triumph is secure, my friends, and the cause which we proclaim is so noble, that, conquerors, we shall be covered with glory; and, happen what may, we shall be honored by our fellow-citizens."

This proclamation was signed by General Valencia. The secret of this was, that events had been so arranged by Santa Anna that the revolution must occur, and Valencia having become aware of this, determined to take such a stand that he would be like the occupant of a manor in dispute, in possession, and force two other litigants to bid for the key, that the ejectment might be brought against, not by him. In Mexico, as well as elsewhere, possession is nine points of the law, and the importance of Valencia's movement will therefore be understood at once.

Paredes, in the interim, marched from Guadalajara upon Guanajuato, and there General Cortazar, just promoted by Bustamente for his courage in resisting Farias and Urrea, proved traitor and sided with Paredes. The two united, advanced on Queretaro, where Juvera sided with them, having previously pronounced *by accident*, just before they received orders to march to assist the president. The united forces of the three now advanced towards Mexico, where Valencia was still persisting that he asked nothing for himself but only the good of the country, and required the deposition of Bustamente.

Santa Anna still remained at Perote, and Bustamente was in the city with Canalizo and Almonte, making head against the revolters. An intelligent Frenchman who was in Mexico during this scene, and subsequently travelled in the United States, thus explained this game of cross purposes. Santa Anna, while in Mexico in July, corrupted all these generals. Almonte, one of his intimates, who has been said to be a relation, was *gefe del plano mayor*, or general staff of the president, and thus it occurred that all things contributed to the fall of Bustamente.

After several days of threats, and marchings and counter-marchings in the capital, Santa Anna wrote that Bustamente had repeatedly violated the constitution, and that he would therefore come immediately to Mexico. The people generally began to desire his presence, as shells passing from the quarters of Valencia to the national palace, were destroying the most beautiful part of the city. On the 19th of September, however, Torrejon, who had kept Santa Anna in check, was ordered to the city, and Bustamente placed himself at the head of the forces thus obtained and those commanded by Canalizo and Almonte, consequently leaving Echavarri at the head of the government. Santa Anna immediately set out for Mexico, taking possession on the way of Puebla; he received large reinforcements on the march, so that his ragamuffins had increased into an army of respectable size. It was then evident that danger to the government was to be expected not from him alone, but from Paredes. Strangely enough, however, the president at the head of his troops, with Canalizo and Norriega, had marched to meet Paredes, leaving Almonte and Echavarri in Mexico, to act in his stead. After some delay the president met Paredes, and after an interview, left him for the seat of government, in which direction Paredes also moved on the 27th.

Santa Anna was not, during the last four or five days idle. He too had been marching, and after an interview with the commissioners from the president, met Almonte on the 27th. What transpired between the two is a mystery, except when the latter left, Santa Anna said simply, "*Es bueno muchacho*"—he is a good boy.

On the 28th, Paredes, Valencia, and Santa Anna met at the palace of the archbishop, at Tacubaya, the result of which conference was the following plan formed on the 29th, consisting of thirteen articles, by which are established the following pacts, not one of them seeming to look to a principle.

The first declared—It is the will of the nation that the supreme powers established by the constitution of 1836 have ceased, excepting the judicial, which will be limited in its functions to matters purely judicial, conformably to the existing laws.

The second—A *Junta* is to be named, composed of two deputies from each department, elected by his excellency the commander-in-chief of the Mexican army, Don Antonio Lopez de Santa Anna, in order that they may be entirely free to point out the person who is to hold the executive power, provisionally.

The third—This person is immediately to assume the executive power, taking an oath in the presence of the junta, to act for the welfare of the nation.

The fourth—The provisional executive power shall in two months evoke a new congress, which, with ample powers, shall engage to re-constitute the nation, as appears most suitable to them.

The fifth—This congress extraordinary shall reunite in six months after it is convened, and shall solely occupy itself in forming the constitution.

The sixth—The provisional executive shall answer for its acts, before the first constitutional congress.

The seventh—The provisional executive shall have all the powers necessary for the organization of all the branches of the public administration.

The eighth—Four ministers shall be named; of foreign and home relations; of public instruction and industry; of treasury; and of war and marine.

The ninth—Each department is to have two trustworthy individuals to form a council, which shall give judgment in all matters on which they may be consulted by the executive.

The tenth—Till this council is named, the junta will fulfil its functions.

The eleventh—Till the republic is organized, the authorities in the departments which have not opposed, and will not oppose the national will, shall continue.

The twelfth—The general-in-chief and all the other generals, promise to forget all the political conduct of military men or citizens during the present crisis.

The thirteenth—When three days have passed after the expiration of the present truce, if the general-in-chief of the government does not adopt these *bases*, their accomplishment will be proceeded with; and they declare in the name of the nation, that this general and all the troops who follow him, and all the so-called authorities which counteract this national will, shall be held responsible for all the Mexican blood that may be uselessly shed; and which shall be upon their heads."

Strange as had been the scenes of this drama, the denouement was yet stranger, Bustamente *pronouncing* on the 30th in favor of the federal system. During four months the Mexican republic had undergone two revolutions, and at the end of that time found itself under a military dictatorship; in relation to which we can but say, what all must confess, that a people who will submit to such a state of things, deserve no better.

Canalizo and Almonte soon followed the example of Bustamente, and left Santa Anna uncontrolled. After seven days of perpetual cannonading, the president did what he should have done, when he pronounced for federation, resigned, and Santa Anna entered Mexico. The people who had not sustained the president were, however, too obstinate to welcome their conqueror; and Madame Calderon says, he entered the city sternly and silently, and after a Te Deum, at which the archbishop officiated, retired to the palace of that dignitary at Tacubaya, which he preferred to the national palace at Mexico. Perhaps in this he was prudent; a new revolution might have unseated him; and a president in Mexico is always formidable as long as he is unchecked by bolts and bars. A conviction of this probably induced Alaman to shoot the brave Guerrero.

Valencia and Paredes had each governments offered them, but the former refused to leave his division, which had enabled him to play the part, on a small scale, of the Warwick king-makers.

The new ministry were: Gomez Pedraza, for foreign

and home relations; Castillo, for public instruction; Tornel, for war and marine; and Dufoo, for the treasury. Paredes, too, insisted on keeping his command, and the only person who seems to have reaped any advantage was Santa Anna. All who know Mexico, however, say that on account of this revolution various indemnities were not paid, and Mexican bonds were far below par in London and New York. Soon after this revolution Mr. Thompson arrived in Mexico, and states that he heard from all, that Bustamente was one of the purest men who as yet had occupied the Mexican executive chair. If so, why was he not able to retain his power? The Mexican people were opposed to him because they were unworthy of him, and Santa Anna was his enemy because he could not make him his instrument. General Bustamente retired at once to Guadalupe, and soon after left Mexico.

Santa Anna was now dictator. How completely he had possession of Mexico the following extract from a letter published in a Boston paper in November 1842, will show:

"Mexico, Sept. 28th.—Yesterday was buried, with great pomp and solemnity, in the cemetery of St. Paul, the foot which his excellency, President Santa Anna, lost in the action of the 5th of December, 1838. It was deposited in a monument erected for the purpose, Don Ignacio Sierra y Roza having pronounced a funeral discourse appropriate to the subject."*

Santa Anna was, during this time, dictator in the fullest sense of the term; a power conferred on him by a vote

* Afterwards, when Santa Anna was exiled, this honored member was exhumed, and dragged through the streets with shouts of derision by the *leperos*.

of the congress of Mexico, until a constitution had been formed. For the first time in the history of the world, the people requested him to terminate the legislative sessions of that congress which was the guarantee of their rights. In the December of the same year, the president complied with their requests, and convened, in the place of the congress, a junta of notables, to prepare a new constitution. The result of their deliberations was, not a new constitution, for they dared not apply that name to their monster generation, but the *Bases of the political organization of the Mexican Republic,* proclaimed June 13, 1843. The following were some of the provisions of this instrument:—

Slavery is for ever prohibited.

The liberty of the press is guarantied; *a guarantee, however, purely theoretical: it is no more free than in France, nor as free.*

Equally theoretical is the provision that no one shall be arrested but by the authority of law.

No taxes to be imposed but by the legislative authority.

Private property not to be taken for public uses but with just compensation.

Mexicans to be preferred for public offices to strangers, if their qualifications are equal.

Persons who have attained the age of eighteen years are entitled to the rights of citizens, if married; if unmarried, twenty-one years; and who have an annual income of two hundred dollars, either from labor or the profits of capital.

After the year 1850, those only are to exercise the privileges of a citizen who can read and write.

By becoming a domestic servant, the privileges of a citizen are suspended: so, also, pending a criminal prosecution, being a habitual drunkard or gambler, a vagrant, or keeping a gaming-house.

The rights of citizenship are lost by conviction of an infamous crime, or for fraudulent bankruptcy, or by malversation in any public office.

The legislative power is composed of a house of deputies and a senate; one deputy for every seventy thousand inhabitants. A supernumerary deputy shall be elected in all cases to serve in the absence of the regular deputy.

The age prescribed for members of congress is thirty years. They must have an annual income of twelve hundred dollars. One-half of the members to be re elected every two years.

The senate is composed of sixty-three members, two-thirds of whom are to be elected by the departmental assemblies; the other third by the house of deputies, the president of the republic, and the supreme court; each department to vote for forty-three persons, and those having the highest number of votes of the aggregate of all the departmental assemblies are elected senators. The judges of the supreme court and the president shall vote in like manner for the remaining third; and out of the names thus voted for by each of those departments of the government, the house of deputies selects the proper number (twenty-one). The first selection of this third of the senators to be made by the president (Santa Anna) alone.

The president of the republic and judges of the supreme court are required to vote only for such persons as have *distinguished* themselves by important public services, civil, military, or ecclesiastical. Amongst others disqualified from being elected members of the house of deputies, are the archbishops, bishops, and other high ecclesiastical officers.

The senators elected by the departments are required to be five agriculturists, and the same number of each of the following occupations — miners, merchants, and manufacturers: the remainder to be elected from persons who have filled the office of president, minister of state, foreign minister, governor of a department, senator, deputy, bishop, or general of division. The age of a senator is thirty-five years, and an annual income of two thousand dollars is required.

One-third of the senate to be renewed every three years.

All laws must originate in the house of deputies.

All treaties must be approved by both houses of congress. Congress has a veto upon all the decrees of the departmental assemblies which are opposed to the constitution or the laws of congress.

Congress are forbidden to alter the laws laying duties on imports which are intended for the protection of domestic industry.

No retrospective law or laws impairing the obligation of contracts to be passed.

The senate to approve the president's nomination of foreign ministers, consuls, and of officers in the army above the rank of colonel.

Members of congress not to receive executive appointments except with certain limitations, amongst which is the consent of the body to which they belong.

The other powers of congress are nearly the same as in our own or other popular constitutions. The president must be a native of the country, and a layman, and holds his office for the term of five years. It is made his duty to supervise the courts of justice, and he may prescribe the order in which cases shall be tried. He may impose fines, not exceeding five hundred dollars, upon those who disobey his lawful commands. Certain large powers are conferred upon him in relation to concordats, bulls, decrees, and other ecclesiastical matters. He possesses a very qualified veto upon the acts of congress. He may call an extra session of congress, and prescribe the only subjects to be considered. The president not to exercise any military command without the consent of congress. Not to leave the republic during his term of office, nor for one year after its expiration, but with the consent of congress, nor to go more than six leagues from the capital, without the like permission. He shall in no case alienate, exchange, or mortgage any portion of the territory of the republic. All his acts must be approved by the secretary of the department to which it properly belongs. He cannot be prosecuted criminally, except for treason against the national independence, or the form of government established by the constitution during his term of office, nor for one year afterwards.

During the temporary absence of the president, his functions devolve upon the president of the senate; if his absence continues longer than fifteen days, a president ad interim shall be elected by the senate. The other grants of power to the executive seem to be pretty much copied from our own constitution.

The different secretaries may attend the sessions of either branch of congress, whenever required by them, or so ordered by the president, to give any explanations which may be desired. The secretaries are responsible for all acts of the president in violation of the constitution and laws which they may have approved.

The council of the president consists of seventeen members, selected by himself. These councillors must be thirty-five years old, and have served at least ten years, without intermission, in some public station.

The judges of the supreme court must be forty years old.

The government may be impleaded in this court by any individual (I think a wise and just provision); as may also the archbishops and bishops in particular cases.

A permanent court-martial is also organized, composed of generals and lawyers, appointed by the president.

Each department has an assembly of not more than eleven, nor less than seven members. Their powers are to impose taxes for the use of the department; establish schools and charitable institutions; make roads and keep them in order; arrange the mode of raising troops which may be required of the department; establish corporations, superintend the police, and encourage agriculture; propose laws to the congress, and fit persons to the president for the office of governor of the department (from the persons thus recommended, the president, except in extraordinary cases, must make the selection); establish judicial tribunals for their departments, with many other powers of a similar character; and constituting the assembly a sort of state legislature, with jurisdiction of matters appertaining strictly to the department.

The whole republic is divided into sections of five hundred inhabitants. Each of these sections selects by ballot one elector. These electors in turn elect others, in the ratio of one for every twenty of the electors thus primarily elected. These last constitute the electoral college of the department, which again elect the deputies of the general congress, and the members of the departmental assembly. All persons who have attained the age of twenty-five years, are eligible as primary electors. The secondary electors must also have an income of five hundred dollars a year. On the first of November preceding the expiration of the term of office of the president, each of the departmental assemblies is required to meet and cast their votes for his successor. A majority of the votes of this assembly decides the vote of the department. On the second day of January, both houses of congress assemble together and declare the election. If no one has received the votes of a majority of the departments, the two houses of congress make the election from the two who have received the greatest number of votes. If more than two have an equal number of votes, the election is made from those who have received such equal number. If one has received a higher number, and two others have received a less and equal number of votes, congress selects, by ballot, one of these last to compete with him who has received a higher number. This election is required to be finished in a single session.

In cases of a tie a second time in these elections, the choice is to be made by lot.

Punishments shall in no case extend to confiscation of property, or to attainder.

No cruel punishment shall be inflicted in capital cases, only such as are necessary to take life.

The judges are responsible for any irregularities or mistakes in their official proceedings. They hold their offices for life.

Amendments of the constitution to be made by a vote of two-thirds of both branches of congress.

The Catholic religion is established to the exclusion of all others. Most of the other provisions of the constitution seem to be almost exactly copied from that of the United States.

Santa Anna was inaugurated under this instrument, January 1, 1841.

This is by no means a constitution, but is calculated to give an idea of Mexico far more exalted than any generally entertained. It could scarcely be expected that a people just emerged from civil war would be able to provide for all things, and foresee all difficulties; but it will appear that most of the requisitions of society have at least been remembered.

This may be considered as the realization of the schemes of which Santa Anna sketched the outlines when he achieved the revolution which deposed Bustamente. Thus again did this chieftain succeed in fastening on the people the central system, which revolution after revolution had each time seemed to throw off. It was his work only, and he only is responsible for its effects. The people, however, seemed satisfied with it; and the reason is, that the people in Mexico are few in numbers, while the populace is immense; and that all power was collected in the hands of a very small number of that people. No one, we fancy, will call Mexico a republic, or Santa Anna a patriot, as Mr. Thompson says he is not a model man, but he is a great one. He has outlived all his early associates, while every man who began life with him is either dead or in exile. He rides above the storm, the very heavings of which he fashions to his will.

The condition of Mexico at the present day recalls a

passage of one of the letters of Jacopo Ortiz, in relation to his own Italy, at the commencement of the present century:

"Italy," says he, "has soldiers, but they are not her defenders; she has friars and monks, who are not priests; she has counts and marquises, but no nobility; and a populace, but not a people." To create this was the mission of the Italian patriots, who failed in driving the strangers from her soil; which the Mexicans have already achieved for themselves. The world has hopes of Italy, which yet writhes beneath the heel of the Austrian; why should it not be hopeful of Mexico, on the soil of which the Spaniard has not stood for twenty years?

Canalizo, it will be remembered, was the confidant of Bustamente when Paredes went over to Valencia on his attacking the president, to whom he had made such professions of attachment in July, 1842. Even after the resignation of Bustamente, Canalizo held out for some time with but three hundred men, and by his valor won the name of "*El Lion de Mejico.*" As soon as all was settled, Santa Anna determined, Richelieu-like, to blot him from the list of his enemies by favors, and appointed him in his absence president *ad interim*; an exhibition of shrewdness which subsequent events have proved prudent. With Valencia he soon quarrelled, and stripped him of his command, and caused Paredes to be arrested at Tula. Paredes was a resident of Guadalajara, a district represented as the best in Mexico in point of wealth, the cultivation of its lands, and information of its inhabitants; and having been permitted to return thither, he set about the organization of his friends, so that it became obvious he was about to pronounce on the first opportunity. Santa Anna too, it is probable, became aware of this, and, anxious to remove him from the scene of his influence, called him to Mexico, and in terms of the greatest conciliation appointed him to the government of Sonora and Sinaloa. On passing through Guadalajara, the friends of Paredes flew to arms, and a pronunciamento was made, which resulted in the downfall of Santa Anna. The affair at the very beginning looked so dangerous that Santa Anna, contrary to one of the provisions of the Organic Bases, placed himself at the head of the troops in the capital, leaving Canalizo to manage the government, and marched to suppress the outbreak. Before, however, he had advanced far on the route, the provinces near the capital also pronounced, and he was forced to return to the city, where Canalizo was altogether unable to manage his numerous opponents. The *pronunciamento* of Paredes complained of the disorganization of the army, the dilapidation of the finances, entire disorder in all departments of the government, and the failure of the various expeditions against Texas, solely on account of the incompetency or neglect of the president. He concluded this manifesto with a demand that all acts of Santa Anna between the 16th of October, 1840, and the end of 1843, should be submitted to the approval of the supreme congress, and the president, in the meantime, be suspended from *his glorious functions of Chief Magistrate of Mexico.* Santa Anna has always handled the pen as readily as the sword, and addressed a proclamation to his army, in which he appealed to their sense of duty, and called on them to support him. The civil war spread through Jalisco, Aguas-calientes, Queretaro, San Luis de Potosi, and Zacatecas, all of which openly declared against Santa Anna. Nor was this all. General Alvarez, who commanded in the southern departments, also *pronounced,* and the disaffection became general. The first act of Paredes was to suspend the imposts levied for the ostensible purpose of invading Texas, which had long been very obnoxious. Vera Cruz finally began to show signs of revolt, which, however, were suppressed by General Quixano.

Things might have remained in this condition for a long time, but on the 2d of December, 1844, Canalizo, the president ad interim, assumed the responsibility of closing the session of congress, and of declaring Santa Anna dictator. For some days, this palpable violation of the constitution apparently attracted but little attention, but on its being reported at Puebla, the commander-in-chief also pronounced against Santa Anna. On the 5th, the garrison and people of the city cast off their torpor, and imprisoned Canalizo and his ministers. The congress immediately assembled and appointed General Herrera president *pro tempore*. A new ministry was appointed by Herrera, to the authority of which the whole country, including Vera Cruz, the strong-hold of Santa Anna, at once yielded obedience. The new ministry was composed of Herrera, president of the cabinet and depository of the executive power; Gonzago Cuevas, minister of foreign affairs; Mariano Riva Palacios, minister of justice; Pedro Jesus Echavarri, minister of finances; and Pedro Garcia Conde, of war and marine.

Santa Anna was left almost alone at Queretaro, with a few troops, already wavering in their attachment, in consequence of an appeal of Garcia Conde, who bade them leave Santa Anna and participate in the advantages of the new regime. Santa Anna was, it will be remembered, deposed from the command, and finally, by the proclamation of Garcia Conde, referred to above, was notified that he still was the constitutional president, and, as such, debarred from command without the consent of congress. His situation thus become drear enough, and it was obvious his chance of regaining power must continue slight, unless some great crisis should occur in which his one idea, self, might have an opportunity to undermine the many-phased Mexican republic.

Santa Anna was a man for great emergencies, and sought out of the "nettle danger to pluck the flower safety," by a coup de main against the capital; when, however, within sight of the city, these men declared against him. He then proceeded towards Vera Cruz, whence he was also repulsed. It was now obvious to him that all was over, as he was deserted by the remnant of his troops, except about two thousand five hundred men of all arms. He, however, made an attack on Puebla, from which he was repulsed, and fled to San Antonio, with one thousand horse. He fled thence at night towards Encerro almost alone, but was recognised by a party of Indians at Mico, three leagues from Jalapa, detained, and subsequently surrendered to the commander of the neighboring city. He addressed, on the 22d of January, a most humiliating petition to the congress, in which he adopts the European maxim, that the king can do no wrong, and offered to substitute his ministers for himself to fulfil the requisitions of justice. His address stated "that after the many privations and mortifications to which he had been subjected, he presumed they would be satisfied in awarding no other penalty against him than perpetual exile."

His address contained this remarkable passage: "Napoleon, after having outraged all Europe, was exiled to Saint Helena, and France, over whom he had long tyrannized, thought herself sufficiently avenged. My services have not equalled his, but I have the advantage over him in other respects. I can show by my mutilated body, that I have suffered for Mexico. The *august* chambers will then, accept my solemn *abdication* of the presidency, and permit me to assume eternal *exile*." It was generally supposed in Mexico, that congress would confiscate his property, especially as it became generally known that from apprehension of some such difficulty, he had sent eight thousand doubloons (one hundred and twenty-eight thousand dollars) by a previous packet to Havana, and had also invested in European funds, more than one million of dollars.

The congress continued to debate on its course in this crisis, and the friends of Santa Anna rallied around him, so that at one time, it became probable he would be able to resume his power. In the long intrigues which took place, he was ably sustained by Almonte, but was, on a final vote, banished for ten years. He was also stripped of a great portion of his money, his estate being suffered to remain in the hands of his *administrador* or agent. This occurred during the early part of June, 1845, and he immediately embarked on board of the English steamer Medway, in the river Antigua, about twelve miles north of Vera Cruz, accompanied only by his wife, a young woman of fortune, of about sixteen years of age, whom he had married not long previously, his nephew and a few personal friends. A general amnesty was then proclaimed, and congress, by a large vote, authorized the conclusion of a treaty recognising the independence of Texas, provided it should not become annexed to the United States. Santa Anna immediately left the country for Havana, and it appeared probable that Mexico would at length be at peace.

There Santa Anna remained, until by the events of the existing war he was, by the unanimous voice of the Mexican people, recalled, and immediately restored to power.

On his return to Vera Cruz, he published a proclamation so strange in itself, but so curious, both as a demonstration of the manner in which he has ever led the Mexican people, that it will not be considered irrelevant, in spite of its length, to reprint it.

Vera Cruz, August 16, 1846.

Mexicans: Called by the people and the garrisons of the departments of Jalisco, Vera Cruz, and Sinaloa, South Mexico, and other points of the republic, I quitted Havana on the 8th inst., at nine in the evening, with the sole object of coming to aid you in saving our country from its enemies, internal and external. Great has been my joy, when, on arriving at this point, I learned that the former had been overthrown by your own forces; and that I was already proclaimed, on all sides, as general-in-chief of the liberating army. A proof of so much confidence will be met by me with the utmost loyalty; but on accepting the plan proclaimed, allow me to enter into some explanation, which I consider necessary, in order to dispel any suspicions founded on a past, the recollections of which are so painful to me.

Desiring to consolidate peace in the interior of the republic, in order to make it flourish and prosper, and to assure by that means the integrity of our immense territory, I devoted all my efforts, in consequence of the events of 1834, to establish an administration endowed with vigor and energy, and capable of keeping down the spirit of turbulence and discord. Without ever going beyond republican forms, I endeavored for this purpose to support myself on property, on high position, on creeds, and even on the few historical memorials existing in our country; hoping thus to moderate, by the *inertia* of conservative instincts, the vehemence of popular masses. But without ascendancy and prestige, as I was, and the elements assembled by me being viewed with distrust, resistance was made on all sides; which I, however, expected to overcome in time. I call on God to witness, that in this I acted with patriotism, with sincerity, and with good faith.

After some years of trial, I began to remark that the republic did not advance; that some departments showed tendencies of separation from the others; and that the public discontent was daily increasing.—Wavering then in my convictions, they afterwards lost all their power, when a part of the country had been occupied by strangers, and our national existence of the whole was endangered. I called on the people to the rescue, and they answered me with threats; as if any other misfortune could have been preferable to that in which the country then was placed. Urged by the firm determination that we should be a sovereign and independent people, and knowing, on the other hand, the vast resources on which we could rely for support, I then became convinced that our government, being organized in a manner by no means conformable with the wishes of the nation, and governed by secondary legislature, not adapted for the advancement of its interests, the people revenged themselves in that way, by seeking for an occasion in which they should be called on to take care of their own good, and to organize their government in a manner which they should consider most proper.

In our time, we have seen another nation, in a similar conflict, employing similar means to oblige its government to promise the representative system which it was anxious to have established, and when that had been obtained, we have seen its moral apathy changed into heroic enthusiasm against the foreign invader who endeavored to subjugate it. Is there anything, therefore, strange in the idea that our people should, in this instance, do as much to recover the full enjoyment of their sovereignty, acknowledged by all governments, though trodden under foot by all, in the practical administration of affairs? On this point I owe to my country, in consideration of the part which I have taken, to declare frankly and honestly, upon this critical and solemn occasion, that it can be saved only by a return to first principles, with entire submission of the minority to the sovereign will of the majority of the nation.

Upon proof so clear and peremptory, of the serious difficulties attending that which I had considered best calculated to secure to the republic respectability abroad, I found it right to recede, and to yield to public opinion, and follow it with the same ardor and constancy with which I had opposed it before comprehending it. To discover the most effective means of raising the spirit of the public, and predisposing it to the war, with which we were threatened on the north, was my employment; and I was beginning to develope the measures for that purpose, when the events of the 6th of December, 1844, occurred, and plunged the republic into the miserable situation in which you now see it.

Expatriated from that time for ever from the national territory, with a prohibition to return to it under the hard penalty of death, the obstacle which I was supposed to present to the establishment of an administrative system, conformable with public exigencies, being removed, I believed that the men who had succeeded in placing themselves in my stead, by calling public opinion to their aid in effecting it, would respect that opinion, and summon the nation to organize its government according to its own wishes. Pained, as I was, not to be allowed to take part in the real regeneration of the country, I still most sincerely desired it; because I believed that whilst our political horizon was daily becoming darker, no other means was left to save us.

My prayers for this were redoubled, on seeing that, in consequence of the development of the invasive policy of the United States, stimulated by the perfidy of the cabinet of General Herrera, on the serious question of our northern frontiers, the European press began to indicate the necessity of a foreign intervention in our domestic concerns, in order to preserve us from the ambitious projects of the neighboring republic. That, however, which raised my uneasiness to the greatest height, was to see in a newspaper of credit and influence, published in the old world, a proposition made in October last, to bring us back, by force, under the yoke of our ancient masters. My conviction was, nevertheless, still strong, that no Mexican, however weak might be his feelings of attachment for his country, would dare to favor such ideas openly, and still less to recommend them to the consideration of the people.

Meanwhile, news reached me of a revolution projected by General Paredes, which revived my hopes; for though he had been the determined enemy of every representative popular government, I supposed that he had altered his opinions, and I honored him so far as to believe him incapable of advancing schemes for European intervention, in the interior administration of the republic. He succeeded, and his manifesto declaring his adhesion to the plan proposed by the troops quartered at San Luis Potosi, increased my uneasiness; because I clearly saw in it a diatribe against the independence of the nation, rather than the patriotic address of a Mexican general, seeking, in good faith, to remedy the evils of his country. His perverse designs were, in fine, fully revealed, as well by his summons [for the assemblage of congress] of the 24th of last January, issued in consequence of this revolution, as by the newspapers showing the tendency of his administration to the establishment of a monarchy, under a foreign prince, in the republic.

As one of the principal chiefs of the independence of our country, and the founder of the republican system, I was then indignant at this endeavor of some of its sons to deliver the nation up to the scoffs of the world, and to carry it back to the ominous days of the conquest. I thereupon took the firm determination to come and aid you to save our country from such a stain, and to avoid the horrible consequences of a measure by which its glorious destiny was to be reversed, carrying it back to what it was, and to what it never should be again. To execute this determination, was to offer up my blood to any one who, in case of failure, might choose to shed it, in compliance with the terms of the barbarous decree which drove me from the republic; but I preferred to perish in this noble attempt, rather than appear indifferent to the ignominy of my country, and see the countless sacrifices made for our independence, and the right to govern ourselves, all rendered illusory.

Mexicans: The real objects of those who, while invoking order and tranquillity, have constantly endeavored to prevent the nation from organizing its government as it chose, have now been laid open; and the time is come when all true republicans of all parties, the body of the people as well as the army, should unite their efforts sincerely, in order to secure entirely the independence of our country, and to place it at liberty to adopt the form of government most suitable to its wishes, each sacrificing his own individual convictions to the will of the majority. How, indeed, can the minority, however wise, opulent, and powerful they may be, pretend to assume to themselves the right to regulate the affairs of the community, or to govern the majority, without an express delegation from the latter, given of their own accord, not presumed, nor still less extorted by force? This may be among people who are ignorant of their own rights, and where the want of the means of independent subsistence subjects the many to the few, who have monopolized everything; but it is not to be effected among us, in whom the democratic spirit, in the midst of so many favoring circumstances, has been developing itself for thirty-six years, and now renders imperious and decisive, the necessity of concentrating by practice, the political axiom of the sovereignty of the nation.

This most essential circumstance has been disregarded and despised in all the constitutions hitherto given to the country; and in the only one which has appeared most popular, the antagonism of the principles adopted, has rendered it ineffective; so that democracy, which alone can serve as a solid basis for our social edifice, has been unable to develope itself, and thus to afford the peace which is its instinctive law, and the other ineffable benefits which it produces. Hence the convulsions which have so long agitated us, and of which some European writers have taken advantage, so far as to depreciate our race; opposing the liberty and independence of the republic; manifesting the necessity of interference, in order to strengthen it against the febrile invasion of the United States; and declaring, in fine, that it would be as easy to conquer Mexico with a portion of the troops now quartered in the island of Cuba, as it was in the time of the native Mexican princes. My blood boils on seeing the contempt with which we are thus treated, by men who either do not know us well, or who, interested in transplanting among us the fruits of their old social systems, and of the times in which they originated, consider America in the same state in which it was in the sixteenth century. Should any attempts be made, as indicated, to carry these mad plans into effect, all interests of race would be silenced, and but one voice would be heard throughout the continent. The one hemisphere would then be seen arrayed against the other, and for the disasters which would fall on the rash aggressor who should thus attempt to interfere with the internal administration of other nations, he alone would be responsible.

To pronounce thus against the many nations which form the great Hispano-American family, to declare them incapable of enjoying republican institutions, is, in fact, to be ignorant of, or to conceal, what is proved by the testimony of Chili, New Grenada, and Venezuela, in contradiction of such assertions. It is to attribute, no doubt with evil intentions, to men of a certain race, defects of administrative forms, which, not being entirely democratic, have produced the bitter fruits of the monarchical forms, engrafted on them, without adverting to the fatal influence of the latter on the lot of the others.

To expect, moreover, to strengthen the nation by

monarchy, under a foreign prince, is to suppose the existence in it of elements for the establishment and maintenance of that system; or that, wearied by its struggle to conquer its liberty, the nation sighs for European masters, or for anything else than the peace which alone it wants. Erroneous, most erroneous indeed is this idea. In the efforts of the nation to emancipate itself from the power of the few, who, in good or in bad faith, have endeavored to rule it in their own way, its democratic tendencies have acquired such a degree of intensity and energy, that to oppose them, to attempt to destroy the hopes to which they gave birth, by a project such as that advanced, would be to provoke a desperate measure; to endeavor to cure an evil by the means calculated to exasperate it. Fascinated by the example of a nation not yet a century old, and which, under its own government, has attained a degree of prosperity and advantages not enjoyed by those of the Old World, notwithstanding their antiquity, and the slow progress of their political systems, our republic aspires only to the management of its own affairs, either by itself, or through representatives in whom it has confidence, in order to develope the vast resources of power and wealth in its bosom.

This being therefore its dominant, its absorbing idea, it would have resisted the other plan with all its might; and if an attempt had been made to change its direction by the employment of foreign bayonets, it would have flown to arms, and war would have burst forth throughout its immense territory, renewing even more disastrously the bloody scenes of 1820 and the succeeding years. From such a state of things, the Anglo-American race would have derived great advantage for the progress of its ambitious schemes, or for forming a new republic from our interior departments, by exciting their sympathies and gratitude for the services rendered them in repelling a project no less injurious to itself. This tendency, which has been excited in some departments by disappointment from not obtaining provincial liberties, which they desired, would have become general throughout all; and no force would have been able to restrain them from carrying such views into effect.

On the other hand, the republic being composed for the most part of young men, who have no knowledge of the past, except from the sinister accounts of their fathers, and who, educated with republican ideas, rely with confidence on a government eminently popular, to lead their country to prosperity and greatness—where are the internal supports which monarchy presented as the means on which our salvation can be founded? That which has disappeared. Habits of passive obedience no longer exist; and if there remains a sentiment of religion, time has undermined the political power of the directors of consciences. An influential aristocracy, so necessary for the permanence of monarchies such as exist in old Europe, the only proper place for institutions of that class, is not to be found, nor can it ever be organized here. In Europe, the misery of the great mass of the overloaded population, which depends on its own labor to obtain what is strictly and merely necessary for its subsistence, in the midst of an industry which is so severely tasked, allows no time to the people to think of their political rights, nor means to free themselves from the tyranny of the patrician families, on whom they depend, all the landed property being in their hands. But no such state of things can be found in our republic; in which all is uncultivated, virgin, rich, and fruitful, offering to man, in the utmost abundance, and with the greatest facility, all that he can ask for his labor—all that can lead to that individual independence which favors the development of democratic instincts.

These difficulties being, therefore, of such a nature as to render nearly impossible the establishment of monarchy in our country, attempts have been made, in order to overcome them, to throw the affairs of the republic into the greatest disorder, preventing the organization of its government within, and aggravating the most serious question of our northern frontiers with another nation.

In this manner the faction which fostered that par ricide project, having attained the first of its ends by many years of artifices and manœuvering, next proposed to carry the second into effect, by provoking, in a manner almost direct, the government of the United States to aggrandize itself by taking our rich department of Texas, and then advancing into the very heart of our country. To involve our people in the evils of a fearful invasion, has been its last resource, in order to force them to accept its painful alternative—obliging them either to become the prey of Anglo-American ambition, or to fly, for the safety of their national existence, to monarchical forms under a European prince.

For this object it was that this party, having the control in the chambers of 1844–'45, refused to the government of that period the appropriations which it asked for maintaining the integrity of the national territory, already seriously jeoparded. It did more: it raised up a revolution, in which the slender allowances made to the government for that object, on its urgent demands, were unblushingly declared to be suppressed: and, on its triumph, it scattered the means collected for the war, and hastened to recognise the independence of Texas. The chief of this revolution, who has always acted under the influence of his own fatal inspirations, then appeared again in insurrection at San Luis Potosi, with the force destined for the defence of the frontiers; and withdrawing that force to the capital of the republic, he there usurped the supreme power, and began to put in operation his scheme of European intervention in our interior administration, whilst the hosts of the Anglo-Americans were advancing to take possession, even of the banks of the Rio Bravo. Having at his disposal considerable forces in the adjoining departments, he allowed the enemy time to advance, without resistance, through our territory; and at length—most tardily—he sent to Matamoras a small body of troops, needy, and unprovided with anything necessary for conducting the campaign with success. Who can fail to see, in these perfidious manœuvres, the bastard design of attracting the forces of the enemy to our central territories, in order there to propose to us, in the midst of the conflicts of war, as the only means of safety, the subjection of the republic to servitude, the ignominy of the country, the revival of the plan of Iguala—in fine, the return to the government of the viceroys.

With this object, and for this fatal moment, which every means was employed to hasten, was a congress assembled, chosen for the purpose, composed only of representatives of certain determined classes, not forming even a sixth of our population, and elected in a manner, perfidiously arranged, to secure a number of voices sufficient to place the seal of opprobrium on the nation. Leaving, with scarcely a single representative, the great majority of the nation, the eleven bishops of our dioceses were declared deputies, and our ecclesiastical *cabildos* were authorized to elect nine others on their parts, giving to the bishops the faculty of appointing such proxies as they might choose, to take their places in case they should not find it convenient to attend in person. Does not this prove abundantly that a decided endeavor was made to supplant the will of the nation, in order to give some species of authority to this scheme of European intervention in the settlement of our internal affairs?

The protestation of republican sentiments made by General Paredes, after these irrefragable proofs so fully condemning him, were only new acts of perfidy, intended to tranquillize the republic, to set its suspicions at rest, and to arrange the occasion for carrying into effect his base designs. He uttered these protestations in the middle of March last, when he saw the public discontent manifest itself against his powers and his plans. But what followed? Did he not continue to protect the Tiempo, a newspaper established in the capital itself, for the sole object of rendering republican forms odious, and recommending the necessity of a monarchy; advancing every argument which could be supposed calculated to lead astray the good sense of the nation? Did he convene another popular congress? Did he retract the summons which he had issued in January, placing the fate of the nation at the mercy of the few men who remain among us of the old colonial regime? Everything continued in the same way; and, when the press was prohibited from discussing forms of government, it was in order to give an amnesty to the writers in favour of monarchy, who were then prosecuted by the judicial power, and to encourage them to continue their criminal publications, while silence was imposed on the defenders of the republican system. Meanwhile he hastened, by every means in his power, the assemblage of the congress destined to carry into effect his monarchical plan; he concentrated his forces, in order to suppress all movements on the part of the people, alarmed by the near approach of such an unpropitious event; abandoning our frontiers to the invaders, or rather surrendering them to the foreign enemy, by the reverses which he had prepared and arranged at Palo Alto and Resaca de la Palma.

No, Mexicans! let there be no compromise with a party whose conduct has been a tissue of cruel treachery towards our country; have nothing to do with it, however flattering be its promises, and whatsoever the forms with which it may in future invest itself.

In the last convulsions of its agony, it sought to assure its safety by its accustomed manœuvres. It proclaimed principles which it detested. It allied itself with bastard republicans, and exhibited itself as the friend of liberty, in order, by that means, to avoid its just punishment, to maintain itself in power, and to continue to undermine the edifice cemented by the illustrious blood of the Hidalgos and Morelos.

The fraudulent schemes of the enemies of our country being thus unfolded, and the true source of its misfortunes being laid open to all, the radical remedy of the whole evil consists in putting an end for ever to the ruinous control of minorities, by calling on the nation honestly to fix its own destiny, and to secure its territory, its honor, and its welfare. Thus placed in entire liberty to act, as it should be, in the midst of the discussions carried on by the press, in the tribune, and even in the streets and squares, it will take into consideration the evils which surround it, and seek the means of resisting them; and satisfied in its desires, mistress of its own fate, it will display the energy peculiar to a free people—will prove equal to the conflicts in which it is to be engaged—and will come out of them, not only honorably, but moreover, entirely regenerated. In this way, the administration, established, resting on, and springing from public opinion, may display all its organized forces, to maintain our territory, instead of quartering them in the central towns, as hitherto, under a government created by seditious movements, constantly at war with the nation, and occupied solely in endeavoring to save itself, without regard for our external dangers.

Fellow-countrymen, never has the situation of the republic been so difficult as at present. Its national existence threatened on one side, on the other an attempt has been to subject it to the hardest of all lots, to European dominion. Such is the abyss to which we have been brought by the endeavor to govern our young society according to the system adopted in the old. This, the true cause of the long struggle in which we have been engaged, which has weakened our forces, and by which the interests of the majority have been sacrificed to the extravagant pretensions of a small minority. This state of things must be ended, in compliance with the wishes of the nation; and by opposing to the former, the union of republicans of true faith, the concert of the army and the people. By this union we shall conquer the independence of our country; thus united, we shall confirm it by establishing peace on the solid basis of public liberty; thus united, we shall preserve the integrity of our immense territory.

But now, with regard to the plan proposed for the

revolution, it is my honor and my duty to observe, that by limiting the congress therein proclaimed to the organization of the system of government, and the determination of what relates to the serious question of our northern frontiers, the provisional government of the nation would find itself required, until the system has been thus organized, to use its own discretion on all other points. This would be investing the provisional government with a dictatorship, always odious, however imperious might be the circumstances rendering it necessary. I therefore propose that the said assembly should come fully authorized to determine with regard to all branches of the public administration, which may be of general interest, and within the attributes of the legislative power; the provisional executive of the nation acting with entire submission to its determinations.

I consider it, moreover, indispensable that a uniform rule be established for the regulation of the interior affairs of the departments; and that for this purpose the constitution of the year 1824 be adopted, until the new constitutional code be completed. By this means we shall avoid that divergency of opinions, at this critical moment, when uniformity is so much needed; the national will which sanctioned that code will have been consulted, and the executive of the nation will have a guide to follow, so far as the present eccentric position of the republic will allow. I submit both measures to the will of the departments, expressed by the authorities, who may be established in consequence of the revolution; proposing, moreover, that the provisional government of the nation should adopt forthwith the second, as the rule of its conduct, until it be determined otherwise by the majority of the departments, in the form already indicated. The slave of public opinion myself, I shall act in accordance with it, seeking for it henceforth in the manner in which it may be known and expressed, and subjecting myself afterwards entirely to the decisions of the constituent assembly, the organ of the sovereign will of the nation.

Mexicans! There was once a day, and my heart dilates with the remembrance, when leading on the popular masses, and the army, to demand the rights of the nation, you saluted me with the enviable title of *soldier of the people.* Allow me again to take it, never more to be given up; and to devote myself until death, to the defence of the liberty and independence of the republic.

ANTONIO LOPEZ DE SANTA ANNA.

His old position he yet occupies, in spite of two signal defeats and a tide of misfortunes, which would justify a more volatile people than the Mexicans, in a popular commotion. Of all the men in that country, he is best calculated to guide her in such an emergency as has befallen her, and he is doubtless wise enough to know that not only the good of the country, but his own selfish ends, can only be attained in a season of peace.

The glance we have thus given of the public events of the life of General Santa Anna, is a meagre sketch, but will suffice to show that he has played no inconsiderable part in the events which have occurred in Mexico, all of which will appear either to have been effected by him or for his benefit. One who occupies so prominent a station, cannot be denied to be great, though it is by no means a consequence that he is good. It is probable no one living is so unpopular in the United States, in some portions of which his name is never mentioned but with execrations. The events of the war with Texas, so disastrous to him, have made him universally known; and so long as English is written, will the massacre of Colonel Fanning be looked on as an atrocity unparalleled, and worthy of the severest punishment. We cannot but look on his violations of his treaty with Houston as being a wilful disregard of his word, but to both the one and the other it may be urged that he followed the example of those whom the world points to as models. Malta is yet in the hands of the English, in spite of a sealed treaty which promised its surrender, and often have the rules of war been violated by the same government, with regard to her prisoners. It may not be amiss to hear what he says himself in relation to the first of these occurrences, as reported by an unquestionable authority.

"As to the affair at the Alamo, he said that it was not expected of any commander to restrain his troops when a place was taken by storm, and still less so when the disproportion of the forces of the besiegers and besieged was so great as to make a successful defence altogether hopeless—that in such a case to protract the defence was a wanton sacrifice of the lives of the assailants, and unjustifiable; that scenes equally sanguinary were enacted by the troops under the command of the Duke of Wellington at the storming of San Sebastian, Ciudad Rodrigo, and Badajos. The Texans who defended the Alamo did not exceed one hundred and fifty men, without artillery, against between four and five thousand Mexicans, with artillery. He added that he had seven different times summoned them to surrender, and offered them quarter, which he would have taken the risk and responsibility of granting, but that they refused to accept it, and fought to the last and died gloriously."

His justification of the shooting of Fanning's men, has been given in an earlier part of this work.

In a career of thirty years, but three events have occurred to cast on Santa Anna the stains of cruelty; and when we remember the sanguinary school in which he grew up, we have more reason to wonder at his moderation than his excesses. Far hence be any design to palliate his faults, which are dark enough to need no fancy touches and misrepresentations to give them theatrical *effect* to suit those who most prefer to sup on horrors.

Santa Anna has amassed a vast fortune; it does not, however, follow that this has been by means of peculation, for his father was an officer of rank, and he has twice married women of estate. The first Senora Santa Anna has been represented by all as kind and gentle, ever exerting her influence for good, and deservedly popular. Much of the consideration and kindness extended to the Santa Fe prisoners was to be attributed to her, and more than one of them have remembered her. She was the mother of a daughter of whom the journals of Mexico have recently made but little mention. The present Senora he married soon after the death of the former, which took place in 1843. The second one is said to be attached to him, has shared his exile, and submitted to much privation with him.

Such is Santa Anna, whether good or bad, what his country has made him. A chapter of his history is yet to be written which will perhaps display him in yet more brilliant colors: or, it may be, record another reverse from which he will be unable to recover himself.

CHAPTER VIII.

VALENTINO GOMEZ FARIAS AND ANASTASIO BUSTAMENTE.

Farias an opponent of Iturbide — Elected vice-president — Attempts to obtain liberal institutions—Congress suspends its sessions—Farias banished—Returns to Mexico—Pronounces against Bustamente's government—His attempt defeated—Early life of Bustamente — Election to the presidency—Banished—Returns to Mexico—His second election to the presidency—Resigns.

VALENTINO GOMEZ FARIAS is one of the most eminent men in Mexico, and has always been found in the same phase of the political world, a partisan of radical reform. His name has appeared in the records of every event since the revolution, having been a *diputado* to the first congresses; always the defender of popular liberties, he opposed Iturbide when the latter made himself a monarch, although one of his partisans at the commencement of his career; supported both Pedraza and Victoria, and has always been willing to stand by any one who would take a step towards the advancement of popular liberty.

He first appears in a prominent position when, at the expiration of Pedraza's presidency, Santa Anna was chosen to succeed him with Farias as his vice-president. The state of affairs in Mexico at this period was most peculiar. Santa Anna was the constitutional president, and sought to destroy the instrument under which he held office so as to extend his authority, while Gomez Farias, a liberal, or "*exaltado*," was anxious to increase the privileges of the people, and assimilate the government to that of the United States his great object of admiration. In the congress of 1833 and 1834, there was a strong majority in favor of the vice-president, and decrees were passed or proposed destroying much of the incubus of oppression, by which the church, heterodox in the eyes of the Catholic world, as it was repugnant to the principles of a free people, would have been removed. Santa Anna long protested against these innovations, and at length began to hint that he would employ force to counteract the views of the reformers. This was a hazardous scheme, the chances of which, however, he had well calculated; and by one of those manœuvres which he so well understood, he began to concentrate his forces around the capital. He proceeded so far as to post a guard at the door of the senate chamber, and gave to the officer in command, Captain Cortez, orders to exclude all but the senators known to be his friends. At this outrage, Cortez, who had been educated in the United States, represented, in a conversation not long afterwards, that though he obeyed his general, he felt as if he were guilty of matricide, knowing that he destroyed the liberties of his country. The consequence was, that the congress immediately declared the freedom of its discussions invaded, and on the 14th of May, 1834, suspended its sessions. This is the last thing a deliberative body should do. It should remember it has no dignity separate from that of its constituents; that it is its duty to do all things, to suffer all things, rather than degrade the character of the nation. A senate should never fly from a foreign enemy; and it may be with some propriety maintained, that it should sit, like the old Romans, calmly in the capitol till Gauls plucked at the beards of the senators.

The senate of Mexico, however, was not Roman. It was not even supported by the prejudices of the people.

It is one of the peculiarities of the Spanish race, on both continents, to love titles. The old Castilian, like the soldier in Kotzebue's "Pizarro," proof to bribes, can be won by an appeal to kindness and vanity. The race is everywhere fond of titles, and consequently jealous of those who possess higher distinction than themselves. Mier y Teran, when he dispersed the congress of Chilpanzingo, said "that instead of attending to the interests of the people, its members were occupied in taking care of themselves, and calling each other *excellentisimos*," and this account seems to exhibit all the characteristics of the legislative assemblies of the country, before or since. The consequence of such a state of affairs could not but be jealousy on the part of the people, the existence of which Santa Anna took advantage of. Immediately on the suspension of its sessions by the congress, Santa Anna appealed to the people by a proclamation, in which he set forth his views in relation to the preservation of religion, order, and law, all of which, he said, were threatened by the vice-president, Farias, and his tyrannical majority in the legislature. How potent this address was, will be understood by a reference to a subsequent chapter, in which is exhibited a statement of the condition of the church. The minds of the people having been prepared by this address, a pronunciamento was effected on the 25th of May, at Cuernavaca, a town of the department of Mexico, about thirty miles from the capital. The plan proposed on this occasion was strange: it put a negative on all prospect of improvement from the extension of religious liberty, by a provision that all laws affecting church property should be repealed; it destroyed liberty of political opinion, by an enactment that all the partisans of the federal system should be banished, that the actual congress had ceased to exist, and that another should be convened, the members of which were to possess full powers to re-organize the government. This plan was almost universally adhered to, and the session of congress finally ceased. The new congress met on the 1st of January, 1835, as has previously been described, and the first act was to declare the vice-president, Farias, disfranchised, and he was accordingly compelled to retire to New Orleans, where he resided as lately as 1838. It then proceeded to a series of discussions, relative to the form of government, &c., the result of which was a declaration that congress might make any alterations it pleased in the organic form of the government, so that a republican constitution existed, and the Catholic religion was not interfered with.

During the presidency of Bustamente, who seems far purer and less vindictive than any other of the public men of Mexico, the prohibition under which Gomez Farias lay was removed, and he returned to Mexico. Bustamente, it will be recollected, had been a friend of Farias, or, at least, at one period of his life, had professed as devoted an attachment to the old federal system; but during the absence of Santa Anna on his expedition against Texas, he had become chief magistrate under the constitution which declared the Mexican republic one and indivisible, and procured the exile of the subject of this notice. All accounts represent Farias as a pure and disinterested patriot, as one who, had he lived in the United States, would have acted with Jefferson and the other defenders of the greatest liberty against all and any usurpations. Bustamente, on the other hand, was a man of peace, a pupil of that school which believes whatever is safest is best, and which would inculcate the maxim that all things are better than a violation of public peace.

Madame Calderon, in her entertaining book, represents him as boldly avowing these opinions, admirable, perhaps, for a private citizen, but altogether unworthy of the chief of a nation. The minister, however, often finds it convenient to renounce the opinions he had professed when seeking power, and Bustamente, under the old and the new constitution, were different beings. The sanction of an oath, also, gave him an excuse for acting as he did.

No sooner had Farias landed in Mexico, which he did in the latter part of 1839, the date it is almost impossible now to ascertain, than he set to work to arrange his plans, and in General Urrea, already somewhat known from his participation in the campaign of Texas, he found a hand ready to execute what his head would suggest. This pronunciamento was made on the 15th of July, 1840. At the head of two regiments, one that *del Comercio*, the commandant of which was the celebrated Count Cortina, now distinguished as being not only one of the wealthiest, but most erudite men in Mexico, but who appears to have sustained Bustamente in this movement, they rushed to the palace *del Gobierno*, and imprisoned the president. The whole circumstances are, however, best explained by the government bulletin, an extract from which follows:

"Yesterday, at midnight, Urrea, with a handful of troops belonging to the garrison and its neighborhood, took possession of the National Palace, surprising the guard, and committing the *incivility* of imprisoning his excellency the president, Don Anastasio Bustamente, the commander-in-chief, the *Mayor de la Plaza*, and other chiefs. Don Gabriel Valencia, chief of the *plana mayor* (the staff), General Don Antonio Mozo, and the minister of war, Don Juan Nepomuceno Almonte, reunited in the citadel, prepared to attack the *pronunciados*, who, arming the lowest populace, took possession of the towers of the cathedral, and of some of the highest edifices in the centre of the city. Although summoned to surrender, at two in the afternoon firing began, and continued till midnight, recommencing at five in the morning, and only ceasing at intervals. The colonel of the sixth regiment, together with a considerable part of his corps, who were in the barracks of the palace, escaped and joined the government troops, who have taken the greatest part of the positions near the square and the palace. His excellency the president, with a part of the troops which had *pronounced* in the palace, made his escape on the morning of the sixteenth, putting himself at the head of the troops who have remained faithful to their colors, and at night published the following proclamation:

"*The President of the Republic to the Mexican Nation.*

"Fellow-Citizens: The seduction which has spread over a very small part of the people and garrison of this capital; the forgetfulness of honor and duty, have caused the defection of a few soldiers, whose misconduct up to this hour has been thrown into confusion by the valiant behavior of the greatest part of the chiefs, officers, and soldiers, who have intrepidly followed the example of the valiant general-in-chief of the *plana mayor* of the army. *The government was not ignorant of the machinations that were carrying on; their authors were well known to it, and it foresaw that the gentleness and clemency which it had hitherto employed in order to disarm them, would be corresponded to with ingratitude.*

"This line of policy has caused the nation to remain

headless (*acefala*) for some hours, and public tranquillity to be disturbed; but my liberty being restored, the dissidents, convinced of the evils which have been and may be caused by these tumults, depend upon a reconciliation for their security. The government will remember that they are misled men, belonging to the great Mexican family, but not for this will it forget how much they have forfeited their rights to respect; nor what is due to the great bulk of the nation. Public tranquillity will be restored in a few hours; the laws will immediately recover their energy, and the government will see them obeyed.

"ANASTASIO BUSTAMENTE.

"MEXICO, July 16th, 1840."

Previous to this the president had escaped. One proclamation in Mexico always produces another, and Farias, who had been proclaimed president by his party, issued the following reply:

"Fellow-Citizens: We present to the civilized world two facts, which, while they will cover with eternal glory the federal army and the heroic inhabitants of this capital, will hand down with execration and infamy, to all future generations, the name of General Bustamente; this man without faith, breaking his solemnly pledged word, after being put at liberty by an excess of generosity; for having promised to take immediate steps to bring about a negotiation of peace, upon the honorable basis which was proposed to him, he is now converted into the chief of an army, the enemy of the federalists; and has beheld, with a serene countenance, this beautiful capital destroyed, a multitude of families drowned in tears, and the death of many citizens; not only of the combatants, but of those who have taken no part in the struggle. Amongst these must be counted an unfortunate woman *enceinte*, who was killed as she was passing the palace gates, under the belief that a parley having come from his camp, the firing would be suspended, as in fact it was on our side. This government, informed of the misfortune, sent for the husband of the deceased, and ordered twenty-five dollars to be given him; but the unfortunate man, though plunged in grief, declared that twelve were sufficient to supply his wants. Such was the horror inspired by the atrocious conduct of the ex-government of Bustamente, that this sentiment covered up and suffocated all the others.

"Another fact, of which we shall with difficulty find an example in history, is the following. The day that the firing began, being in want of some implements of war, it was necessary to cause an iron case to be opened, belonging to Don Stanislaus Flores, in which he had a considerable sum of money in different coin, besides his most valuable effects. Thus, all that the government could do, was to make this known to the owner, Senor Flores, in order that he might send a person of confidence to take charge of his interests, making known what was wanting, that he might be immediately paid. The pertinacity of the firing prevented Senor Flores from naming a commissioner for four days, and then, although the case has been open, and no one has taken charge of it, the commissioner has made known officially that nothing is taken from it but the implements of war which were sent for. Glory in yourselves, Mexicans! The most polished nation of the earth, illustrious France, has not presented a similar fact. The Mexicans possess heroic virtues, which will raise them above all the nations in the world. This is the only ambition of your fellow-citizen,

"VALENTIN GOMEZ FARIAS.

"God, Liberty, and Federalism.

"MEXICO, July 17th, 1840."

Besides this, a circular was sent to all the governors and commandants of the different departments, from the "Palace of the Federal Provisional Government," to this effect:

"The citizen José Urrea, with the greater part of the garrison of the capital, and the whole population, pronounced early on the morning of this day, for the re-establishment of the federal system, adopting in the interim the constitution of 1824, whilst it is reformed by a congress which they are about to convoke to that effect; and I, having been called, in order that at this juncture, I should put myself at the head of the government, communicate it to your excellency, informing you at the same time, that the object of the citizen Urrea, instead of re-establishing the federal system, has been to reunite all the Mexicans, by proclaiming toleration of all opinions, and respect for the lives, properties, and interests of all.

"God, Liberty, and Federalism.

"VALENTIN GOMEZ FARIAS.

"NATIONAL PALACE OF MEXICO, 15th July, 1340."

Thus the ball opened, and as proclamations are valueless everywhere without force, and especially so in Mexico, the several documents were sustained by arms. Gomez Farias, though no military man, exhibited himself every where, and it was clearly enough shown that his cause was popular with the people and almost with the military, by the impunity with which he rode through the city. Mexico was, however, devastated; there was almost a want of the necessaries of life in the capital, and the lives of inoffensive citizens were lost in the public squares and private dwellings of the national capital.

On the 19th, the following proclamation was issued:

"*Address of His Excellency, Señor Don Valentin Gomez Farias, charged provisionally with the government of Mexico, and of the General-in-Chief of the Federal army to the troops under his command.*

"Companions in arms: No one has ever resisted a people who fight for their liberty and who defend their sacred rights. Your heroic endeavors have already reduced *our unjust aggressors* almost to complete nullity. Without infantry to cover their parapets, without artillery to fire their pieces, without money, without credit, and without support, they already make their last useless efforts. On our side, on the contrary, all is in abundance, *(sobra)* men, arms, ammunition, and money, and above all, the invincible support of opinion;—while the parties which adhere to our *pronunciamento* in all the cities out of the capital, and the assistance which within this very city is given by every class of society to those who are fighting for the rights of the people, offer guarantees which they will strictly fulfil to all the inhabitants of the country, natives as well as foreigners. Our enemies, in the delirium of their impotence, have had recourse to their favorite weapon, calumny. In a communication directed to us, they have had the audacity to accuse you of having attacked some property. Miserable wretches! No—the soldiers of the people are not robbers; the cause of liberty is very noble, and its defence will not be stained by a degrading action. This is the answer given to your calumniators by your chiefs, who are as much interested in your reputation as in their own. Soldiers of the people! let valor, as well as all other civic virtues, shine in your conduct, that you may never dim the renown of valiant soldiers and of good citizens.

"VALENTIN GOMEZ FARIAS.
"JOSE URREA."

Thus stood affairs for several days; and *Mexico la hermosa* was becoming a ruin. The palace of the archbishop was made a fortress by the party of Farias, a circumstance which, added to the fact that he had required, as one of the bases of any new organization of government, that the lands in possession of ecclesiastical bodies should be liable to alienation, and should pay taxes, as did the property of individuals, enabled the government to make representations that he had required the confiscation of the holy vessels of the cathedrals, and other churches, and thereby to alienate from him the people, whose superstition was more powerful than their patriotism.

At this juncture, came a letter from Santa Anna, dated Mango de Clavo, July 19, in which he professed his willingness to assist the president in allaying this commotion. This letter is remarkable; as Farias and Urrea, the latter of whom was never known to act but as the lieutenant of Santa Anna, had everywhere represented the last as their friend: and Bustamente at once took advantage of the circumstance, by publishing this *adhesion*, and others received from Valencia, Galendo, &c., in a bulletin, which, moreover, stated that it would be seen, in spite of all misrepresentations, how devoted Santa Anna was to the *national cause.*

The people of Mexico were not deceived. They saw in this Janus-faced policy, that Santa Anna, whatever might have been his professions, now made a catspaw of the pure Farias, and was seeking to grasp the fruits of a contest his high-minded contemporary had entered into for the good of his country.

On the 15th of July, it is well enough here to state, the following proclamation was made:—

"Ministers: I protest that I find myself without liberty and without defence, the guards of the palace having abandoned me. Under these circumstances, let no order of mine, which is contrary to the duties of the post that I occupy, be obeyed; since, although I am resolved to die before failing in my obligations, it will not be difficult to falsify my signature. Let this be made known by you to the congress, and to those generals and chiefs who preserve sentiments of honor and fidelity.

"ANASTASIO BUSTAMENTE.

"NATIONAL PALACE, July 15th, 1840."

The object of this was, that as Farias and his friends stated that Bustamente had been released, on condition that he would restore federalism, the public might be aware, either that such a promise had been extorted, or even if made in good faith, would be disregarded. On the same day, Urrea, who had command of the troops of the federalists, proposed the following terms for a cessation of arms:—

"Article 1st. It not having been the intention of the citizen, José Urrea, and of the troops under his command, to attack in any way the person of the president of the republic, General Anastasio Bustamente, he is replaced in the exercise of his functions.

2d. Using his faculties as president of the republic, he will cause the firing to cease on the part of the troops opposed to the citizen Urrea; who on his side will do the same.

3d. The president shall organize a ministry deserving of public confidence, and shall promise to re-establish the observance of the constitution of 1824, convoking a congress immediately, for the express purpose of reform.

4th. Upon these foundations, peace and order shall be re-established, and no one shall be molested for the opinions which he has manifested, or for the principles he may have supported, all who are in prison for political opinions being set at liberty."

All of which were rejected by the party of Bustamente.

On the 23d, the archbishop, acting in the capacity of mediator, which his social rank and functions entitled him to do, invited all parties to a conference in his palace, a proposition unanimously acceded to; but unfortunately, the truce was broken, and a bloody contest ensued; during the course of which, the *calle de Monterillo,* in which were the head-quarters of Bustamente, since he had left the palace *del gobierno,* ran with blood.

In spite of the rejection of the terms proposed by Urrea, Gomez Farias, on the same day, offered the following:—

"1st. The forces of both armies shall retire to occupy places out of the capital.

2d. Both the belligerent parties shall agree that

the constitutional laws of 1836 shall remain without force.

3d. A convention shall be convoked, establishing the new constitution, upon the basis fixed in the constitutive act, which will begin to be in force directly.

4th. The elections of the members of the convention will be verified according to the laws by which the deputies of the constituent congress were directed.

5th. His actual excellency, the president, will form a provisional government, he being the chief, until the foregoing articles begin to take effect.

6th. No one shall be molested for political opinions manifested since the year 1821 until now: consequently, the persons, employments, and properties of all who have taken part in this or in the past revolutions, shall be respected.

7th. That the first article may take effect, the government will facilitate all that is necessary to both parties."

These propositions were refused, and every means was used to prejudice the people against those who would have saved them; at the same time it was stated that Santa Anna was approaching the capital.

The more the revolution progressed, the more disgusting it became: evidently aware they were acting falsely to the interests of Mexico, every opportunity was taken to misrepresent the leaders of the revolt in the eyes of the people. A yet more unworthy system was pursued; the taxes were lowered to gain the support of the *leperos*, who thronged the capital. The consequence of this was, that on the 27th the president was enabled to say:

"We have the grateful satisfaction of announcing,

that the revolution of this capital has terminated happily. The rebellious troops having offered, in the night, to lay down arms upon certain conditions, his excellency, the commander-in-chief, has accepted their proposals with convenient modifications, which will be verified to-day; the empire of laws, order, tranquillity, and all other social guarantees being thus re-established."

Similar documents were sent to all the departments of the republic, and thus terminated the abortive but honest attempt of Farias to reform the government of his country.

The following letter of Santa Anna may be considered its finale:

"The triumph which the national arms have just obtained over the horrible attempts of anarchy, communicated to me by your excellency, in your note of the 27th, is very worthy of being celebrated by every citizen who desires the welfare of his country, always supposing that public vengeance (*la vindicta publica*) has been satisfied; and in this case, I offer you a thousand congratulations. This division, although filled with regret at not having participated on this occasion in the risks of our companions in arms, are rejoiced at so fortunate an event, and hope that energy and a wholesome severity will now strengthen order for ever, and will begin an era of felicity for the country. The happy event has been celebrated here, in the fortress, and in Tepeyahualco, where the first brigade had already arrived (and whom I have ordered to countermarch), with every demonstration of joy. I anxiously desire to receive the details which your excellency offers to communicate to me, so that if the danger has entirely ceased, I may return to to my *hacienda*, and may lay down the command of those troops which your excellency orders me to preserve here.

"With sentiments of the most lively joy for the cessation of the misfortunes of the capital, I reiterate to your excellency those of my particular esteem.

"God and Liberty.

"ANTONIO LOPEZ DE SANTA ANNA.

"PEROTE, July 29, 1840."

This plan had for its object the political regeneration of the republic, and stated that six years previously a constitution had been adopted arbitrarily, which destroyed the lawful government of 1824, and which appropriated to a very few all the advantages of the social compact. The time, it stated, had come, when nothing but the exertions of the whole nation would win its ultimate salvation, and place Mexico in the position she should occupy among the nations of the earth. The first and fundamental article restored the constitution of 1824, and called for a congress to be composed of four deputies from each state. The constitution, after a scrutiny by this body, was to be submitted to the people of each state for approval. The third promises that the Catholic church shall be respected (*respectada*); the form of government was guarantied to be popular, representative, and liberal, and absolute equality was insured. The fourth provided for a temporary government in the capital, whose functions were to be limited exclusively to foreign affairs. Other clauses provided for the refunding of taxes illegally levied, the closing of all internal custom houses, and the prohibition for ever of all taxes having such an object as the odious *Alcabala* of the Spanish rule. All political offences since the revolution were absolutely pardoned. Where is the fault of this plan? It has not even one selfish clause; yet it did not succeed. Farias also published a letter denying any design to touch the cathedral plate, and appended to this was a letter from the archbishop, stating explicitly that there had been no outrages committed in any of the ecclesiastical buildings occupied by his followers.

On the night of the 18th of August, articles of capitulation were signed on both sides; and Gen. Andrade, in the *absence* of Urrea, led the *pronunciados* from the city to Tlanapantla, whence they dispersed. When all was evidently lost, Gomez Farias disappeared; and Madame Calderon says, he was supposed to be concealed in the city.

His party did not, however, lay down their arms but on the following terms:—

"1st. Their lives, persons, employments, and properties are to be inviolably preserved.

2d. General Valencia engages to interpose his influence with the government, by all legal means, that they may request the chambers to proceed to reform the constitution.

3d. All political events which have occurred, since the fifteenth up to this date, are to be totally forgotten; the forces who adhered to the plan of the fifteenth being included in this agreement.

4th. A passport out of the republic is to be given to whatever individual, comprehended in this agreement, may solicit it.

5th. The troops of the *pronunciados* are to proceed to wherever General Valencia orders them, commanded by one of their own captains, whom he shall point out, and who must answer for any disorders they may commit.

6th. General Valencia, and all the other generals of his army, must promise, on their honor, before the whole world, to keep this treaty, and see to its exact accomplishment.

7th. It only applies to Mexicans.

8th. Whenever it is ratified by the chiefs of both parties, it is to be punctually fulfilled, hostilities being suspended until six in the morning of the twenty-seventh, which gives time to ratify the conditions."

Gomez Farias thus for a time disappeared from the history of Mexico. When Bustamente was expelled from his country he went to Europe, and amid the double-faced court of Louis Philippe, was highly feted and honored. It is a matter of some self-congratulation that Farias sought the shores of the United States. Far be from us the design to impugn the motives of Bustamente, who seems to have won the hearts of all who came near him. The aristocratically disposed Madame Calderon, altogether English in her views, and consequently disposed to support with her ready and powerful pen that clique which would favor the interests of her country, and as the wife of a Spanish ambassador necessarily remembering that the representative of the Spanish crown who preceded him, was a king in power and almost in station; and the democratic ambassador (comparatively speaking), all unite in giving testimony in favor of his honesty. Of this there is incontestible proof in the facts, that he laid down his public honors and his high power, poorer than when he entered the national palace as president, and in his long exile was indebted for all the civility he received, not to wealth, but worth. It may not be unsuitable here to refer to some of the incidents of the life of Bustamente.

When, in September 1810, Hidalgo and Allende raised the cry of independence, which gathered around them most of the true hearts of Mexico, Bustamente was about thirty years of age, a physician in the city of Guadalajara, which is about fifty leagues west of Mexico. He was already in possession in that career of some reputation, when he felt himself called on to abandon it to participate in the efforts being made against his countrymen, the insurgents, by Spaniards. During the four months which followed the first pronunciamento, he had under the orders of Calleja fought against the cura Hidalgo, Allende, Aldama, and Abasolo, the four principal figures of the great scene of Mexican liberty. He was a participator as a subaltern, it is said, at the battle of Calderon, and acted so bravely as to attract general attention to him. The result of this sad battle has already been described, and we will not now follow Bustamente through the bloodstained episodes of this cruel war, every page of the history of which is interesting as it is horrible. Suffice it to say that at length he joined the patriots, disgusted at the outrages of Calleja and Vanegas, and became a general in the republican ranks. It is a pleasant task to say that one of the first efforts of his authority was to take down from the stakes to which they had been affixed, the heads of Hidalgo and his comrades, whom he had opposed, and have them buried with the rites of the church; for they had been inhumanly treated as persons heretical and accursed. This was the year of the revolt of Iturbide, to whom Bustamente was always loyal, and in which for the first time he found himself in direct opposition to Santa Anna, who was the first to declare against, as he had been the first to hail him the emperor.

Don Anastasio Bustamente.

From this time to 1828, when the constitutional presidency was terminated, Bustamente participated in all affairs of state. On the 30th of November, an insurrection broke out in the capital, for the purpose of annulling the election of Pedraza, who had succeeded Victoria, the consequence of which was the sacking of the seat of government, the expulsion of Pedraza, and the accession to power of Guerrero, who, though called vice-president, was the chief magistrate *de facto*. In the next year, Guerrero shared the fate of his predecessor, except that death, not exile, was his portion.

In December, 1829, Bustamente commanded a division encamped at Jalapa, when, as happened often in that portion of the Roman republic Mexico has ever seemed to imitate, the soldiers proclaimed their general the ruler of their country. On the 18th of December, he set out for the capital, which he approached with his indefatigable soldiers with such rapidity, that Guerrero was unable to collect a sufficient force to oppose him, and deserted the seat of government, the defence of which he confided to a subordinate officer. Mexico cannot be approached from Jalapa without a great detour, except over a long and exposed bridge across the lakes which are on the western side of the city. This causeway existed in the time of Montezuma, and across it Cortes marched to destroy the Aztec empire. Its communication was at the barrier of Gaudelupe, where, as well as at the national palace, earthen defences were hastily erected. The merchants who remembered that in the same month of the preceding year, Mexico had been pillaged, made other preparations for defence, and fortified their warehouses. All who have ever been in any city of Spanish America, are aware that every building is a castle, and in the hands of brave men, would be a serious impediment to an enemy.

Parties of *civicos* (armed citizens) also patrolled the streets. This body was created in imitation of the national guard of France; but instead of being the protectors, like them, of public liberty, are composed, generally, of the dregs of the populace; and always have been found ready to follow any enemy of public peace.

Bustamente had marched to within a few leagues of Mexico between the 18th and 24th. The night of the 22d and 23d was very dark, and a thick mist hung, like an impenetrable veil, over the causeway, and concealed, from the sentinels at the barrier of Guadalupe, a black mass, which advanced rapidly towards this outlet of the city. At length, the body of men, for such was this mass, was discovered.

"*Quien anda?*" cried the sentinel. "*Amigos,*" was the reply. "*Que gente?*" cried the sentinel again. "*Tropas de Mejico.*" They were suffered to pass in under the impression that they were partisans of Guerrero; and as they passed, the drowsy guards asked, "*Donde han vmdes dejado Bustamente?*" (Where have you left Bustamente?) and were amply satisfied by being told, at Cordova.

Another, and yet another body of troops, were suffered to pass in a similar manner.

At daybreak, these parties united into one column, and proceeded rapidly down the streets of San Francisco and Plateros, to the *plaza del palacio,* of which, as well as of the terraces of the great palace, they took possession. In but a short time, a rumor was spread through the city, that a regiment of insurgents had passed the defences in disguise; and crowds collected in time to see them commence an attack on the startled garrison. Shot flew over the heads of the crowd; but all were too anxious about the result to leave. Bustamente at last entered the palace, and by energetic measures restored tranquillity, and prevented any recurrence of the scenes of 1828.

Thus was accomplished the victory of the Yorkinos over the Escoceses, referred to in the account of the presidency of Guerrero. Bustamente was for three years at the head of the government, which was in fact administered by Don Lucas Alaman.

During his government he sought to endow Mexico with the benefits of art and manufactures, and established the *banco de avio* to protect them, and employed eminent artisans of other countries to instruct the natives. Mexico continued, however, in a condition of turmoil, in consequence of the hostilities of Guerrero with Alvarez and Armijo, in the south of the republic, a state of affairs only terminated by the death of the unfortunate president. Of all participation in this the world has acquitted Bustamente, and attributed it to his minister Alaman, in the life of whom will be fully detailed all its circumstances.

In 1833, when Bustamente was replaced by Pedraza, and Santa Anna become president, after the expiration of Pedraza's term, congress was induced by Santa Anna to banish a number of his enemies, among whom Bustamente had the honor to be included, and was sent under an escort to Vera Cruz, whence he expected to go to France. The ship which he purposed to sail in, was not however ready, and Santa Anna caused him to be confined in a hulk beneath the castle with the vilest criminals, an indignity base as it was useless.

In 1836 he visited Europe, where he attracted much

attention, and it is said devoted himself to the studies of the peaceful career he had adopted in early life.

When Texas revolted he crossed the Atlantic, and asked to be permitted to draw his sword in defence of the rights of the Mexican nation he had once governed. He was more fortunate than he expected; the imprisonment of Santa Anna having allowed the nation to act as it pleased, he was chosen president on the 25th of January, 1837, and was inaugurated on the 20th of April of the same year. His opponents were General Bravo, his old minister Alaman, and Santa Anna. The latter, on his return, was accused of having sacrificed the interest of the nation by an onerous treaty he had concluded at Washington, but found Bustamente had forgotten all his private wrongs in the high functions of his office.

A few days after his accession to power, Bustamente, to allay the impatience of his troops, who had long been unpaid, and the demands of whom the treasury was unable to meet, paid to them from his own funds, ten thousand dollars. He also concluded a definitive treaty with Spain on the 8th of May, by which that power finally consented to recognise the independence of Mexico, and renounced all hopes of conquering it.

A severer ordeal for any ruler cannot be conceived than that to which Bustamente was subjected. The Mexican people have ever been prone to attribute to the government all their misfortunes; and the capture of San Juan by the French won for him many enemies. The penury of the country also added to his difficulties. Two years after this event, congress levied an impost of fifteen per centum on all articles brought into the city of Mexico. Commerce was already depressed, and this circumstance but added to the public distress; the many murmurs which were raised by the people, were eagerly taken advantage of. There has always been in Mexico a party of sincere men, lovers of the system of government of the United States, who neglect no opportunity to achieve their country's independence, who were on this occasion headed by Farias. A series of fights occurred, which filled up the whole space between the 12th and the 27th of July, the result of which has been already described in the preceding part of this chapter, and the effect of which was that Farias was driven into exile. There is, however, one episode which deserves particular mention. On one occasion the cannon had beaten in the wall of the national palace, and it was evident all would soon be over. The staff and friends of Bustamente besought him to fly, but he refused, saying that honor and duty required him to remain. Just then a band rushed into the room, crying, "Death to Bustamente!" The president advanced towards them, threw off his cloak, and showed them his glittering uniform. This intrepidity saved his life, for the insurgents withdrew without daring to lift a hand against the representative of their nation. The popular cause, however, was but partially successful; congress removed the new tax, and Bustamente retained his power. In the course of but a few months, a new revolution broke out which changed the state of affairs. Bustamente, disgusted with power, resigned and returned to Europe in the months of September and October, 1842. He passed some time in travelling, and finally established himself in Genoa, where he remained until the new troubles of 1844 and 1845 induced him again to seek his native land.

In June, 1845, Santa Anna arrived at Havana, in the English steamer Medway, and met Bustamente on his way to Mexico. Had the ex-dictator gone to New Orleans, he would have met Farias on a similar voyage. In the two victims of his last ambitious intrigue, he read a lesson that honesty is the best policy, for, though widely differing in opinions, both Bustamente and Farias are equally honest.

Both Bustamente and Farias have since participated in public affairs in a civil capacity; the one having been president of the congress at the time of Paredes' inauguration, and the other having contributed to the revolution which restored Santa Anna.

Events have recently occurred which change the whole aspect of affairs, and have produced a state of things which may conduce ultimately to the salvation of Mexico, provided that country does not blindly shut her eyes to the demonstrations of experience, and confide in the pretence of a false republicanism, which must fade before the truth of institutions more liberal in character and faithfully executed.

The president, Bustamente, must not be confounded with his kinsmen Don Carlos Bustamente, celebrated as the author and editor of many works on Mexican history and the memorials of the Aztec race, and Don Jose Maria Bustamente, well known as a botanist and contributor to the natural history of his country. The whole family are said to be distinguished by high talent and devotion to Mexico.

Don Mariano Paredes.

CHAPTER IX.

MARIANO PAREDES Y ARRILLAGA AND DON JUAN NEPOMUCENO ALMONTE.

Election of Herrera—Paredes pronounces against him—Herrera deposed—Paredes elected President—Deposed—Imprisoned—Escapes to Europe—Almonte—Battle of San Jacinto—Almonte sent minister to England and France—His character.

General Paredes is a new man in the history of Mexico, though one of its oldest soldiers, having participated in all the events which have occurred since the days of Iturbide. He first appears in the history of his country when the revolution of 1840, the one which overthrew Bustamente, occurred.

General Paredes was one of the persons whom Bustamente had especially trusted, yet he was one of those who first pronounced against him, and evidently was one of the prime movers of the revolution; having been referred to pointedly by General Valencia, in his proclamation of August 30, 1841, in the same paragraph in which he mentions Santa Anna and Cortazar, who avowedly planned the whole movement.

At this time Paredes commanded at Queretaro, nearly north of the city, and in the direction of Guanajuato, and Bustamente marched against him, but was forced to return on account of intelligence he had received that Santa Anna was advancing to the capital from the direction of Jalapa and Vera Cruz.

There is little doubt that Paredes was very influential in this whole movement; and was understood to speak the sentiments of the people of Jalisco, Zacatecas, Aguas Calientes, Queretaro, and the other mining districts, which had become aware that their mineral wealth could only be turned to advantage by the employment of foreign capital, and were eager for a repeal of those organic laws which prohibited foreigners from acquiring real estate (which, by-the-by, he has always been anxious to effect), religious toleration, &c. Whether he was sincere in this has appeared a mystery, as in the revolt of Farias, two months previously, he was known to have opposed that person with all his power. When the crisis, however, came, Paredes refused positively to accept the executive office, and insisted on its being conferred on Santa Anna. His reasons for this have been supposed to be that he was aware, as a general in command of a strong division, he would always be able to exert much influence, and at least take care of himself; while as president, he might, at any moment, be unseated, and driven into exile. On the 7th of October, the revolution terminated, leaving Santa Anna, where every change had contributed to place him, in power. One thing here occurred, which shows that both Santa Anna and Paredes estimated alike the value of the army at Guanajuato. It was proposed to make Paredes minister of war and marine; a compliment he declined, as he was aware its intention was to separate him from his division.

As previously stated, Santa Anna continued at the head of affairs as dictator until the first of January, 1844, when he was installed as president. In the course of less than one year, a revolution broke out, the result of which was his deposition, and the election of Herrera to replace him.

Santa Anna has always been in advance even of the

most enlightened of his countrymen, and was aware of the power of the United States. As soon as he saw that the annexation of Texas was inevitable, he prepared to submit to it, and sought gradually to bring over the Mexican people to his opinion. The consequence was, that towards the end of 1844, the views he had gradually begun to promulgate, were received with marked disfavor; and Paredes placed himself at the head of a spontaneous movement which pervaded the whole of Mexico, and resulted in the deposition and banishment of Santa Anna. When Paredes commenced this revolt he had twenty-five thousand men at his orders, to oppose which Santa Anna could muster but about six thousand, and thirty pieces of artillery, a proof the people sided with the former.

We will not repeat here the details of this *emeute*, which have been fully given in the life of Santa Anna, but will content ourselves with referring briefly to the immediate consequences of this one of the many changes of the Mexican government.

Many years since, a band of Indians of the Ojibway race, were sent by their tribe to Washington city, to arrange some of the many difficulties perpetually occurring where the white and red man come in contact. It need not be said that on their journey, every care was taken that the sons of the forest should see all that passed around them, and all the wonders of the pale faces. They finally returned home, having settled the business on which they had been sent, loaded with presents, but, as their brethren thought, having betrayed their interests. A general council of the nation was called, and the envoys were required to account for their acts. They told of the wonders of the city of St. Louis, with its thousand wigwams and twelve thousand inhabitants (this was twenty years ago); of Louisville, of the steamboats, and of the vast cities of the east, and were listened to with astonishment, but were believed. While the envoys were in the United States there chanced to be exhibiting himself, along the frontier, an eastern juggler, who, among other feats, amused the audience by swallowing a sword, and pulling ribbons from his mouth, by some peculiar legerdemain. The Ojibway council had believed all the astonishing accounts in relation to the power of the government; it had swallowed the histories by which the envoys had been imposed on, but would not hear one word in relation to the steam engines which manufactured cloth and ribbon, for they had seen the juggler pull them from his mouth. Arguing *a posteriori*, they disbelieved all former tales, said that the envoys were liars and unfit to live, and by the summary judgments of the Indian territory, put them at once to death. This was natural enough, for the world always measures what it hears by the events of its own experience.

So it was with Santa Anna; previous to the war of Mexico, he used to talk gravely of taking, some day, the city of New Orleans from the United States, and was not a little surprised when he found himself a prisoner, and at the mercy of a mere abrasion of that people.

On his way through the United States, he had learned how vain it was to contend against it, and sought on his return to import to his countrymen the rational views he had imbibed. The people of Mexico believed that his army had been routed in Texas; they had seen the fugitive and maimed soldiers, but they could not realize the information he bore them, that it was better for the magnanimous Mexican people to lose Texas irretrievably, than engage in war with a nation the people of which would possibly not be satisfied till they had reached as far south as San Luis Potosi, if they did not insist on unfurling their banner over the halls of Mexico. This information, gathered by so painful an experience, could not be appreciated by the people of Mexico, and enabled Paredes to commence his revolt.

Those who have followed us in this rambling sketch of the revolutions of Mexico, have become aware that nowhere has power so little security, or does office hold forth less inducement, than in the Mexican nation. The supreme power has, since the first outbreak of Hidalgo, been occupied by more than forty persons, who, with the exception of those who have died by the bullet and the bayonet, have seemed determined to make good Mr. Jefferson's description of office-holders in other countries, "that few die, and none resign."

Herrera was unable long to keep possession of the presidency. Paredes pronounced against him, and in union with Arista contrived to depose him. The pretext for this movement was a charge that Herrera sought to dismember the Mexican union by treating with the United States; and the army of reserve, stationed at San Luis and Monterey, was advanced to the city of Mexico, and the troops of Herrera gave in their adhesion to the more successful Paredes.

This resolution was momentous to Mexico, the American minister immediately leaving the country, and Mexico proceeding to adopt a line of policy which made inevitable that war which, in spite of all occurrences, must terminate by placing her at the mercy of a more powerful adversary.

After having for some six months exercised the supreme power, the congress convened and proceeded to re-organize the executive branch, which had not been legally occupied since the ejection of Herrera, and on the 12th of June Paredes was elected president, receiving fifty-eight out of eighty-three votes. General Bravo received thirteen, and Herrera seven. Bravo was then elected vice-president. After having been installed on the 13th, Paredes obtained permission to take command of the army, confiding the administration of the government to Bravo, who was recalled from Vera Cruz. The events of the war belong to another story than this; and it only remains to state that various pronunciamentos were made during the month of July, 1846, to which, on the 31st, the garrison of Vera Cruz, headed by Generals Landero and Perez, acceded, thus permitting Santa Anna to return, which he immediately did. Bravo assumed at once the title of provisional president. General Salas almost immediately seized on Paredes and imprisoned him in the citadel of Mexico, where he was confined until the latter part of September, when he escaped and proceeded to Havana. It is said that in Europe he is now perseveringly attempting to induce the governments of France and England to interfere in the existing war, in behalf of Mexico.

The motives of this pronunciamento have been much discussed, and it is unfortunate that the interruption of intercourse prevents its being more fully understood, by means of information from Mexicans, who alone could solve the mystery which hangs around it. The government of the United States, there is no doubt, contributed to effect it, by suffering Santa Anna to pass, on his return, through a blockading squadron, a thing now not denied, if it ever was. Why it did so seems obvious. This distinguished chieftain would doubtless be a formidable antagonist at the head of the Mexican army; but there was no doubt that the men who conquered at Palo Alto, Resaca de la Palma, and in front of Matamoras, the Mexican troops commanded by Ampudia, could conquer again the same men, commanded by Santa Anna; while it was obvious, that by the return of the latter to Mexico, a cabal which was headed by Paredes, who, for that purpose, had deposed Herrera, to place at the head of the Mexican government a Spanish or French prince, would certainly be frustrated. The event justified the means: the Bourbonists were defeated, and Paredes forced to seek protection among the kings for whom he would have sacrificed the independence of Mexico.

Don Juan Nepumoceno Almonte, so favorably known in this country, where he has long resided, is said to be a natural son of the distinguished General Morelos. In Mexico, where some time since the celibacy of the priests was scarcely a matter of profession even, the fact has never been denied; and the picture of the priest of Nucupetaro is said by travellers to have hung in the house of Almonte, and to have been treated with that respect which would scarcely be elicited by the picture of one not a relation. When Santa Anna marched against Texas, we first find the name of Almonte occupying a prominent position. In the massacres which will long serve to render the name of the Mexican soldier an approbrium, and which disgrace that campaign, we do not find, for a long time, any account of Almonte, and when we do, it is in the act of performing a military duty, and exhibiting a presence of mind which seemed to have deserted all others.

At the battle of San Jacinto, when the Texans made the famous charge with their clubbed rifles and bowie-knives, which won the day, so utterly unused were the Mexicans to such an attack, that it never occurred to them either to resist or surrender. Trusting exclusively to flight, they were soon overtaken by the hardy western hunters who composed the mass of Houston's force, and indiscriminately slaughtered. General Almonte, seeing that the fight was over, called around him a few officers, and by great efforts contrived to surrender the remnant of that army with which Santa Anna had boasted he would encamp on the Sabine. By the terms of the capitulation, Almonte returned to Mexico, where he found all things in disorder, the cause of his friend and patron, Santa Anna, ruined, and Bustamente seated in the chair of state. He was, it is said, very poor, but had by his talents made himself so well known, that the new government was glad to avail itself of his talents as minister of war. When the pronunciamento of Urrea and Farias occurred, Almonte adhered to the president, and on one occasion distinguished himself by the same courage which was so pre-eminent at San Jacinto. When the first overt act was made, Almonte chanced to be in the street, and was met by Urrea at the head of few soldiers, who asked for his sword, saying, at the same time, the president was arrested. Almonte drew his sword, but instead of surrendering it cut his way through the insurgents, and reached the citadel, where he concerted the measures which enabled Bustamente to repress the revolution of July. Urrea immediately retraced his steps, and passing the house of Almonte, discovered his lady at the window, of whom, as quietly as if nothing had occurred, he asked after her husband's health. Her astonishment may well be conceived, when, not long afterward, she heard what had happened. When the revolution in the fall of the year

Street in Mexico during the Revolution of 1840.

deprived Bustamente of power, Almonte left office with a great portion of his salary undrawn, and was so poor that, previously to his appointment as ambassador to the United States, he supported himself by delivering popular lectures in the capital on scientific subjects.

General Almonte resided long in this country, making many personal friendships, which have not been interrupted by the occurrence of national difficulties; and finally returned to Mexico. When diplomatic intercourse was terminated by the retirement of Mr. Shannon from the city of Mexico, he continued high in favor with Santa Anna, until the cabal arose which exiled him; and even while the dictator was in prison, worked in his favor with such zeal, that more than once it was doubtful if he would not be removed from the citadel, where he was a prisoner, to the national palace as president. These efforts, however, were unavailing; and, when all was over with his friend, Almonte was sent, in a diplomatic capacity, to the courts of France and England. He repaired thither by way of Havana, where he saw and had much intercourse with General Santa Anna. Whether it be that the appointment he had received was a *ruse* to remove him from Mexico, or that Herrera had become alarmed at the results of his conference with the ex-dictator, cannot now be determined; but his mission was immediately revoked. He returned to Havana, where he remained until the recall of Santa Anna, under whom he has filled important functions.

Few men in Mexico are more favorably known. He is brave, cultivated, and intelligent; and is likely to rise to a more exalted position than he has yet reached, having now the respect and support of the better class of his countrymen, of all phases of political opinions.

CHAPTER X.

DON MARIANO ARISTA AND OTHER GENERAL OFFICERS.

Arista—*Jarochos*—Campaign in the department of Vera Cruz—Duran's insurrection—Insurrection quelled—Arista ordered to the Rio Grande—Ampudia—Battle of Mier—Naval action—La Vega.

When Santa Anna was governor of Vera Cruz, in 1828 (the crisis of the cabals between the Yorkinos and Escoceses), Arista was a colonel and his aid-de-camp, and participated in the attempt made with success, on the castle of Perote. When the congress, in consequence, declared Santa Anna an outlaw, Arista was also included in the decree, and for a long series of years participated in all his fortunes. To Arista, who has the reputation of being one of the best cavalry officers in the world, it is not improbable Santa Anna was indebted for the formation of that famous corps of men, with whom he commenced the rambling campaign over the whole department of Vera Cruz, which first established the future dictator's reputation as a soldier, and in spite of all other checks he may have experienced, will place Santa Anna's fame as an officer and brave man, beyond all dispute.

These men were all from the tierra caliente, of mixed Spanish, Aztec, and negro blood, as we have said before, proof against weather and fever, very Arabs in constitution, while, from their vicinity to the mountains of the tierra templada, they are enabled to acquire the agility of the chamois hunters of the alps. Their horses

Don Mariano Arista.

were like them, wild looking and small, but hardy as their riders. Their arms were the lance and carbine, and their food, whatever they could find. The head of this corps, which, in emergencies, could always be increased indefinitely by all the rancheros or herdsmen of the district it chanced to occupy, was Arista. Emphatically a *hombre de caballo*, or horseman he was, it is said, able to perform feats of horsemanship amid the battle when squadrons were charging around him, that one of Franconi's pupils, with the readiest eye and boldest seat, would scarcely attempt in the arena.

The result of this campaign we have already described, and we will only say here, that though the forces of Santa Anna were finally driven into Oaxaca, and almost destroyed, yet he had distracted the attention of Pedraza's government so long that Guerrero was ultimately enabled to triumph. When Santa Anna became secretary of war under Guerrero, Arista was not neglected, and was made use of to keep up his influence in the tierra caliente, until Santa Anna thought proper to instal Pedraza again.

In the expedition against the last Spanish invaders, Arista also figured, and received a large portion of the rewards of the success. When Bustamente was deposed, Arista was yet the main-spring of all the plots of the period, though apparently occupied solely with the discharge of his duties as brigadier and commander of a department. In this movement Arista also figured as chief of the *Jorochos*, or men from the tierra caliente, who exalted Santa Anna to power in 1832. Towards the end of 1833 happened one of those ridiculous scenes, which, like the ecclesiastical *nolo episcopari*, or Cæsar's refusal of the crown, have occurred in every country. General Duran, who commanded in Vallidolid or Morelia, having commenced an insurrection for the purpose of proclaiming Santa Anna dictator, the latter patriotic and self-sacrificing individual was stirred with the greatest indignation, and as the depository of law and power, immediately marched to give the world an example of that superhuman virtue which made old Rome so illustrious. He was of course accompanied by his *fidus Achates*, General Arista. The latter, however, was no Roman, but a genuine Mexican, and immediately proposed to the president to let General Duran have his way, and to accept the greatness thrust upon him. Santa Anna was indignant, and told Arista that an acquaintance of so many years' standing should have taught him to appreciate his public virtue, and ordered him to be silent for ever on the subject. Arista immediately declared that he would not obey him; that his first duty was to his country, and that if Santa Anna would not consent to be the savior of Mexico willingly, he would make him serve her.

Arista immediately joined Duran with a large body of troops, many of whom, strangely enough, were *Jarochos*, or men from the tierra caliente, to whom we have previously referred as being so devoted to Santa Anna. In the course of this contest, in which there were many manœuvres and no men killed but a few known to adhere to the republican vice-president, Gomez Farias, Santa Anna was made prisoner and returned to Mexico, whither the revolt of Duran had extended, the garrison of the citadel and the city having given their adhesion to it. Farias opposed it; but the honor of suppressing it was reserved for Santa Anna. This *bene merito* of the country then marched against Arista and Duran, whom he forced to capitulate (need we say the terms were not severe), and retired to Mango de

Clavo, intrusting the administration to Farias until new events occurred.

We here lose sight of Arista for a long time, during which he was at Cincinnati, in the United States, in exile. In connexion with this period of his life, an interesting anecdote is told. Having been disappointed in the receipt of funds, he was in great distress, and worked for some time as a journeyman tinman, until circumstances relieved him from necessity. When the French landed at Vera Cruz, Arista, the story goes, was found in Santa Anna's house, and surrendered to the Prince de Joinville, who is, by the French authorities, said to have headed the party directed especially against Santa Anna. In the rest of the career of the dictator until his exile, Arista remained with him; and when war became imminent, having been assigned to the command of the army of Mexico on the north, was ordered with reinforcements to the Rio Grande, where Ampudia commanded. The two acted in concert, and contrived to lose battle after battle in the most unprecedented manner, and to march and countermarch between Monterey and the Rio Grande without opposing even a momentary check to the American general. This circumstance gives us the clue to the character of Arista. He had not, in all his early career, exercised any important command, and his master-mind, Santa Anna, being absent, he was altogether inadequate to the emergency of his situation. The quarrel between Arista and Ampudia consequent on the battle of La Resaca, might explain these events to the advantage of the former and to the Mexican people. This, however, is a task incumbent on a Mexican, and cannot be done satisfactorily till the war shall have ended.

Don Pedro de Ampudia has very long been an officer of the Mexican army, and became a general after Santa Anna had deposed Bustamente in 1840. He participated in many of the events of the Mexican expeditions against Texas. His first prominent service was in 1842, when a Mexican foray, headed by General Wohl, was made against the frontier of Texas, and many citizens were imprisoned and carried off. It has been said that this expedition was never authorized by the Mexican government, but was composed entirely of rancheros, who were collected by the hope of plunder. Houston, the president of Texas, immediately ordered out eight hundred volunteers to rendezvous at San Antonio, on the 27th of October, to oppose the force of Wohl, which consisted of thirteen hundred men. The command of this expedition belonged to General Summerville, who, however, on his arrival at San Antonio, found many persons willing to dispute the command with him. The troops, however, finally obeyed him, and he marched to the Rio Grande and took possession of the town of Loredo. Before reaching this place, many symptoms of mutiny occurred, and after he had left it, two hundred Texans, in open defiance of his authority, marched back and pillaged the inhabitants of everything worth being carried off. This occurrence, so very disgraceful, and which would have placed Texas and her people on a level with the brigands of Wohl, had it been approved of, determined General Summerville to retrograde, which was certainly the course otherwise dictated by policy, as it was obvious that the people of the Rio Grande were too poor to support his forces, and he had not men enough to make any permanent impression on Mexico.

At this juncture the excitement became universal, and the men so clamorous, that a council of officers was convened to decide on the course of the expedition, the result of which was, that a few already disgusted by what had occurred, returned home, but the majority continued their march. It is much to be regretted that Summerville did not accompany those who returned. He, however, continued as far as Guerrero, with no other intention than plunder. This was a miserable village where the people are poor and starving, without mines, agricultural wealth, or any other inducement, yet it was besieged. This circumstance so terrified the people that they sought by presents to propitiate the officers of the expedition, to prevent the recurrence of such a scene as had taken place at Loredo. There was much dissatisfaction among the men, who, however, resolved to continue on to Mier, a town of considerable importance.

Here, General Summerville became disgusted; and, as ammunition had begun to fail, did what he should have done long before, called on his men to return. One hundred obeyed him; and the rest, under another commander, resolved to attack Mier. The force which remained consisted of about two hundred and seventy men; and it is a mystery how they contrived to keep together, as their ideas of military obedience were of the rudest kind. Who really commanded is even now uncertain. A message was sent to the alcalde, calling for a contribution of five thousand dollars; and, when informed that all the money that could or would be be extorted was one hundred and seventy-three dollars, the officers determined to attack the town, though aware that Don Pedro de Ampudia was within it, at the head of a large force.

On Christmas day, the town was attacked; and, when night came on, the Texan force, under a heavy fire, was slowly forcing its way into the streets. It cannot be denied, unholy as the object of the expedition was become, the mass of its members being attracted by the desire of plundering the Mexican churches, and by the lawless pleasures of a partisan war, the officers and men fought with that courage and perseverance which have been conspicuous through the whole war of Texan independence. They at last reached a house where they were protected from the ordnance of Ampudia, and the contest was suspended until the next morning.

The Mexicans then advanced to the attack, and assault after assault failed, the officers being conspicuous by their insignia, and falling, one after the other, before the deadly aim of the Texan rifle. Ampudia at last sent an officer with a white flag to offer terms, which, after much deliberation, were accepted. The terms were, that they were to be surrendered as prisoners of war. The loss of Ampudia in this action is said to have exceeded five hundred men; a thing likely enough, as he acknowledged to have lost two hundred. The Texans had twelve men killed and eighteen wounded; and the survivors no sooner were in his power, than they were chained two together, and every stipulation of the surrender, except that which secured their lives, violated.

The events of this expedition have been the subject of much comment. The captured Texans were taken to various prisons, and a large party were long employed in laboring on the streets of Tacubaya. While on their march to the city of Mexico, they, on one occasion, overpowered the guard, and seized its arms, a circumstance of which advantage was taken by Santa Anna, to order them all to be shot. This sentence was afterwards relaxed, and every tenth man was made an example of.

Ampudia was, for his conduct on this occasion, much applauded; and we almost lose sight of him until the army of the United States approached the Rio Grande, when he was placed in command of the district around Matamoras, in which were Loredo and Mier, the scenes of his former triumphs.

Ampudia has, however, made himself infamous by an act of brutality, unequalled for many centuries in a civilized country. In the summer of 1844, the Mexican General Sentmanat, exiled by Santa Anna, made a rash attempt on the town of Tobasco, at the head of but fifty men, so confident was he of being supported by the population. The vessel which bore them was taken by a Mexican man-of-war, and this forlorn hope was surrendered to Ampudia. The unfortunate general was, with fourteen of his companions, shot; and their heads, the monster Ampudia states in his despatch, he caused to be *boiled in oil*, and hung in iron cages to the walls of the town.

General Sentmanat had lived long in New Orleans, where he married, and had many friends; and the news of his death was received with a burst of indignation, which may account for the prejudice entertained in the United States against Ampudia more than against any other Mexican general.

Immediately after the battle of Mier, which took place in December 1842, General Ampudia assumed command of the army, more than ten thousand strong, which had been for two months besieging the city of Campeche, (Yucatan), which port was also blockaded by the entire naval force of Mexico, consisting of three steamers, two brigs, and two schooners, under the command of Admiral Lopez. Campeche held out nobly, and on the following April, 1843, that port was relieved by the arrival of Commodore E. W. Moore, of the Texan navy, who had been detained in New Orleans for the want of means to fit out; which, although they had been appropriated by the Texan congress in July, 1842, were most unaccountably withheld by President Houston at that time, who controlled the destiny of Texas.

The government of Yucatan furnished Commodore Moore with means to get to sea, with which and the aid of friends in New Orleans, he sailed from that port on the 15th of April, 1843, in command of the sloop-of-war Austin, mounting *eighteen* (medium) twenty-four-pounders, and two eighteens, accompanied by the brig Wharton, Captain Lothrop, mounting sixteen (medium) eighteen-pounders. With these two vessels, which were well manned and thoroughly equipped, Commodore Moore sailed for Campeche, where he arrived on the 30th of April, and attacked the whole Mexican fleet, which after an action of over an hour, hauled off—but renewed the fight again during the interim of calm between the land and sea breeze; their steam giving them great advantage, besides their great superiority in weight of metal. Commodore Moore had in the meantime been joined by four gun-boats, which came out from Campeche; the action this time lasted but little over half an hour, when the Mexicans again hauled off. On the 16th of May another engagement took place, which lasted more than four hours, the particulars of which would exhibit, in the Texan naval forces, the existence of the gallantry which has ever characterized the same arm of the public service of the United States.

Commodore Moore made repeated efforts to engage the enemy prior to the last action, (May 16th), which was fought by Commodore Don Thomas Marine, Admiral Lopez having been arrested and sent to Vera Cruz for trial, for not capturing the two Texan vessels. Commodore Moore had one-fourth of his force killed and wounded, but he made repeated efforts to bring on another battle, which Commodore Marine, the Mexican commander, avoided, his steam enabling him to do so whenever he chose.

On the night of the 26th of June, the Mexican army embarked on board of their vessels of war and a few transports (it having been reduced full one-half by the vomito and desertions), and fell back to Tobasco, where General Ampudia remained until the summer of 1844; whence he was transferred after his barbarous course towards the gallant Sentmanat.

The following was the force of the Mexican navy:

Steamer Montezuma, two sixty-eights and six forty-twos, Paxihan guns.

Steamer Guadalupe, two sixty-eight Paixhans and two long thirty-twos.

Steamer Rejenerador, one long thirty-two and two long nines.

Schooner Eagle, one long thirty-two and six eighteens, all Paixhans.

Brig Yucateco, one long eighteen and sixteen eighteen-pound carronades.

Brig Yman, one long twelve and eight six-pounders.

Schooner Campecheano, one long nine and two six-pounders.

This is the first time that steam and sail vessels had ever come in contact, and Commodore Moore beat these three steamers (two of them armed with heavy Paixhan guns), they having a sail force co-operating with them, fully equal to the force of the two Texan vessels. It was also the first time that Paixhan guns had been used in a naval combat.

The reason why Commodore Moore ventured on such an unequal contest, was to save Galveston, the principal port of Texas, from an attack as soon as Yucatan had surrendered, which she was on the eve of doing, the preliminaries having been agreed on between General Ampudia and Governor Meredez, of Yucatan, who was in command of the troops at Campeche, and the articles of compromise were to have been signed the *very* day, April 30th, 1843, that Commodore Moore arrived off Campeche, and defeated the Mexican squadron.

Comment is useless upon the value that the little navy of Texas was to that republic, in her struggle for independence, by keeping her ports open, and the entire coast clear of all Mexican cruisers, from the year 1839 to the treaty of annexation, when the Texas navy was laid up in ordinary, (protection having been then guarantied by the government of the United States.) Although *two* proclamations of blockade of the ports of Texas were published by the Mexican authorities, one in 1839 and the other in 1840, the Mexican vessels of war were kept in their own ports, and many of their merchant vessels were captured by the Texan cruisers under Commodore Moore, who was all the while off the Mexican coast with some of the vessels under his command, up to the summer of 1842. At this time he went into New Orleans to refit, which he was prevented from doing by the extraordinary course of President Houston, already mentioned, who withheld the appropriations of congress for that purpose, and left Commodore Moore to keep up the navy with his own means and resources, which he did for upwards of nine months, and finally fitted them out for a cruise without a dollar from his government. He was proclaimed a traitor and pirate by the presi-

ment of Texas for this course, but nobly sustained by the people and congress of the republic.

This proclamation of Houston's was published in Texas the same day that Commodore Moore fought the overwhelming force of the enemy for more than four hours, and chased them, as Commissioner Morgan says in his testimony before the court martial ordered by the congress of Texas at the urgent request of Commodore Moore, "so far to sea that he could not see us from the top of the house he was on in Campeche."

The resolutions of the people of Matagorda and Galveston counties contain some interesting statements and show the feelings of the people. Meetings were also held in many of the other counties of the republic, and the disapprobation of the people expressed in strong terms, of the course pursued by President Houston towards the commodore of the little navy of Texas.

The conduct of Ampudia since the war, has been much censured by his countrymen, and in the United States many have been found willing to decry him. He has had, undeniably, great difficulties to contend with, and has scarcely had an opportunity to act otherwise than he has done. He was in command of men prepared to be conquered, who had a great disinclination to meet the American army, and who had, it will be remembered by all, mutinied at San Luis, when first ordered to the frontier. He appears, in spite of all *evidence*, to have done his duty as long as any of his brethren. He has since been arrested, and though released, now occupies no prominent position.

Don Romulo de la Vega is a soldier by profession, and when the war broke out only occupied the rank of colonel of infantry, with the title or brevet of general of brigade. He has won much reputation in this country since the war, having previously been entirely unknown. He has been stationed for many years on the northern frontier of Mexico, and was for a long time *xefe militar* of the department in which Monclova is situated. At the battle of the 9th of May he was taken prisoner while fighting, and having been exchanged, was again captured at Cerro Gordo during the present campaign. It has been stated that General La Vega has not made the return which might have been expected from so brave a man, for the hospitality and consideration extended to him, and that on his return to Mexico he suffered American officers who had been captured to continue in prisons not fit receptacles for military men. It may be doubted, however, if he has ever had the power to change their situation. He is, it will be remembered, only a brigadier, with many superiors, and with little influence. His gallantry has, it seems, been appreciated in Mexico, where he has since his return received promotion, and had confided to him an important command, a rare compliment to be bestowed on an unfortunate soldier. Whether he deserves this applause, may be doubted; for many have always been disposed to think, that when victory is hopeless, the bravest soldier may be permitted to think of himself.

General La Vega is young and handsome, with an appearance altogether prepossessing, and manners that won at once the sympathy and friendship of the officers of the army of the United States, into the society of whom he was cast. The last advices from Mexico represent him as a prisoner at Jalapa, where, however, he is not, and probably will not be subjected to restraint, unless a guerilla war should force upon the government of the United States a course of reprisals, and a more severe system than has hitherto been adopted by them towards prisoners of war. General La Vega, it is said, while in the United States, became engaged to be married to a lady of New Orleans, to whom on the termination of the war he will be united. He no doubt devoutly prays for this consummation of his wishes.

CHAPTER XI.

DON LUCAS ALAMAN AND DON JOAQUIN HERRERA.

Alaman—His personal appearance—Character—Visits Europe —Appointed minister of foreign affairs—Reforms in the government of Mexico—Execution of Guerrero—*Banco de avio* —Revolution—Alaman again elevated to office—Bustamente deposed—Alaman establishes a cotton manufactory—His failure—Made minister of foreign affairs in 1842—Herrera —His character.

"ABOUT the end of eighteen hundred and thirty," says a French writer, "there occurred at Mexico a mysterious circumstance, which kept public curiosity long awake. About daybreak the body of the Corregidor Quesada was found near one of the corners of the cathedral. He was lying in the midst of a pool of blood, with a wound in the side, evidently given with great earnestness, for the marks of the guard were deeply impressed on the edge of the wound, and many of the spectators seemed to look with jealousy at the trace of the handiwork of a person who was master of his business. No one was aware that the corregidor had any personal enemies, but all knew that he had declared himself to be an enemy of the government. For some days the body, in grand costume, was exposed, as is the custom of the country, to public view, and great exertions were made, but in vain, to discover the assassin.

"A short time afterwards, an event not less strange occurred at Jalapa. A senator generally considered hostile to the government, was poisoned in a manner not less strange than Quesada had been stabbed. One day

Don Lucas Alamán.

immediately after he awoke, this senator took up a cigar which lay on the table near his bed, and ringing for his *valet-de-chambre*, bade him bring him a light. The Mexicans smoke much more scientifically than any other people, and never think of lighting a cigar with a blaze, but always from living coals, which are kept in a *brazero*, which, in this instance, was of silver. Scarcely had he begun to smoke when he was seized with a violent sneezing, in consequence of which, in a short time, a hæmorrhage ensued, of which he died. His body was examined, and it appeared that the nasal passages and brain were violently inflamed, that the cigar must have been poisoned and killed him, as described. No one could tell what hand had placed the cigars on the senator's table, and the appearance of his servant, when he told what had happened, would have convinced the most sceptical that he was guiltless of this assassination of his master. Who, then, was guilty? People insisted on connecting together these two inexplicable murders, and fancied that the hand which drove the dagger so deep into Quesada's side, was the one which had placed the cigars on the senator's table, and belonged to Don Lucas Alaman.

"This may be, and probably is, all calumny, for the story of the poisoned cigar is too elaborate, and is evidently copied from the days of the Borgia and La Brinvilliers, but will serve to show the estimate put on the morals of Don Lucas Alaman, whom all the world confessed to be a true patriot, yet who, to secure the good of his country, would not hesitate to trample in the dust, the rights of its citizens and of itself, with a courage which is the more heroic as it neither receives the reward of public approbation nor is sustained by the inspiration of the hope of fame."

This paragraph of comment is taken from the same writer who records the anecdotes which, true or false, are characteristic of what was considered Alaman's disposition.

Alaman has already been said to have governed Mexico, in fact, during the presidency of General Guerrero, but at that time had given little evidence of the energy he afterwards exhibited. The Mexican people had, however, already conceived a presentiment that ere long a firm hand would hold in check the evil passions which then under the impetus of the absence of government, incident to the revolution, had devastated their country. The appearance of Alaman certainly would not indicate him to be that person. His stature is low, his forehead broad, wide, and unwrinkled. His hair is black and silky, his eyes keen and piercing, and his complexion certainly would not betoken him to belong to the Spanish race, but to be a child of some colder climate than Mexico. One would think him feeble, irresolute, and indolent. In doing so a great error would be committed. He is possessed, in fact, of great determination, of a moral energy capable of anything, and of ceaseless perseverance. His activity of mind prompts him to undertake all conceivable schemes, even those which would be thought most incompatible with his inclinations. He is said to speak perfectly well French, Italian, and English, and what is yet more rare among his countrymen, to speak pure Spanish and to write it correctly.

Alaman is a mere man of the bureau, and therefore it is that he has never been able to participate in the realization of any of the plans he has dictated. One thing is sure, that he ever maintained, that patriotism justified any excesses, and that whosoever wills the attainment of any object, approves of the necessary means to accomplish his wishes. For this reason his political opponents have not hesitated to accuse him of the two strange assassinations referred to above; while his admirers have maintained that, in pure and unshrinking patriotism, devotion to the cause of human enlightenment, and farsight into the tendency of the future, he has had an equal only in our own Jefferson.

Don Lucas Alaman must now be fifty-three or four years of age. He is a native of Guanajuato, of good family, and was educated at the college of La Mineria. Those who knew him there, say, that but for the revolution, he would have been one of the most expert *administradores* of mines in Mexico. As it was, he only became the most skilful of her politicians. He entered the army when the war of independence broke out, but soon discovered he had no talents for such scenes. His enemies say he proved himself on all occasions to be a most arrant coward. He soon laid aside his sword to study the laws of his country, that he might participate in political affairs. His political career was curious, and an autobiography from him would be invaluable as a sketch of men and things in Mexico for the last thirty years. A circumstance especially creditable to him is, that he had nothing to do with Iturbide's plans, but immediately after his deposition became minister of foreign affairs, a post he occupied when the ex-emperor returned to Soto la Marina, in 1844. The manner of Iturbide's death has already been described. It is worth while, however, to state, that in Mexico political offences have almost always been pardoned, except when Alaman has been at the head of affairs, by whom they have been severely punished.

After he retired from the ministry, he visited Europe, and remained there for a long time. This was the most promising aspect of the star of Mexico, when the English were beginning their explorations of the mines, and when the United Mexican Mining Company originated. The early studies of Alaman, and his intimate knowledge of Mexico, procured for him the position of director, with magnificent emoluments of office. At the same time he became *administrador* of the *Duca di Monteleone*, a noble of Sicily, who, as the representative of Hernando Cortes, the conqueror, is in possession of an extensive Mexican territory and of immense wealth.

While in England he became thoroughly imbued with English prejudices, and conceived an aversion to France and America, and exhibited, on all occasions when Mexico was not concerned, the greatest predilection in favor of England. To this may be attributed the fact that most of the valuable mines of Mexico are in the hands of British subjects, and the patents for the great majority will be found to date from Alaman's subsequent administration.

It is probable that when he returned to Mexico, Alaman purposed to interfere no more in political affairs; for he devoted himself exclusively to the many private trusts confided to himself. The administration of Guerrero was overthrown in December, 1829, when Bustamente insisted on his taking office under him as minister of foreign affairs, an honor Alaman sought to decline on the plea of his many engagements. He however accepted it, and afforded to the world another example of the *nolo episcopari*, which, though common to Mexico, is by no means peculiar to it.

When he again took charge of the administration of the government, Mexico was in a strange position.

But one year previously it had been devastated by civil war, and almost become the captive of the bow and spear of the clique that sheltered themselves under the cloak of Guerrero's honesty. Public confidence was not restored; and Guerrero himself was still in arms in the south. Santa Anna was at Mango de Clavo, biding his time. Finances were exhausted, and all classes of the army were calling lustily for some years of pay, while the treasury was empty. Robbers infested the high-roads; and more than once magisterial offices were purchased by *ladrones* with money obtained by red-handed plunder. The custom-house officers were partners in smuggling adventures; and, repeatedly, *alcaldes* and magistrates were proved to be partners of robber bands. The people were taxed beyond all endurance, while it was notorious that not one-tenth of the revenue collected ever reached the puplic coffers.

Smuggling was carried on .on the broadest scale. Ships would arrive from France, England, or the United States, with the richest and most costly goods, packed in cases side by side with coarse cottons or other articles of little value, each of which was numbered in the manifest, 1, 2, 3, 4, &c. The manifests would be sent at once to the custom-house, and a single tide-waiter be placed on board. At night a launch was put off from one of the remote quays of Vera Cruz unobserved, whether the night were bright and starlit or the reverse, from the fact that no one passes through the streets of a Mexican city after the posting of the watch. The cases were opened,—each one was found to contain two smaller ones: the one filled with costly silks and dutiable articles, the other with articles which were free. Morning came; the valuable articles were on shore, and the tide-waiter watched over the remains of the cargo.

A half dozen ounces to him, and a rich present to the *commandante* of Vera Cruz, made all right, and hushed any suspicions as to why a large ship should be sent across the Atlantic with a few hundred dollars worth of goods.

Such a state of things obviously rendered it impossible for the government to meet its obligations, and its soldiers necessarily became associates of highway robbers. In this year, 1828, a German gentleman on his way to the South Sea for the purpose of pursuing some botanical inquiries, was attacked by the *dragones* of his escort, and only escaped from the fact that his pistols being new, were water-tight, and did not fail, while the dilapidated fire-arms of the Mexicans could not be discharged, in a slight rain which chanced to be falling. Every road leading to and from the capital was infested by robbers, who were strong enough to set almost any safeguard at defiance.

"Such bands," says a writer who seems to understand Alaman thoroughly, "may almost every day be met with in the arid plains of Tepeyahualco, so aptly named *mal pais*, in the fearful gorges of Pinal, or the icy woods of the *Rio Frio*. They are all admirably mounted, and seem the best horsemen in the world. With their faces shaded by their large hats and covered with handkerchiefs which permit nothing to be seen but their sparkling eyes, they hold in one hand the deadly *lazo*, while with the other they restrain their fiery steeds, husbanding their energies until the time shall come when they must either leap a precipice to escape, or dash forward at speed to strike their prey. The lonely traveller, who has no baggage but his *poncho* and lance, may pass quietly among them, exchanging the amicable *buenas dias*, as if he were under the protection of a fortress wall, unless he should look so closely at them as to indicate any recognition." He is safe, for they are on the alert for a richer prey, and have not come out to rob a beggar of his cloak. When they find their prey, if resistance is made, they become pitiless murderers. If not, they suffer the traveller who surrenders to pass on with the courteous *adios caballero*, or *Dios guarda vmd.* (Good day, sir; God watch over your worship); and return to their *ranchos* to play with their children, and it may be to give the alcalde a portion of their plunder.

Such people are not to be judged by the rules of every-day life, having been corrupted by a bad government, which defiles all things, and superinduces a forgetfulness as well of the laws of man as of God; and a German traveller, referred to above, who is familiar with the people, states, that the only wonder to him is, that they have not long ago dissolved all the bonds of society, and become mere savages; and attributes their existence as a nation to the influence of the younger clergy, who, grown up since the revolution, see that the high position of the church can only be enjoyed while the body politic is at least entire.

Alaman was the very person to put down such disorders; and when he found the power to do so in his possession, he would not pause for the many obstacles which would have terrified a man of less moral courage. When once enlisted in such a cause, he was not a man to draw back.

Alaman, when he assumed the direction of foreign affairs, resolved to make financial and political reform march *pari passu*, and to make the second contribute to the first. The most obvious means to be adopted was the employment of honest men, with ample salaries

Such was the apparent corruption of the community, that it was by no means easy to find such in sufficient number, and he had to limit his endeavors in a great degree to repressing the peculation of such as he was forced to keep. By this means smuggling was prevented, the treasury became replenished by a stream of wealth which previously had been exhausted by tide-waiters and collectors, and the soldiers, well paid and equipped, were really what they were intended to be, the defenders of the nation. The disbursements did not exceed the receipts, and the treasury, under the able Mangino, was able to meet all demands on it. For the first time since the revolution, Mexico had a government.

The highway robbers shared the fate of the peculators in public office, many having been taken by patrols of cavalry, and either summarily shot, or *garroteado, to encourage the others*, who proceeded to hang up their bruised armor and seek subsistence by honest industry. The red crosses which marked the place where murders had been committed, one after the other decayed, and no newer ones replaced them, so that the roads around Mexico were as safe as in any other part of the world. Alaman said that he would not stop in this career until he could lay his *serape* on the plaza in Mexico, and on his return in the morning find it untouched; and but for interruptions in his course he could not foresee, he would have accomplished it.

There yet remained to be chastised the disturbers of public peace, and for them the punishment was death.

Unfortunately, however, for the prosperity of Mexico, a civilian had to deal with men of the sword, and though he had the sinews of war at his command, the polished steel often more than balanced gold and the interests of Mexico. Santa Anna was probably in his eye constantly, but that general was as wily as Alaman, and preferred that he should waste himself in efforts against other eminent men, and thus prepare an open field for him, than to measure himself against an adversary dangerous as he was. The man who had murdered a senator, would no doubt strike at a general, and therefore with his political prudence Santa Anna remained at Mango de Clavo in perfect quiet, aware that the long arm of Alaman would reach him even amid his Jarochos. Guerrero was still in arms in the south, surrounded by his faithful Pintos, and defied all efforts against him and his authority, which after all was constitutional. Fever and the climate protected the latter against any army which could be marched against him, and recourse was had to treason to obtain possession of him.

An Italian named Picaluga, a native of Genoa, at that time was in the port of Acapulco, the head-quarters of the general. This man, with the tact peculiar to his countrymen, contrived to insinuate himself in the confidence of Guerrero, who was frank and soldierlike in his bearing. One day Guerrero, who detested the *faste* and parade of which most Mexicans seem so fond, went without any suite to breakfast with Picaluga, who received him with the greatest apparent cordiality. The general was a little fond of good wine, and after a hearty meal went on deck and discovered that the black-hearted villain had weighed his anchor and was then entering a neighboring port, which was in the possession of the enemy. He was at once overpowered and surrendered to the officers of the government.

A form of trial was soon gone through with, and on the 14th of February, 1831, near the city of Oaxaca, the general was shot. It is said that at the place of execution he wept bitterly. He had in defence of his country fought so bravely, that on such an occasion he might give vent to his feelings, and weep at her ingratitude. Public opinion attributes this act to Alaman exclusively, and he is also suspected of having, by means of others, induced the gallant Iturbide to return to Mexico to meet a similar fate. Picaluga, it is said, received for this foul treason $50,000, and the order for that sum is now preserved in the treasury—an authentic autograph of Alaman. The vessel of Picaluga, commanded by another, returned to Genoa, when the story was told, and such was the universal disgust at it, that his name was blotted from the roll of Genoese citizens, and became in Spanish a term to express one dyed in the deepest villany. Picaluga afterwards, it is said, apostatized from Christianity, and in 1840 was in the service of a Mahometan prince. Two other chieftains were subsequently taken in other parts of the country and mercilessly shot, in spite of the influence of their friends; the brother of one of them, Codallos, was governor of Mexico, and the other, Victoria, was the only brother of Guadalupe Victoria, first president of Mexico. This much good and evil was effected by Alaman during 1830 and 1831.

Then commenced for Mexico a new era, that of manufacturing industry, its resources having been previously merely agricultural and pastoral. Alaman wished to place the people he governed on a level with those of Europe, and this was his great motive in the establishment of peace. Nature has conferred on Mexico three different climates, the tropical, temperate, and cold, (comparatively speaking.) It has also given to these three latitudes inexhaustible fertility, a cloudless sky, and mountain ridges from the summits of which the rains bring down sands of gold, where silver is found everywhere, and, as if to force it to rely on its own industry, has refused to it only navigable rivers and good ports. Its topographical peculiarities are such, that it must ever be almost impossible to contrive any system of railroads through it; in a word, Mexico is deprived of that facility of communication with which nature recompenses less favored regions for the curse of sterility. The question of industry is then more vital to it than to any other in the world, since it cannot transport its raw material to the shore of either sea.

At the instance of Alaman, who was the president of the council, as an encouragement to industrial undertakings, a large portion of the customs collected was appropriated, under the name of *banco de avio*, bank of succor, to be loaned to persons employed in manufacturing enterprises of certain kinds: as, cotton, iron, silk, wool, and paper. Another portion was expended in machinery purchased in Europe, and loaned gratis to manufacturers. This was an admirable scheme, worthy of imitation in other countries boasting of a more extended civilization; and the consequence was, that industry received a new impulse, there seemed less desire for revolution, and the roads and public buildings began to exhibit strong evidence of the fostering care of a government. Amid all this prosperity, however, one man contrived to disturb this promise, at the very time that measures were being taken to call him to account for his past misconduct. Santa Anna had remained quiet as long as Alaman would not interfere personally with him; but having learned from some of the numerous agents his private fortune enabled him always to maintain that he would soon be arraigned, he pronounced against Bustamente and destroyed the influence of

Alaman, which certainly was working wonders for Mexico in one point of view, while it is equally sure that he was not to be considered a model either of honor, honesty, or obedience to the behests of religion.

On this occasion Santa Anna acted with his peculiar decision and promptness. He called around him his *Jarochos*, induced the garrison of Vera Cruz to revolt, and seized on the sum of five hundred thousand dollars, which had been collected by Alaman, and which served to ruin him. It was in vain, during this contest, that Alaman gave his generals the most exact orders, money, and disciplined troops; they were unable to realize the plans he had conceived in his bureau. The secretary at war took the command of the army, but had no better success; and Alaman being unable to place himself at the head of troops to repair their errors, Bustamente capitulated. The man who had caused Iturbide, Guerrero, Codallos, and Victoria to be shot, had reason to fear a similar fate for himself, for a similar offence, the failure of his plans; and disappeared not only from the political but the social world, and none knew where he sheltered himself.

Fifteen months afterwards, during the presidency of Santa Anna, who was aware of all the details of Alaman's plans against him, the ex-minister made his appearance in the capital as mysteriously as he had left it. All that ever transpired was, that becoming frightened about his safety, whether with reason or not, Santa Anna best knew, Alaman had sheltered himself amid the inviolable seclusion of a convent. In this retreat he learned to restrain his political enmities and ambition, and his secret was so well kept, that even now, when all motive for it is lost, the seal of secrecy has never been broken as to what altar concealed him. He was completely isolated from public affairs until 1837, when, on the return of Bustamente to power, he began gradually to exert his power and influence again. At the election, which resulted in favor of Bustamente, Alaman obtained the next largest number of votes, and so high was his reputation for capacity, that Bustamente forgot all feeling of jealousy, and confided to him almost all the functions of government.

The central constitution, called the plan of Tagle from the name of the person by whom it was proposed, had created a third power of the government, called *consejo del gobierno*, or council of government, and had assigned singular powers to it. This body was empowered to review all laws passed by the chambers, to originate decrees itself, and its consent was necessary before any act could be submitted to the president; it was an institution like the English star-chamber, and the Venitian council of ten, which deliberated in secret, and changed a democracy into an oligarchy. The presidency of this body was offered to Alaman, who, however, objected to the conspicuous nature of the appointment though he had no objection to the power. The post was therefore conferred on General Moran, an invalid in whose frequent absence, and by the influence he had over him, Alaman was the president *de facto*. Alaman contrasted in his mind his present position, in which he was totally irresponsible and sheltered by the secret discussions, with the state of affairs when he was a minister—he could but congratulate himself on the change which permitted him to do so much for his country with such safety to himself.

This state of things did not last long, for in 1840 Alaman was again living in a private station, having been driven from power by the dissolution of the plan of Tagle on the deposition of Bustamente.

When Santa Anna a second time regained supreme authority, the great men of the country fled from it; Farias came to the United States, and Bustamente sought to forget his adversity in Genoa and Rome. Alaman, aware that he was now for a long time destined to be excluded from public affairs, resolved to realize for his own advantage some of the benefits he sought to confer on his countrymen by the *banco de avio*. He therefore established a vast cotton manufactory at Orizaba, in the state of Vera Cruz. The scheme, however, was scarcely promising; the competition of England and the United States being sure to repress such enterprises in Mexico, where labor is difficult to be had, and cotton by no means plenty—where broken machinery must either be repaired by foreign artisans, or sent from the country—and last of all, where any day may witness the transformation of the peaceful warehouse into a barrack. Smuggling enterprises also could be undertaken under the administration of Santa Anna, encouraged by countless harbors unwatched, the absence of any marine force, and the vicinity of New Orleans with its boundless supplies; so that it has become almost to be confessed, in spite of the success of a few factories at Jalapa, that no similar enterprise can prosper near the coast of the Gulf of Mexico.

The administration of Santa Anna was spendthrift as that of Alaman had been careful; and consequently the manufacturers everywhere became involved, and Alaman was forced to suspend payment. It is said that he failed for the sum of $1,200,000, an event which created consternation throughout Mexico. His painful situation he bore with *sang froid;* and it was natural that a man who had ordered the execution of an emperor, a president, and countless generals, should not shrink from having caused the ruin of a few hundred operatives.

Alaman then was merely the administrador of the Duke of Monteleone, and though Santa Anna was aware if he had fallen into his hands in the days of his power, he would have been shot summarily, he rather protected him; and not unfrequently, it is said, consulted him in his fiscal difficulties when he first succeeded to power. In 1842 he became again minister of foreign affairs; and, strangely enough, men who but a few years before would have shot each other without compunction, used to embrace most cordially when they met. Alaman was not, however, so attached to Santa Anna, as to be unable to console himself for his exile; and, since the latter's return, has again occupied a prominent position. There is, it is said, however, but little doubt that Alaman on the first opportunity would shoot the dictator with as little compunction now as he would have done during the administration of Bustamente, when Guerrero, Codallos and Victoria fell.

Don Lucas Alaman was a member of the general cortes of the Spanish empire in 1820; and has never been in favor of the restoration of the Spanish system. He has, however, always been opposed to democratic tendencies; and has been one of the bitterest enemies of the United States in Mexico.

The plan proposed in the preparation of this book has its advantages, but in many respects is not so convenient as might be wished. Its greatest disadvantage consists in the fact that in the sketch of the more important individuals, reference to others is made so frequently, that when we touch on their lives the material is exhausted, and it becomes necessary to repeat or to give but a meagre account of men who have occupied a large space of public attention. This is especially the case with General Herrera. In the sketches of General Paredes and of Santa Anna, the details of the revolution have been given, which broke out in Queretaro, headed by the former, the consequence of which was the destruction of Santa Anna's prospects, and the reduction of one who had boasted that he was the Napoleon of the west, to the humble state of a suitor for life and safety to a congress he had trampled on and contemned. The government of Herrera was, no doubt, correct, and seemed calculated to advance the great interests of the country. There is little doubt that he foresaw the consequences which were likely to result to Mexico from a war with the United States, and sought by conciliatory means to avert it. It was, however, in vain, for the whole army under Paredes pronounced against him, and he was deposed in November, 1845.

The strongest evidence of the purity of Herrera's conduct in this case, 'is the fact that the pronunciamento against him was purely military, and a conspicuous part was played in effecting it by Arista. The consequence of this revolution was the installation of Paredes as president, and the certainty that Santa Anna only could restore quiet. No sooner was Paredes installed than reports arose of a counter-revolution by Arista, likely enough when we take into consideration the events which have subsequently occurred, and the evident coquetting of Santa Anna and Almonte.

Paredes' power was but short lived; Santa Anna returned, and Herrera was excluded from military command until the last struggle of the president at Cerro

Gordo, when, with La Vega, and the best men of the Mexican army, he was taken prisoner in the entrenchments from which Santa Anna fled. He was there paroled by General Scott, and returned to the capital. His military career is therefore over, but it is not unlikely he may yet be called to serve Mexico in some civil capacity. The avowed reason of his deposition, after the exile of Santa Anna, was, that he was suspected of wishing to receive the American minister and consenting to the final relinquishment of Texas. Should he be installed, we may expect the same course to be advocated by him.

General Thompson speaks of Herrera as a man confessedly of high character, but in no other respect remarkable. Madame la Barca says as much. Can there be higher praise in Mexico, where some strength of mind is required to withstand the temptations to corruption?

There are other eminent men in Mexico, of a reputation scarcely less than those who have been the subjects of this book, and the names of whom have frequently occurred. A minute sketch of General Bravo and of Valencia would no doubt throw much light on the military history of Mexico, while a life of Rejon would unfold much of the tortuous policy which has been so peculiar to that country. At some other day a history of the events that produced the present war may be written, which the author believes will expose a waste of the blessings of nature in a manner unprecedented in the annals of any era, or any degree of barbarism.

CHAPTER XII.

The City and Valley of Mexico—The Church.

If we may believe the accounts of the old chronicler Bernal Diaz, who, like Sir John Mandeville, wrote what he had seen, Mexico at the time of the conquest by Cortes was a western Venice. It had its palaces and gardens, its temples and market-places, filled with a population of three hundred thousand souls. As Chevalier aptly says, population is an index of a certain stage of civilization; but it must be remembered, that the age when Bernal Diaz wrote was that when all the world believed the stories of the Great Cham, and when the King of the Cannibal Isles was devoutly believed to exist. Popular tradition told of the existence of an island where demons hovered above every hill, and pictured the prototype of Shakspeare's Caliban and Prospero as stern realities. While Cortes and Pizarro were waging war in Mexico and Peru, Gonsalvo of Cordova, in Italy, was winning laurels at the head of his troops, by the side of which nothing but exaggeration could place the conquests in America.

The book of Bernal Diaz tells of vast temples, of costly edifices, and of all the comforts of private life; yet, strange to say, not one relic of those times has reached us. The halls of Montezuma have left no more trace than the palace of Aladdin, and of all the buildings of hewn stone that Diaz and his contemporaries and immediate successors speak of, not one remnant

City of Mexico.

exists. Yet all these stories tell us of no ruin of Mexico, but would induce the belief that the people merely changed their ruler; that the Aztecs obeyed a viceroy of Charles V., instead of Montezuma.

It is not, however, to be denied, that there are vast ruins in Mexico—pyramids and temples that speak of a highly cultivated race, certainly acquainted with the arts of civilization. These ruins yet remain, and the traveller, when he gazes on them, is satisfied he looks on the wreck of a cultivated race, whose antiquity is more venerable than that of the Pharaohs or Brahminical rulers. It no more follows, however, that the Mexican or Aztec races were the authors of these, because Europeans found them beneath their shadows, than that the colossal remains of Egypt, or the beautiful columns of Tadmor and Palmyra, are to be attributed to the Ishmaelite or Turk who rules the country where they are. Near the Rock River in Michigan, and Chilicothe in Ohio, are vast ruins, which no one will attribute to the Shawnee and Wyandotte races, but which bear all the internal evidences of a cultivation quite equal to that of the Aztec and Tlascalan. The probability is, that the continent had been ruled by a more powerful race, possessed of a civilization of its own, with which the Mexicans had no more to do than the Iroquois or Sioux.

It is, however, ascertained, that at the time of the conquest, Mexico was surrounded by the waters of the lake; for Cortes, before he could subdue it, was compelled to build brigantines of burden sufficient to support the shocks of heavy ordnance. The Aztecs fought long and well, but without a knowledge of the use of iron they gave way before the chivalry of Cortes. The trenchant steel of Toledo shivered the weapons of *vol-*

canic glass of Montezuma's and Guatimozin's array, and the conquest soon became a slaughter. Positive proof of this is afforded by the fact that battles occurred in which the Spaniards fought from sunrise to sunset, and not one man was killed in their ranks, while hecatombs of Indians fell. Let it not be understood, that any effort is made to detract from the credit of the conquistator, whose achievements recall to us the Bible history of the slaughter of the hosts of Philistines with the jaw-bone of an ass.

The *tierras calientes* and *templadas* of Mexico are both a succession of platforms or steps which terminate in the lofty mountain of Popocatapetl. On the descent from the brow of a mountain about twenty-five miles east of Mexico, a view of the countless towers and domes of the city are first discovered. Far in the distance is seen the snow of Popocatapetl reflecting the brilliancy of a vertical sun. More remote is seen the brow of Iztaccihuatl. The valley is now a barren waste; for the canals which, rude as they were under the last Indian princes and the first viceroys, sufficed to irrigate the land, are now choked up; and the lakes themselves are rapidly disappearing. Hundreds of villages, which they tell us were once cities, are seen around the capital. The road descends the western declivity into the valley of the lake about sixteen miles from Mexico, passing over a narrow neck of land, on one side of which are the salt waters of Tezcuco, and on the left the fresh water of Chalco.

The cities from each of which they took their names nave now disappeared, and even the acute Mr. Oldbuck would find difficulty in identifying one stone of their walls. At a high piñal, or cliff, six miles from the city, the traveller first meets the causeway, and sees around him a new sandy soil, partially covered with water from the lakes of Tezcuco, Chalco, Hochimilco, Zumpango, and San Christoval, pointing out the area of that inland sea from which Mexico arose. Forty years ago, when Humboldt wrote, the waters were supposed to cover one-tenth of the valley, which now in the rainy season is one vast marsh. When in the arid months of summer the waters subside, the surface of this marsh is covered with coarse salt, generally used in all the surrounding country.

The city of Mexico is in the north-western part of this valley, about three miles from the village of Guadalupe, of which more anon. The valley itself is a vast oval basin, surrounded by mountains and cliffs of various heights, from those of but a hundred feet in height, to Popocatapetl, with its ever burning fires and eternal snows, lifted more than ten thousand feet above the loftiest domes of the city. On the road from Vera Cruz are a few low hills of volcanic origin, but everywhere else the valley is one vast plain. It is a usual thing to attribute to the disappearance of the lake the sterility of the country, and to the choking of the canals, which were but amplifications of the natural water-courses. But need we look further than the still-burning summits of Iztaccihuatl and Popocatapetl, the countless extinguished craters, for a reason why the waters have partially disappeared? The Mexican nation is sufficiently impotent, and feeble enough, and inflicts evil enough on the beautiful country it occupies, without our attributing to it things dictated by a higher providence and more august wisdom than mortality can comprehend. The soil is now uncultivated, yet yields a copious return for the sweat expended on it. Wheat, corn, and vegetables are produced in great abundance, and the *agave*

Mexicana, that plant which, like the cocoa-nut in the South Sea, is bread, apparel and drink, are produced in great plenty, while countless herds roam over the expanse unchecked, as are their fellows in the newest country of this continent, the prairie of New Mexico, or in the venerable *campagna di Roma*, the classic land of Europe. The city of Mexico, however, does not receive its supplies from this plain, which is so peculiarly endowed that every product of every land would grow there in rich abundance. Vegetables of all kinds are brought either on the backs of Indians, or in panniers on asses, from beyond the valley; wagons being used exclusively by the mining companies. On asses, too, are borne to the city the freights disgorged by the many vessels at Vera Cruz. French clocks, jewelry, velvets, hats, and European wines, all are thus transported to the capital, and thence diffused over the whole republic in a similar manner. At Monclova and in the secluded towns of Sinaloa, clocks are seen with alabaster columns transported in this manner; and Brequet returns his lepine watches on the backs of mules, not unfrequently to the employees of the very mines whence the gold of which they were made was taken.

The entrance from the north and west into the city of Mexico, does not greatly differ from the route to Vera Cruz, except that the roads are worse and more lonely, and the *posadas* or inns fewer and worse in quality. Here and there are strewn miserable Indian hamlets, with wretched half-starved inmates, who it is impossible to believe are the descendants of the polished races whom Cortes and Bernal Diaz have described. It is possible they are not; for north, in the mountains of Santa Fe, are a race, who boast that when all was lost, they emigrated northward as their fathers had come south,

Plaza and Cathedral in the City of Mexico.

and amid the inaccessible hills found safety. In the dark caves of these hills they still keep up a belief in the milder divinities of Aztec mythology, humanized, but similar to that which Montezuma entertained.

Mexico is, beyond a doubt, the most magnificent city on the American continent, and contains more rich and beautiful buildings than any other. As has already been said, it contains not one remnant of the old race who began the city, but is instinct with the taste which promoted the erection of the monuments of the cities of the peninsula, the majority of which were built when the arts, revived by the Medici, were extending themselves over the world. The houses in the principal streets are built in the purest taste, and many of the most splendid are even now owned by the descendant of Cortes, the Duke of Monteleone. The plaza grande is a vast area, paved with stone, with the cathedral on one side and on the opposite a row of fine houses, with projecting balconies. On one of the other side is the *palacio nacional*, the old vice-regal dwelling, built on the site of the far-famed halls of the Montezumas. This building is utterly tasteless, a vast mass of stone and mortar, with small windows, and badly arranged. The president occupies but a small portion of this building, in which are the halls of the senate and deputies, and the bureaus of the various ministers. At the end of a dark passage is a massive door opening into a court called the botanical garden, in which are a few stinted trees, among which, however, is the strange *manita* tree, but one other of which species is known to exist, and which is curious from bearing a blossom resembling the human hand. Mr. Thompson, Madame Calderon, Gilliam, the French and German travellers, all unite in one account, which all who have seen it will endorse, that it looks more like a ruinous barrack or deserted factory than the home of the chief magistrate of one of the great divisions of the world. The cathedral has no equal in North America, and is built in the florid Gothic style which the Spaniards have always been so fond of. It too is historical, and stands on the site of the temple of one of the Mexican blood-stained divinities, ALMITZOTLI. The walls are of solid stone.

The wealth of our own country is inadequate to give any idea of the splendor of its interior, filled with paintings and statues. On entering the building the eye is attracted to the high altar of solid silver, its massive candelabra of gold, and a balustrade extending on each side of it, cast from a metal of the color of gold, the component parts of which are copper, silver, and brass, in such proportions that it is worth far more than its weight in silver. The separate pieces of which it is formed are four feet high, and several inches thick; and its whole length is three hundred feet. Several years ago a silver smith of Mexico offered to replace it with a railing of the same form and weight in solid silver, and to pay into the fund of the cathedral $500,000 besides.

On every side are smaller chapels richly decorated, where all the utensils are silver, besides vast store-rooms filled with plate, rarely or never produced, but there in its sterling value.

This seems exaggeration, and recalls to our minds things we have dreamed of in childhood, but never realized as existing; and whether Cortes deceived the emperor Charles V. in his account of Montezuma's wealth, matters not, for the viceroys realized all his promises.

Here also is the calendar of Montezuma, a round stone inserted in the wall, covered with hieroglyphics of that mysterious kind, so far even more impenetrable than the mystic writing of the obelisks of Egypt. On the great plaza there was, in 1844, a column being erected surmounted by a figure of Liberty, in commemo ration of Mexican independence.

The square of the cathedral is not the only beautiful public place in Mexico. The Alameda, in all the elements of physical beauty, will compare with any public walk in Europe, not excepting the parks of London and the Prado of Vienna. The beautiful *paseo* of Havana cannot compare with this luxurious spot, redolent with the shrubs and flowers of which nature has been so prodigal in Mexico. Leading to the Alameda, is the noble street of St. Francis, with its rich edifices, not the least interesting of which is the palace of Iturbide, both on account of the richness of its architecture and the associations connected with it. There are other interesting buildings in Mexico, the most prominent of which are the convents of La Profesa, of St. Augustin, and San Francisco, of vast wealth and great influence, the colleges of Biscay and La Mineria, and hosts of others.

In the university is much that is attractive, not the least of which is the equestrian statue of Charles IV. by Tolsa, a native artist, who has left behind him works in bronze, worthy of the artists of the best days of Italy. It also contains the sacrificial stone, from the great Teocalli of the Aztec days. The palaces of Cortina, of Regla, of Count Beneski, the friend of Iturbide, and multitudes of other splendid residences, will compare with the private dwellings of most cities, but unfortunately in close proximity are the hovels of the miserable leperos, so wretched, that at the contrast we can but exclaim, "Can these be thy children, oh Mexico, and the fellow-citizens of those?"

The first singularity which attracts attention in Mexico, however, is the character of the people in the street;

priests and friars in their strange garbs, *canonigos* in their immense hats, military men in brilliant uniforms, and Indians and leperos in the costume chance offers them. Naples with its lazzaroni, Calcutta with its hordes of pariahs, St. Giles in London with all its abominations, are decent in comparison with the place of assemblage of these wretches—the lame, halt, and the cripple, the maimed soldier and disabled robber, the victim of leprosy. Words cannot express the horror of the scenes to be met with in the streets, and which strike with equal disgust the soldier who has served on the battle-fields of Europe, and the scientific naturalist, who wonders how a land so blessed by nature can be suffered by God to be so deformed with crime. Madame Calderon records having met with beggars everywhere—in her private house, in the Alameda, in the very temple. Everywhere, and amid wealth beside which that of the Califs becomes insignificant, is heard the cry, *Caridad por el nombre de Jesus; una media por los santos.* If these be the consequences of all the gold and silver of Mexico, if its wealth be not able to prevent them, far better were it if the land, doomed to absolute sterility, should force its children to starve or live by the sweat of their brows.

The strongest argument to justify the occupation of America by the Europeans, has ever been, that God never intended so fair a land to be occupied by howling savages; and if this be true, what inference may we draw from the present condition of Mexico?

In any account of Mexico, however, in which the church was omitted, an inexcusable oversight would be made. It is an important element of the Mexican social system, and many go so far as to say that it is the government. When Cortes conquered Mexico, he was under the influence of the spirit of loyalty and military obedience not more than of the fervor of the crusader He devoutly believed that he was conquering a kingdom for his earthly master, beside which the crowns of Castile and Aragon become insignificant, and for his God the souls of generations, otherwise doomed, according to the harsh theology of the age, to interminable perdition. Everywhere we see the traces of this spirit, from the day when he threw down the idols from their pedestals, to the great conflagration of Mexican and Tezcucan manuscripts by the Spanish Arab, Juan de Zummoraga, first archbishop of Mexico, in the great market-place. The consequence was, that vast sums were appropriated to the priesthood, and more than an ecclesiastical tithe of the fruits of the conquest was appropriated to the honor of religion. The course of the early missionaries was strange: we read of baptisms which recall to us the conversions of apostolic days; of thousands made, in the words of the old chroniclers, "children of Christ from priests of the devil." The vast wealth of the Aztec priests was appropriated to their successors, and the endowments of the richest days of the old church, "when pontiffs placed their sandalled feet on the necks of mailed kings," were exceeded by this its youngest conquest.

The riches thus acquired by the church have perpetually been increased by endowments and bequests. Scarcely a will is made in Mexico, that does not contain a clause in favor of some shrine or ecclesiastical corporation; and the plate in its convents, like that of the mess of a European regiment, is of so many patterns and such various forms, that it would seem to have been gathered from the sacking of a hundred cities.

There is a selfishness about the Mexican church which is strange indeed, and finds a parallel nowhere else. In England, when Richard I. was taken prisoner by the archduke of Austria, the abbeys and convents brought their plate to ransom their monarch; in the wars of the league, the mitred princes and bishops contributed to support their army, and during the invasion of the Peninsula by the orders of Napoleon, the ecclesiastics were foremost in their contributions. This, however, has never been the case in Mexico. In all the wars which have occurred the church has not contributed one *media*, and now, while the stranger is a master in her cities, and an enemy's foot presses the sentinel's walk on her ramparts, the church and its dignitaries yet refuse to pay one farthing to defend their altars and their flocks. No president except Gomez Farias has ever dared to advocate the confiscation of one cent of the ecclesiastical property, and on three occasions that he has sought to effect such a reform, he has been driven from power. Mr. Thompson says that a small sum has been realized by the sale of the property of the Jesuits, but it must be remembered the church itself first cast them from its bosom. The general impression (and those who have had an opportunity of judging, say it by no means exaggerates the fact) is that one-third of the real property of Mexico is in the hands of the church, not counting a vast amount of money invested in mortgages on the remainder.

No college of theologians in the world would call the Mexican church orthodox. The ceremonies are certainly those of the Roman Catholic church, but even in the minds of the priesthood are engrafted such a host of Aztec superstitions, that it may even now be doubted if the mass of the people merit the name of Christian more than do the Abyssinians, or the few worshippers found by the Portuguese in the fourteenth century in the neighborhood of Goa, in India. Worshipping at the shrines of the saints, a vast portion of the Indian population believe implicitly that some day Montezuma will return to rule his people and restore the glory of his realm. Even now, on the pyramid of Cholula is a chapel dedicated to the Virgin, attended by a lowly and sincere Indian monk, who, as he points out to the traveller the traces of the ruins around him, gives satisfactory evidence that he is not without faith in the gods of the ancient Teocalli, which his altar has replaced.

From all America it is believed that the Catholic church has admitted into her calendar but three saints. St. Tammany, from Canada; St. Rosa, from Lima, in Peru; and one other from Mexico, the name of whom escapes us, and scarcely one of the many miracles said to have occurred, have stood the test to which the authorities of Rome have subjected them. This circumstance does not, however, prevent the every-day occurrence of a new beatification and the admission into the faith of Mexico of countless new candidates for veneration, from many of whom the church derives a great portion of its wealth. The two most striking instances of this fact are the following.

On the 8th of December, 1531, a poor and humble Indian, whose name was Juan Diego, sate on a rock, on the summit of Tepeya. Having sunk to sleep, he saw in a vision the Blessed Virgin, who bade him go to Mexico and command the archbishop to build a chapel where she then stood. The Indian went immediately to the city; but being refused admission into the archiepiscopal palace, returned the next day to the lonely rock, where the Mother of God again appeared to him.

She bade him immediately return and insist on the attention of the bishop. Diego did so, but was not more successful; and when he returned asked from the Virgin some token that what he said was true. At the command of the holy Mary, he went out on the mountain, and gathered a handful of roses from a barren rock that neither before or since has nourished vegetation. The Virgin blessed the flowers, and threw them on the cloak of Diego, and bade him take them to the bishop. Diego obeyed; he met the bishop at the gate of the palace, unfolded his *serape*, and exhibited to him not only the mountain flowers but a portrait of the Blessed Virgin. The archbishop was convinced, called the image on the cloak the Blessed Virgin of Guadalupe, and ordered a beautiful church to be built where the Mother of God appeared to the lonely Indian.

That chapel now stands, and is a spot of pilgrimage from all parts of Mexico. The shrine is as rich as any in the world, and the Indian's cloak now hangs in a case of gold amid a wilderness of candelabra of the same metal, worshipped by the faithful. On the festival day of the Virgin of Guadalupe, all Mexico rushes to its shrine, and the long causeway of the Aztec metropolis is thronged with persons of every grade. Mr. Gilliam, an intelligent traveller, saw there in 1843 the President Canaliza and all his cabinet, ecclesiastics of high rank, *ladrones* and leperos, all come to worship at the wonderful altar. It is scarcely necessary to say to the well informed reader, that this is one of the miracles of the church of Mexico, altogether unrecognised by the authorities of Rome.

Next in the veneration of the present Mexican people to the Lady of Guadalupe, is our lady *De Los Remedios*—the origin of the worship of whom is not less strange. Cortes, the conqueror of Montezuma, was originally ordered to Mexico by Velasquez, the governor of Cuba, who, soon becoming jealous of him, revoked his commission before he had left the island. In this little episode of Cortes's life, we see the traces of all the events of the revolution and of the intellectual vivacity he afterwards displayed. El Conquistador was the last man in the world to exchange for a prison the privileges of an independent command, and therefore boldly set sail in defiance of Velasquez's orders. The success of Cortes was soon related in Cuba, and an expedition under Narvaez was sent to dispossess him of his conquest, which rendered it obligatory on him to confide the garrison of Mexico to his subordinate, and to march to overpower Narvaez in person. How he did so is a matter of history. On his return he found yet a new danger to be confronted. Alvarado had outraged the inhabitants, and Cortes found the whole nation in arms and was obliged to retreat. This he determined to do across the causeway of Tacuba, along which, amid the darkness of *la noche triste*, he cut his way to a lonely hill, about twelve miles from Mexico, where he fortified himself.

In this sad retreat he had lost the flower of his army, and the remnant was dispirited and mutinous. It was one of those conjunctures, when the lion's skin having failed, recourse was to be had to the fox's, and by a daring imposture Cortes contrived to reanimate his army. One of his soldiers had brought far off from Castile a little image of the Virgin in alabaster, it is not unlikely some memento of the friends he had left at home. In the lonely hours of the camp Cortes had seen it, and determined to have recourse to it, to effect the restoration of the morale of his men. The soldiers of Spain in America at that age, were crusaders in spirit, and prepared to believe his story, that it had fallen from heaven and had brought a promise from on high, that all their troubles would be miraculously healed, and that they would be brought back in triumph to Mexico. The stout hearts of his men-at-arms accomplished this, and the merit was attributed to *la santisima Virgen de los Remedios.*

When his triumph was secure, El Conquistador erected a chapel on the hill on which he had encamped after *la noche triste*, in which was placed the wonderful image. There it has remained for three hundred years in a magnificent shrine, attended on by nuns. It is now one of the richest shrines in Mexico, and in seasons of plague, pestilence, and famine, the image is borne in procession through the streets of the neighboring capital, with a devout faith that by the intercession of the miraculous image, all evil will be arrested. This occurred but a few years since, on the occasion of the illness of the first wife of Santa Anna, when a grand procession took place, and all that was distinguished in Mexico, generals, statesmen, and ecclesiastics, followed the miraculous image.

The manner in which the cathedral at Puebla was built, the devout belief entertained that the angels of heaven came by night to work at its walls, and a hundred other superstitions, are all received in Mexico, by not only the mass, but by many of the most enlightened classes, and go to show, that if the religion of Mexico is not Protestant, it is surely not Roman Catholic.

At the head, however, of this vast ecclesiastical establishment, is the archbishop of Mexico, with seven suffragans. At the time of the revolution, Don Pedro Fonte withdrew from Mexico with many of his bishops, and resided in Spain until the time of his death, during which time their benefices, estimated as being worth $371,148, were sequestered by the government. The present incumbent, the Doctor Posada, is one who has won golden opinions from all, and who by his benevolence and humanity merits them. "*No es dios el Señor Posada,*" said a Mexican gentleman, several years since, to the writer of this book, "*pero un hombre muy bueno.*" It may be worth while here to compare the statements of two travellers who have very little sympathy for each other—Mr. Thompson and Madame Calderon de la Barca—and see how they agree in the praise of the archbishop. The latter says:

"Were I to choose a situation here, it would undoubtedly be that of archbishop of Mexico, the most enviable in the world to those who would enjoy a life of tranquillity, ease, and universal adoration. He is a Pope without the trouble, or a tenth part of the responsibility. He is venerated more than the Holy Father is in enlightened Rome, and like kings in the good old times, can do no wrong. His salary amounts to about one hundred thousand dollars, and a revenue might be made by the sweetmeats alone which are sent him from all the nuns in the republic. His palace in town, his well-cushioned carriage, well-conditioned horses and sleek mules, seem the very perfection of comfort. In fact, *comfort*, which is unknown among the profane of Mexico, has taken refuge with the archbishop; and though many drops of it are shed on the shaven heads of all bishops, curates, confessors, and friars, still in his illustrious person it concentrates, as in a focus. He himself is a benevolent, good-hearted, good-natured, portly and jovial personage, with the most *laissez-aller* air and expression conceivable. He looks like one on whom the good things of this world have fallen in a constant and benignant shower, which shower hath fallen on a rich and fertile soil. He is generally to be seen leaning back in his carriage, dressed in purple, with amethyst cross, and giving his benediction to the people as he passes. He seems engaged in a pleasant revery, and his countenance wears an air of the most placid and *insouciant* content. He enjoys a good dinner, good wine, and ladies' society, but just sufficiently to make his leisure hours pass pleasantly, without indigestion from the first, headaches from the second, or heartaches from the third. So does his life seem to pass on like a deep untroubled stream, on whose margin grow sweet flowers, on whose clear waters the bending trees are reflected, but on whose placid face no lasting impression is made.

"I have no doubt that his charities are in proportion to his large fortune; and when I say that I have no doubt of this, it is because I firmly believe there exists no country in the world where charities both public and private are practised on so noble a scale, especially by the women, under the direction of the priests. I am inclined to believe that, generally speaking, charity is a distinguishing attribute of a Catholic country.

"The archbishop is said to be a man of good information, and was at one time a senator. In 1833, being comprehended in the law of banishment, caused by the political disturbances which have never ceased to afflict this country since the independence, he passed some time in the United States, chiefly in New Orleans, but this, I believe, is the only cloud that has darkened his horizon, or disturbed the tranquil current of his life. His consecration, with its attendant fatigues, must have been to him a wearisome overture to a pleasant drama, a hard stepping-stone to glory. As to the rest, he is very unostentatious; and his conversation is far from austere. On the contrary, he is one of the best tempered and most cheerful old men in society that it is possible to meet with. . . ."

Mr. Thompson says almost in the same words: "The archbishop of Mexico is a stout, healthy-looking and very agreeable old gentleman, the personification of a burly and jolly priest. He is a man of learning and well spoken of by every one. I took a great fancy to the archbishop of Cesarea, and I believe that it was in some degree mutual. I might almost say with the romantic German girl who met another over a stove, at an inn on the roadside, that at the first sight we swore 'eternal friendship to each other.' When I was about to leave the room he came to me and asked where I lived, and said that he intended to call upon me. I begged that he would not do so, but allow me to make the first visit (for that is the custom in Mexico), the stranger making the first call upon the resident. But the next day, the good old man called at my house, and as I happened not to be at home he would not leave his card, but told my servant that he would call again, as he did not wish me to regard his visit as one of mere form. This, of course, brought about a great intimacy between us, and I often visited him at his country house on the borders of the city. I shall never forget the pleasant hours which I have spent there, nor cease to remember the venerable and good old man with gratitude and affection. He is a man of learning, especially on all matters connected with the church and its history."

To the Santa Fe and other Texan prisoners, he was uniformly kind, and no man in Mexico has been heard to say one word to the discredit of the good old archbishops of Mexico and Cesarea.

The following are the several sees and the amount of their revenues in 1805, since when, by the increase of the mining operations, they have probably doubled in value.

Mexico - - -	$130,000
Puebla - - - -	110,000
Valladolid - - -	100,000
Guadalajara - - -	90,000
Durango - - -	35,000
Monterey - - - -	30,000
Yucatan - - -	20,000
Oaxaca - - - -	18,000
Sonora - - -	6,000

The above dignitaries preside over the religion of Mexico, which permits no dissent; so much so that it was long impossible to procure even the right of burial but by bribery, for a person not a Catholic. In 1825, even the capital of Mexico was not exempt from this barbarous prohibition, from which there would now be no escape but for a singular speech of Senator Canedo. The matter being under discussion, that gentleman said:

"I perfectly assent to the principles of my colleagues remarks, but only regret they cannot be reduced to practice, and therefore would vote against their propositions. It could not be denied there were many foreigners in Mexico, and as a necessary consequence, some of them must die. What, then, shall we do with their bodies? I see but four modes of disposing of them; to bury, to burn, to eat, or to export them. To dispose of them in the first manner my reverend colleagues would not consent; the second is too expensive; the third I have no objection to, provided I am not called on to officiate;

and dead heretics are not included in the last tariff. I vote, therefore, for burial, as the least of four evils."

The senate agreed with Señor Canedo, and heretics may be buried in Mexico in a separate cemetery.

The council of the Indies contributed more than any other cause to the corruption of religion in Mexico, from the fact that it allowed no direct intercourse with the Holy See; permitted no delegate or nuncio to visit the new world, and no bull or rescript to be published until fortified by the placet of the king or council. To this may be attributed the corruption of the faith by Aztec traditions, and that independence which makes the Mexican church what it is, a mass of corruption, with but little dependence on the Pope.

ADDITIONAL CHAPTER.

Causes of the present war—Mexican spoliations—Annexation of Texas to the United States—Palo Alto—Resaca de la Palma—Monterey—Buena Vista—Vera Cruz—Cerro Gordo.

Almost from the commencement of the Mexican republic, outrages on the persons and property of American citizens have been committed in Mexico, and redress has always been either positively refused, or so delayed that both there and in the United States the idea became current that such violations of the laws of nations were to be overlooked and unpunished.

This course on the part of Mexico was especially disgraceful, as the United States had been the first nation to recognise her separate existence, and American citizens had fought well in more than one of the battles of her revolution. The many changes of the executive brought no change of policy, and our countrymen began to look on the state of things as hopeless.

Often trivial pretexts were made use of to justify these acts, and a shadow of provocation sometimes found in the adventurous character of American merchants and seamen, who, altogether unused to civil war at home, could not be brought to respect blockades where both parties fought under the same flag, and were equally loud in their professions of love to a common country.

This state of things was endured patiently by the

government and people of this country, because both the one and the other were unwilling to add to the burdens of Mexico, and hoped that a calmer day would break over the sister republic, and a season of peace at home enable her to attend to her foreign obligations.

On the 5th of April, 1831, a treaty of amity and navigation was concluded between the republics; but almost before the ink on the parchment was dry, fresh outrages were perpetrated, so that within six years after that date, General Jackson, in a message to Congress, declared that they had become intolerable, and that the honor of the United States required that Mexico should be taught to respect our flag.

He declared that war should not be used as a remedy "by just and generous nations confiding in their strength for injuries committed, if it can be honorably avoided;" and added, "it has occurred to me that considering the present embarrassed condition of that country, we should act with both wisdom and moderation, by giving to Mexico one more opportunity to atone for the past, before we take redress into our own hands. To avoid all misconception on the part of Mexico, as well as to protect our national character from reproach, this opportunity should be given with the avowed design and full preparation to take immediate satisfaction, if it should not be obtained on a repetition of the demand for it. To this end I recommend that an act be passed authorizing reprisals, and the use of the naval force of the United States, by the executive, against Mexico, to enforce them in the event of a refusal by the Mexican government to come to an amicable adjustment of the matters in controversy between us, upon another demand thereof, made from on board of one of our vessels of war on the coast of Mexico."

Both houses of congress coincided with him; but the senate recommended, the house of representatives concurring, that another demand be made, which, should it be disregarded, would justify the United States in taking into their own hands the redress of the many injuries they had received.

Immediately, a special messenger was despatched to Mexico, to make a final demand for redress; and on the 20th of July, 1837, the demand was made. The reply of the Mexican government on the 29th of the same month, contains assurances of the "anxious wish" of the Mexican government, "not to delay the moment of that final and equitable adjustment which is to terminate the existing difficulties between the two governments;" that "nothing should be left undone which may contribute to the most speedy and equitable determination of the subjects which have so seriously engaged the attention of the American government;" that the "Mexican government would adopt, as the only guides for its conduct, the plainest principles of public right, the sacred obligations imposed by international law, and the religious faith of treaties;" and that "whatever reason and justice may dictate respecting each case will be done." The assurance was further given, that the decision of the Mexican government upon each cause of complaint, for which redress has been demanded, should be communicated to the government of the United States by the Mexican minister at Washington.

These solemn assurances, in answer to demands for redress, were never fulfilled. By making them, however, Mexico obtained further delay.

During the whole administration of Mr. Van Buren a similar state of affairs existed, and though the president urged the adoption of decisive measures, yet from feelings of forbearance, and a disposition to avoid the presentation to the civilized world, of the two greatest republics of the universe, following the example of monarchical rulers, wrangling in forgetfulness of their true interest, congress hesitated.

On the 11th of April, 1839, a joint commission was appointed, which, however, was not organized until August 11th, 1840. The powers of the commission by the act creating it, terminated in February, 1842, and Mr. Polk, in his last annual message, thus characterizes its conduct:

"Four of the eighteen months were consumed in preliminary discussions on frivolous and dilatory points raised by the Mexican commissioners; and it was not until the month of December, 1840, that they commenced the examination of the claims of our citizens upon Mexico. Fourteen months only remained to examine and decide upon these numerous and complicated cases. In the month of February, 1842, the term of the commission expired, leaving many claims undisposed of for want of time. The claims which were allowed by the board, and by the umpire authorized by the convention to decide in case of disagreement between the Mexican and American commissioners, amounted to two millions twenty-six thousand one hundred and thirty-nine dollars and sixty-eight cents. There were pending before the umpire when the commission expired additional claims which had been examined and awarded by the American commissioners, and had not been allowed by the Mexican commissioners, amounting to nine hundred and twenty-eight thousand six hundred and twenty-seven dollars and eight cents, upon which he did not decide, alleging that his authority had ceased with the termination of the joint commission. Besides these claims, there were others of American citizens, amounting to three millions three hundred and thirty-six thousand eight hundred and thirty-seven dollars and five cents, which had been submitted to the board, and upon which they had not time to decide before their final adjournment.

"The sum of two millions twenty-six thousand one hundred and thirty-nine dollars and sixty-eight cents, which had been awarded to the claimants, was a liquidated and ascertained debt due by Mexico, about which there could be no dispute, and which she was bound to pay according to the terms of the convention. Soon after the final awards for this amount had been made, the Mexican government asked for a postponement of the time of making the payment at the time stipulated. In the spirit of forbearing kindness towards a sister republic, which Mexico has so long abused, the United States promptly complied with her request. A second convention was accordingly concluded between the two governments on the 30th of January, 1843, which upon its face declares, that 'this new arrangement is entered into for the accommodation of Mexico.' By the terms of this convention, all the interest due on the awards which had been made in favor of the claimants under the convention of the 11th of April, 1839, was to be paid to them on the 30th of April, 1843, and the 'principal of the said awards, and the interest accruing thereon,' was stipulated to 'be paid in five years, in equal instalments every three months.' Notwithstanding this new convention was entered into at the request of Mexico, and for the purpose of relieving her from embarrassment, the claimants have only received the interest due on the 30th of April, 1843, and three of the twenty instalments. Although the payment of the sum thus liquidated, and confessedly due by Mexico to our citizens as indemnity for acknowledged acts of outrage and wrong, was secured by treaty, the obligations of which are ever held sacred by all just nations, yet Mexico has violated this solemn engagement by failing and refusing to make the payment. The two instalments due in April and July, 1844, under the peculiar circumstances connected with them, have been assumed by the United States and discharged to the claimants, but they are still due by Mexico. But this is not all of which we have just cause of complaint. To provide a remedy for the claimants whose cases were not decided by the joint commission under the convention of April the 11th, 1839, it was expressly stipulated by the sixth article of the convention of the 30th of January, 1843, that "a new convention be entered into for the settlement of all claims of the government and citizens of the United States against the republic of Mexico which were not finally decided by the late commission, which met in the city of Washington, and of all claims of the government and citizens of Mexico against the United States.'

"In conformity with this stipulation, a third convention was concluded and signed at the city of Mexico on the 20th of November, 1843, by the plenipotentiaries of the two governments, by which provision was made for ascertaining and paying these claims. In January, 1844, this convention was ratified by the senate of the United States with two amendments, which were manifestly reasonable in their character. Upon a reference to the amendments proposed to the government of Mexico, the same evasions, difficulties, and delays were interposed which have so long marked the policy of that government towards the United States. It has not even yet decided whether it would or would not accede to them, although the subject has been repeatedly pressed upon its consideration."

By failing to carry out the stipulations of this last convention, Mexico again outraged the government of the United States.

This long series of outrages was no doubt a reason for war, but it may be doubted if it produced the existing hostilities with Mexico. It has ever been the policy of the United States to recognise all governments existing *de facto*, a rule which induced Mr. Monroe to recommend the institution of diplomatic intercourse with Mexico, and all the South American republics, as soon as they had exhibited to the world their capacity to defend themselves. Mexico should not complain that the United States pleased to recognise Texas as free and independent, since it followed as a corollary from the conduct of the same government towards herself. On the 21st day of April, 1836, Santa Anna had been defeated by Houston, since when a Mexican soldier has never been in Texas; and in May, 1836, the president of Mexico, in a solemn treaty, recognised the independence of that republic. It is not pretended that that treaty is binding on Mexico, which never ratified it, except so far that it estops her from complaining if other nations follow the example of the chief magistrate of Mexico, and look on the rebel province as a sovereign state.

On the 29th day of December, 1845, Texas was admitted into the North American Union, as the government understood it, embracing all the territory ceded to Spain by the Florida treaty of 1819, and also that territory beyond the Neuces over which the republic of Texas had exercised sovereign rights.

Mr. Polk, in his message, thus defines the pretensions of the United States:

"The congress of Texas, on the 19th of December, 1836, passed 'an act to define the boundaries of the republic of Texas,' in which they declared the Rio Grande, from its mouth to its source, to be their boundary; and by the said act they extended their 'civil and political jurisdiction' over the country up to that boundary. During a period of more than nine years, which intervened between the adoption of her constitution and her annexation as one of the states of the Union, Texas asserted and exercised many acts of sovereignty and jurisdiction over the territory and inhabitants west of the Neuces. She organized and defined the limits of counties extending to the Rio Grande. She established courts of justice, and extended her judicial system over the territory. She established a custom-house, and collected duties, and also post offices and post roads, in it. She established a land office, and issued numerous grants for land, within its limits. A senator and a representative residing in it were elected to the congress of the republic, and served as such before the act of annexation took place. In both the congress and convention of Texas, which gave their assent to the terms of annexation to the United States proposed by our congress, were representatives residing west of the Neuces, who took part in the act of annexation itself. This was the Texas which, by the act of our congress of the 29th of December, 1845, was admitted as one of the states of our Union. That the congress of the United States understood the state of Texas which they admitted into the union to extend beyond the Neuces, is apparent, from the fact that on the 31st of December,

1845, only two days after the act of admission, they passed a law 'to establish a collection district in the state of Texas,' by which they created a port of delivery at Corpus Christi, situated west of the Neuces, and being the same point at which the Texas custom-house, under the laws of the republic, had been located, and directed that a surveyor to collect the revenue should be appointed for that port by the president, by and with the advice and consent of the senate. A surveyor was accordingly nominated, and confirmed by the senate, and has been ever since in the performance of his duties. All these acts of the republic of Texas, and of our congress, preceded the orders for the advance of our army to the east bank of the Rio Grande. Subsequently congress passed an act 'establishing certain post routes,' extending west of the Neuces."

It is not unlikely there would have been no war, at least immediately, had not the United States occupied the country west of the Neuces, which was done by General Taylor, who encamped at Corpus Christi in August, 1845, where the army remained until March 1846, when it moved westward to the east bank of the Rio Grande, opposite Matamoras. While these movements were being made, an agent of the United States, Mr. Slidell, was in Mexico insisting on being received as a plenipotentiary, while Mexico would only recognise him as a commissioner, a circumstance which produced much acrimonious discussion in both republics.

On the 4th of March, Paredes, then president, through his secretary of war ordered the Mexican general on the Texan frontier to attack the army of the United States.

General Arista at once obeyed his orders by rendering

it no longer doubtful that the two armies were in a state of hostility. After several skirmishes, in one of which Captain Thornton was captured with a squadron of dragoons, in another, Lieutenant Porter, of the fourth infantry, was killed, and a gallant officer of Texas troops had a narrow escape, Fort Brown, a strong work thrown up by General Taylor opposite Matamoras, was attacked by a powerful force under cover of the ordnance of the city, and a strong battery erected by the Mexicans during the night of the 4th. The bombardment lasted during the 6th (when the commander of the fort, Major Brown, was killed); and during the 8th, when under the command of Major Hawkins, the garrison continued to make good their defence. They were successful; and during the day the firing told them General Taylor was engaged with the main Mexican army.

During the events which transpired in front of Fort Brown, both armies had been busy, General Taylor having gone to the assistance of Point Isabel, which was menaced by the Mexican force, and from which he expected to obtain supplies for the rest of his troops. The force of the American general was small; but rarely has any commander led better troops to battle than Taylor, on the 8th of May, arrayed in front of the opposing force; on the right was the light artillery of Ringgold, a battalion of fifth and third infantry, on the left another light battery, commanded by Duncan, and battalions of the fourth and eighth infantry, all veteran troops, which, during the war in Florida, had undergone the baptism of fire, and been subjected to all the ordeals incident to a partisan war. The cavalry was held in reserve.

The enemy numbered six thousand men. The first prominent movement they made was an attempt to pass around the *chapparal* which protected the right of the American forces, and attack the train with supplies. This effort was foiled by the fifth foot, which wheeled into square, received the charge of the Mexican lancers, and sent them to the right-about with a volley which did no little execution. The lancers were, however, again rallied and brought to the attack, when the third infantry, in column of divisions, met them. They immediately retired after receiving the fire of a section of light artillery commanded by Lieutenant Ridgely, which had been detached from Ringgold's battery.

The left of the enemy was mowed down by the American artillery, though the eighth foot suffered much from the Mexican fire. The result of the day was that the American right occupied the ground on which the enemy had originally stood. This was the result of the battle of Palo Alto.

On the 9th of May, Gen. Taylor collected his own and the enemy's wounded into one hospital, among whom were many gallant officers; and moved in pursuit of the retreating enemy towards Resaca de la Palma.

This battle was essentially one of the bayonet and sabre, assisted by the artillery. Here it was that May made his famous charge, which already has become celebrated as the deeds of Cromwell's ironsides, and the assaults of Lee's legion. He lost at least one-half of his men, but was lucky enough to take the battery he assaulted, and with it the Mexican General Romulo de la Vega. The enemy subsequently retook this battery; but, at the end of the day, it was in possession of the fifth regiment of United States infantry, which captured it at the point of the bayonet, a second time.

The following are General Taylor's despatches, giving an account of these battles:—

HEAD-QUARTERS ARMY OF OCCUPATION,
Camp at Palo Alto, Texas, May 9, 1846.

SIR: I have the honor to report that I was met near this place yesterday, on my march from Point Isabel, by the Mexican forces, and after an action of about five hours, dislodged them from their position and encamped upon the field. Our artillery, consisting of two eighteen pounders and two light batteries, was the arm chiefly engaged, and to the excellent manner in which it was manœuvred and served, is our success mainly due.

The strength of the enemy is believed to have been about 6000 men, with seven pieces of artillery, and 800 cavalry. His loss is probably at least one hundred killed. Our strength did not exceed, all told, twenty-three hundred, while our loss was comparatively trifling —four men killed, three officers and thirty-seven men wounded, several of the latter mortally. I regret to say that Major Ringgold, 2d artillery, and Captain Page, 4th infantry, are severely wounded. Lieutenant Luther, 2d artillery, slightly so.

The enemy has fallen back, and it is believed has repassed the river. I have advanced parties now thrown forward in his direction, and shall move the main body immediately.

In the haste of this report, I can only say that the officers and men behaved in the most admirable manner throughout the action. I shall have the pleasure of making a more detailed report when those of the different commanders shall be received.

I am, sir, very respectfully,
Your obedient servant,
Z. TAYLOR,
Brevet Brigadier-General U. S. A., Commanding.

The ADJUTANT-GENERAL, U. S. Army,
Washington, D. C.

HEAD-QUARTERS ARMY OF OCCUPATION,
Camp at Resaca de la Palma, 3 *miles from*
Matamoras, 10 *o'clock*, *P.M.*, *May* 9, 1846.

SIR: I have the honor to report that I marched with the main body of the army at two o'clock to-day, having previously thrown forward a body of light infantry into the forest which covers the Matamoras road. When near the spot where I am now encamped, my advance discovered that a ravine crossing the road had been occupied by the enemy with artillery. I immediately ordered a battery of field artillery to sweep the position, flanking and sustaining it by the 3d, 4th, and 5th regiments, deployed as skirmishes to the right and left. A heavy fire of artillery and of musketry was kept up for some time, until finally the enemy's batteries were carried in succession by a squadron of dragoons and the regiments of infantry that were on the ground. He was soon driven from his position, and pursued by a squadron of dragoons, battalion of artillery, 3d infantry, and a light battery, to the river. Our victory has been complete. Eight pieces of artillery, with a great quantity of ammunition, three standards, and some one hundred prisoners have been taken; among the latter, General La Vega, and several other officers. One general is understood to have been killed. The enemy has recrossed the river, and I am sure will not again molest us on this bank.

The loss of the enemy in killed has been most severe. Our own has been very heavy, and I deeply regret to report that Lieutenant Inge, 2d dragoons, Lieutenant Cochrane, 4th infantry, and Lieutenant Chadbourne, 8th infantry, were killed on the field. Lieutenant-Colonel Payne, 4th artillery; Lieutenant-Colonel McIntosh, Lieutenant Dobbins, 3d infantry; Captain Hooe and Lieutenant Fowler, 5th infantry; and Captain Montgomery, Lieutenants Gates, Selden, McClay, Burbank, and Jordan, 8th infantry, were wounded. The extent of our loss in killed and wounded is not yet ascertained, and is reserved for a more detailed report.

The affair of to-day may be regarded as a proper supplement to the cannonade of yesterday; and the two taken together, exhibit the coolness and gallantry of our officers and men in the most favorable light. All have done their duty, and done it nobly. It will be my pride, in a more circumstantial report of both actions, to dwell upon particular instances of individual distinction.

It affords me peculiar pleasure to report, that the field work opposite Matamoras has sustained itself handsomely during a cannonade and bombardment of 160 hours. But the pleasure is alloyed with profound regret at the loss of its heroic and indomitable commander, Major Brown, who died to-day from the effects of a shell. His loss would be a severe one to the service at any time, but to the army under my orders it is indeed irreparable. One officer and one non-commissioned officer killed, and ten men wounded, comprise all the casualties incident to this severe bombardment.

I inadvertently omitted to mention the capture of a large number of pack-mules left in the Mexican camp.

I am, sir, very respectfully,

Your obedient servant,

Z. TAYLOR,

Brevet Brigadier-General U. S. A. Commanding.

The ADJUTANT-GENERAL of the Army,
Washington, D. C.

In the interim Fort Brown had been summoned, and the garrison been informed that Taylor was defeated. The lie was, however, unproductive, as both officers and men knew better, having served with Taylor in the everglades, and knew he was emphatically one of those who might die, but never surrender.

The following is the bulletin of the Mexican commander to his superior, a strange contrast to the simplicity and terseness of the successful general:

GENERAL-IN-CHIEF,

MOST EXCELLENT SIR: Constant in my purpose of preventing General Taylor from uniting the forces which he brought from the Fronton of Santa Isabel, with those which he left fortified opposite Matamoras, I moved this day from the Fanques del Raminero, whence I despatched my last extraordinary courier, and took the direction of Palo Alto, as soon as my spies informed me that the enemy had left Fronton, with the determination of introducing into his fort wagons loaded with provisions and heavy artillery.

I arrived opposite Palo Alto about one o'clock, and observed that the enemy was entering that position.

With all my forces, I established the line of battle in a great plain, my right resting upon an elevation, and my left on a slough of difficult passage.

Scarcely was the first cannon fired, when there arrived General Pedro de Ampudia, second in command, whom I had ordered to join me after having covered the points which might serve to besiege the enemy in the forts opposite Matamoras.

The forces under my orders amounted to three thousand men, and twelve pieces of artillery; those of the invaders were three thousand, rather less than more, and were superior in artillery, since they had twenty pieces of the calibre of sixteen and eighteen pounds.

The battle commenced so ardently, that the fire of cannon did not cease a single moment. In the course of it, the enemy wished to follow the road towards Matamoras, to raise the siege of his troops; with which object he fired the grass, and formed in front of his line of battle a smoke so thick, that he succeeded in covering himself from our view, but by means of manœuvres this was twice embarrassed.

General Taylor maintained his attack rather defensively than offensively, employing his best arm, which is artillery, protected by half of the infantry, and all of his cavalry—keeping the remainder fortified in the ravine, about two thousand yards from the field of battle.

I was anxious for the charge, because the fire of cannon did much damage in our ranks, and I instructed General D. Anastasio Torrejon to execute it with the greater part of the cavalry, by our left flank, while one should be executed at the same time by our right flank, with some columns of infantry, and the remainder of that arm [cavalry].

I was waiting the moment when that general should execute the charge, and the effect of it should begin to be seen, in order to give the impulse on the right; but he was checked by the fire of the enemy, which defended a slough that embarrassed the attack.

Some battalions, becoming impatient by the loss which they suffered, fell into disorder, demanding to advance or fall back. I immediately caused them to charge with a column of cavalry, under the command of Colonel D. Cayetano Montero; the result of this operation being that the dispersed corps repaired their fault as far as possible, marching towards the enemy, who, in consequence of his distance, was enabled to fall back upon his reserve, and night coming on, the battle was concluded—the field remaining for our arms.

Every suitable measure was then adopted, and the division took up a more concentrated curve in the same scene of action.

The combat was long and bloody, which may be estimated from the calculations made by the commandant-general of artillery, General D. Thomas Requena, who assures me that the enemy threw about three thousand cannon-shots from two in the afternoon, when the battle commenced, until seven at night, when it terminated—six hundred and fifty being fired on our side.

The national arms shone forth, since they did not yield a hand's-breadth of ground, notwithstanding the superiority in artillery of the enemy, who suffered much damage.

Our troops have to lament the loss of two hundred and fifty-two men, dispersed, wounded, and killed—the last worthy of national recollection and gratitude for the intrepidity with which they died fighting for the most sacred of causes.

Will your excellency please with this note to report to his excellency the president, representing to him that I will take care to give a circumstantial account of this deed of arms; and recommending to him the good conduct of all the generals, chiefs, officers, and soldiers under my orders, for sustaining so bloody a combat, which does honor to our arms, and exhibits their discipline.

Accept the assurances of my consideration and great regard.

God and Liberty!

HEAD-QUARTERS, PALO ALTO, *in sight of the enemy, May* 8, 1846.

MARIANO ARISTA.

MOST EXCELLENT SIR,
Minister of War and Marine.

Many were the incidents of humanity which occurred and relieved the sternness of the battle-field, but which it scarcely belongs to our plan to relate.

The result of these battles was, that Matamoras surrendered, and General Taylor having been reinforced was enabled to march to Monterey, which he reached on the 19th of October, encamping at the Walnut Springs, within three miles of the city.

The attack was made, and after four days' continual fighting, General Ampudia, on the 24th of October, sent a commission proposing to surrender; and finally terms were agreed on by the representatives of the two generals, as follows:

Terms of capitulation of the city of Monterey, the capital of Nuevo Leon, agreed upon by the undersigned commissioners, to wit: General Worth, of the United States army, General Henderson, of the Texan volunteers, and Colonel Davis, of the Mississippi riflemen, on the part of Major-General Taylor, Commander-in-chief of the United States forces, and General Requena and General M. Llano, Governor of Nuevo Leon, on the part of Señor General Don Pedro Ampudia, commanding in chief the army of the north of Mexico.

ARTICLE I. As the legitimate result of the operations before this place, and the present position of the contending armies, it is agreed that the city, the fortifications, cannon, the munitions of war, and all other public property, with the undermentioned exceptions, be surrendered to the commanding general of the United States forces now at Monterey.

Article II. That the Mexican forces be allowed to retain the following arms, to wit: the commissioned officers their side-arms, the infantry their arms and accoutrements, the cavalry their arms and accoutrements, the artillery one field battery, not to exceed six pieces, with twenty-one rounds of ammunition.

Article III. That the Mexican armed forces retire, within seven days from this date, beyond the line formed by the pass of Rinconada, the city of Linares, and San Fernando de Parras.

Article IV. That the citadel of Monterey be evacuated by the Mexican and occupied by the American forces to-morrow morning at ten o'clock.

Article V. To avoid collisions, and for mutual convenience, that the troops of the United States will not occupy the city until the Mexican forces have withdrawn, except for hospital and storage purposes.

Article VI. That the forces of the United States will not advance beyond the line specified in the 3d article, before the expiration of eight weeks, or until orders or instructions of the respective governments can be received.

Artice VII. That the public property to be delivered, shall be turned over and received by officers appointed by the commanding generals of the two armies.

Article VIII. That all doubts as to the meaning of any of the preceding articles, shall be solved by an equitable construction, or on principles of liberality to the retiring army.

Article IX. That the Mexican flag, when struck at the citadel, may be saluted by its own battery.

Done at Monterey, Sept. 24, 1846.

W. J. WORTH,
Brigadier-General United States Army.
J. PINKNEY HENDERSON,
Major-General commanding the Texan Volunteers.
JEFFERSON DAVIS,
Colonel Mississippi Riflemen.
MANUEL L. LLANO,
T. REQUENA,
ORTEGA.
Approved,
Z. TAYLOR,
Major-General United States Army, commanding.
PEDRO AMPUDIA.

Rarely has it ever happened that any surrender has been made with which so much fault has been found. For yielding up Monterey, General Ampudia has been arraigned, and virtually suspended from command, because he did not properly support the interests of Mexico, while a large party in the United States have sought to censure General Taylor, and have by implication, done so, because he did not insist on an unconditional surrender. The probability is that injustice was done to both generals.

For want of troops and supplies, General Taylor was long detained at Monterey.

In the mean time the general-in-chief of the army had been ordered to assume the command of a large force prepared for the purpose of attacking Vera Cruz and the powerful fort of San Juan de Ulloa, with orders from Washington city to withdraw from General Taylor the regulars under his command. who had fought so gallantly at Monterey and in the previous battles, the number of which was six hundred men. General Taylor, somewhat chagrined at the circumstance, immediately detached General Worth with them to join General Scott, and having learned that an attempt was about to be made to cut off his communication with Matamoras, he determined to advance and meet the Mexican president. On the 20th of February he was encamped at Agua Nueva, about eighteen miles south of Saltillo, where he learned that Santa Anna, at the head of twenty thousand men, was about twenty miles from him.

The American general at once fell back to an admirable position about seven miles from Saltillo, called Buena Vista.

On the 22d the American troops were in position with the Mexican cavalry in front of them.

General Taylor thus describes it: "Our troops were in position, occupying a line of remarkable strength. The road at this point becomes a narrow defile, the valley on its right being rendered quite impracticable for artillery by a system of deep and impassable gullies, while on the left a succession of rugged ridges and precipitous ravines extends far back toward the mountain which bounds the valley. The features of the ground were such as nearly to paralyze the artillery and cavalry of the enemy, while his infantry could not derive all the advantage of its numerical superiority. In this position we prepared to receive him. Captain Washington's battery (4th artillery) was posted to command the road, while the 1st and 2d Illinois regiments, under Colonels Hardin and Bissel, each eight companies (to the latter of which was attached Captain Conner's company of Texas volunteers), and the 2d Kentucky, under Colonel McKee, occupied the crests of the ridges on the left and in rear. The Arkansas and Kentucky regiments of cavalry, commanded by Colonels Yell and H. Marshall, occupied the extreme left near the base of the mountain, while the Indiana brigade, under Brigadier-General Lane (composed of the 2d and 3d regiments, under Colonels Bowles and Lane), the Mississippi riflemen, under Colonel Davis, the squadrons of the 1st and 2d dragoons, under Captain Steen and Lieutenant-Colonel May, and the light batteries of Captains Sherman and Bragg, 3d artillery, were held in reserve."

At eleven o'clock, Santa Anna sent the following summons to General Taylor, which, with the reply, is subjoined:

Summons of General Santa Anna to General Taylor.

You are surrounded by twenty thousand men, and cannot, in any human probability, avoid suffering a rout, and being cut to pieces with your troops; but as you deserve consideration and particular esteem, I wish to save you from a catastrophe, and for that purpose give you this notice, in order that you may surrender at discretion, under the assurance that you will be treated with the consideration belonging to the Mexican character, to which end you will be granted an hour's time to make up your mind, to commence from the moment when my flag of truce arrives in your camp.

With this view, I assure you of my particular consideration.

God and Liberty. Camp at Encantada, February 22d, 1847.

ANTONIO LOPEZ DE SANTA ANNA.

To General Z. TAYLOR,
Commanding the forces of the U. S.

HEAD-QUARTERS ARMY OF OCCUPATION,
Near Buena Vista, February 22, 1847.

SIR: In reply to your note of this date, summoning me to surrender my forces at discretion, I beg leave to say that I decline acceding to your request.

With high respect, I am, sir,
Your obedient servant,
Z. TAYLOR,
Major General U. S. Army, Commanding.

Senor Gen. D. ANTONIO LOPEZ DE SANTA ANNA,
Commander-in-Chief, La Encantada.

At night-fall many brave men had fallen. General Taylor was in possession of the field, and when morning came the enemy had retreated.

Among the dead none were more lamented than Captain George Lincoln, of the army, an assistant adjutant-general, and Colonels Hardin, McKee, and Yell, and lieutenant-colonel Clay, of the volunteers.

Santa Anna retreated, but he contrived to raise a report which represented him as victorious, too curious to be omitted. Even the Mexicans, however, did not believe it. The extracts which follow will suffice to show its tenor:

"On the 26th, after I had ordered General Minon to follow the movement, the army commenced its retreat with the view of occupying the first peopled localities, where resources might be obtained, such as Vanegas, Catorce, El Cadral, and Matehuala, as also Tula; but I doubt if in those places proper attention can be given to the sick and wounded—or the losses we have sustained in those laborious movements be remedied.

"The nation, for which a triumph has been gained at the cost of so many sufferings, will learn that, if we were able to conquer in the midst of so many embrrassments, there will be no doubt as to our final success in the struggle we sustain, if every spirit but rallies to the one sacred object of common defence. A mere determined number of men will not, as many imagine, suffice for the prosecution of war; it is indispensable that they be armed, equipped, disciplined, and habituated, and that systematized support for such an organized force be provided. We must bear in mind that we have to combat in a region deficient of all resources, and that everything for subsistence has to be carried along with the soldiery: the good-will of a few will not suffice, but the co-operation of all is needed; and if we do not cast aside selfish interests and petty passions, we can expect nothing but disaster. The army, and myself who have led it, have the satisfaction of knowing that we have demonstrated this truth.

"Your excellency will be pleased to report to his excellency, the vice-president of the republic, and to present to him my assurance of respect.

"God and Liberty! Rancho de San Salvador, February 27th, 1847.

(Signed)

ANTONIO LOPEZ DE SANTA ANNA.

To His Excellency, the Minister of War and Marine."

Santa Anna was beaten shamefully, and was glad to take advantage of a pronunciamento, to quell which he went to Mexico.

In the mean time General Scott, aided by the naval forces, had landed his men, and after a bombardment of six days the city of Vera Cruz surrendered, with the castle of San Juan and all other dependencies, to his arms. The Mexican troops, commanded by Generals

Landero and Morales, laid down their arms and were paroled, and the American flag was raised over the city which never before had been in the power of an invader.

General Worth was appointed temporary governor of Vera Cruz, from which General Scott at once set out towards Mexico. On the 17th of April he approached the defile of Cerro Gordo, always reputed impregnable, and defended by Santa Anna with twenty thousand men, to oppose whom were twelve thousand Americans.

The following orders and despatch express the events of this day better than any other account or description can, and will place General Scott at the head of the great commanders of the age.

HEAD-QUARTERS OF THE ARMY,
Plain Del Rio, April 17, 1847.

(General Orders, No. 111.)

The enemy's whole line of intrenchments and bat teries will be attacked in front, and at the same time turned early in the day to-morrow—probably before ten o'clock, A. M.

The second (Twiggs's) division of regulars is already advanced within easy turning distance towards the enemy's left. That division has orders to move forward before daylight to-morrow, and take up position across the National Road to the enemy's rear, so as to cut off a retreat towards Jalapa. It may be reinforced to-day, if unexpectedly attacked in force, by regiments—one or two taken from Shields's brigade of volunteers. If not, the two volunteer regiments will march for that purpose at daylight to-morrow morning, under Brigadier-General Shields, who will report to Brigadier-General Twiggs on getting up with him, or the general-in-chief, if he be in advance.

The remaining regiment of that volunteer brigade will receive instructions in the course of this day.

The first division of regulars (Worth's) will follow the movement against the enemy's left at sunrise to-morrow morning.

As already arranged, Brigadier-General Pillow's brigade will march at six o'clock to-morrow morning, along the route he has carefully reconnoitred, and stand ready as soon as he hears the report of arms on our right—sooner, if circumstances should favor him—to pierce the enemy's line of batteries at such point—the nearer the river the better—as he may select. Once in the rear of that line, he will turn to the right or left, or both, and attack the batteries in reverse, or if abandoned, he will pursue the enemy with vigor until further orders.

Wall's field battery and the cavalry will be held in reserve on the National Road, a little out of view and range of the enemy's batteries. They will take up that position at nine o'clock in the morning.

The enemy's batteries being carried or abandoned, all our divisions and corps will pursue with vigor.

This pursuit may be continued many miles, until stopped by darkness or fortified positions towards Jalapa. Consequently, the body of the army will not return to this encampment, but be followed to-morrow afternoon, or early the next morning, by the baggage trains for the several corps. For this purpose, the feebler officers and men of each corps will be left to guard its camp and effects, and to load up the latter in the wagons of the corps.

As soon as it shall be known that the enemy's works have been carried, or that the general pursuit has been commenced, one wagon for each regiment, and one for the cavalry, will follow the movement, to receive, under the directions of medical officers, the wounded and disabled, who will be brought back to this place for treatment in the general hospital.

The surgeon-general will organize this important service and designate that hospital, as well as the medical officers to be left at that place.

Every man who marches out to attack or pursue the enemy will take the usual allowance of ammunition, and subsistence for at least two days.

By command of Major-General Scott,
H. L. SCOTT, A. A. A. General.

HEAD-QUARTERS OF THE ARMY,
Plain del Rio, fifty miles from Vera Cruz,
April 19, 1847.

SIR: The plan of attack sketched in general orders No. 111, herewith, was finely executed by this gallant army, before two o'clock P. M. yesterday. We are quite embarrassed with the results of victory—prisoners of war, heavy ordnance, field-batteries, small arms, and accoutrements. About three thousand men laid down their arms, with the usual proportion of field and company officers, besides five generals, several of them of great distinction: Pinson, Jarrero, La Vega, Noriega, and Obando. A sixth general, Vasquez, was killed in defending the battery (tower) in the rear of the whole Mexican army, the capture of which gave us those glorious results.

Our loss, though comparatively small in numbers, has been serious. Brigadier-General Shields, a commander of activity, zeal, and talent, is, I fear, if not dead, mortally wounded. He is some miles from me at the moment. The field of operations covered many miles, broken by mountains and deep chasms, and I have not a report, as yet, from any division or brigade. Twiggs's division, followed by Shields's (now Colonel Baker's) brigade, are now at or near Jalapa, and Worth's division is in route thither, all pursuing, with good results, as I learn, that part of the Mexican army—perhaps 6000 or 7000 men—who fled before our right had carried the tower, and gained the Jalapa road. Pillow's brigade, alone, is near me, at this depot of wounded, sick, and prisoners, and I have time only to give from him the names of 1st Lieutenant F. B. Nelson, and 2d C. C. Gill, both of the 2d Tennessee foot (Haskell's regiment), among the killed, and in the brigade 106, of all ranks, killed or wounded. Among the latter, the gallant brigadier himself has a smart wound in the arm, but not disabled, and Major R. Farqueson, 2d Tennessee; Captain H. F. Murray, 2d Lieutenant G. T. Sutherland, 1st Lieutenant W. P. Hale (adjutant), all of the same regiment, severely, and 1st Lieutenant W. Yearwood, mortally wounded. And I know, from personal observation on the ground, that 1st Lieutenant Ewell, of the rifles, if not now dead, was mortally wounded, in entering, sword in hand, the intrenchments around the captured tower. Second Lieutenant Derby, Topographical Engineers, I also saw, at the same place, severely wounded, and Captain Patton, 2d United States infantry, lost his right hand.

Major Sumner, 2d United States dragoons, was slightly wounded the day before, and Captain Johnston, Topographical Engineers — now lieutenant-colonel of infantry — was very severely wounded some days earlier, while reconnoitering.

I must not omit to add that Captain Mason and 2d Lieutenant Davis, both of the rifles, were among the very severely wounded in storming the same tower.

I estimate our total loss in killed and wounded may be about 250, and that of the enemy 350. In the pursuit towards Jalapa (twenty-five miles hence), I learn we have added much to the enemy's loss in prisoners, killed, and wounded. In fact, I suppose his retreating army to be nearly disorganized, and hence my haste to follow, in an hour or two, to profit by events.

In this hurried and imperfect report, I must not omit to say that Brigadier-General Twiggs, in passing the mountain range beyond Cerro Gordo, crowned with the tower, detached from his division, as I suggested before, a strong force to carry that height, which commanded the Jalapa road at the foot, and could not fail, if carried, to cut off the whole, or any part of the enemy's forces from a retreat in any direction. A portion of the first artillery, under the often distinguished Brevet-Colonel Childs, the 3d infantry, under Captain Alexander, the 7th infantry, under Lieutenant-Colonel Plymton, and the rifles, under Major Loring, all under the temporary command of Colonel Harney, 2d dragoons, during the confinement to his bed of Brevet Brigadier-General P. F. Smith, composed that detachment. The style of execution, which I had the pleasure to witness, was most brilliant and decisive. The brigade ascended the long and difficult slope of Cerro Gordo, without shelter, and under the tremendous fire of artillery and musketry, with the utmost steadiness, reached the breastworks, drove the enemy from them, planted the colors of the 1st artillery, 3d and 7th infantry—the enemy's flag still flying—and, after some minutes of sharp firing, finished the conquest with the bayonet.

It is a most pleasing duty to say that the highest praise is due to Harney, Childs, Plymton, Loring, Alexander, their gallant officers and men, for this bril liant service, independent of the great result which soon followed.

Worth's division of regulars coming up at this time, he detached Brevet Lieutenant-Colonel C. F. Smith, with his light battalion, to support the assault, but not in time. The general, reaching the tower a few minutes before me, and observing a white flag displayed from the nearest portion of the enemy towards the batteries below, sent out Colonels Harney and Childs to hold a parley. The surrender followed in an hour or two.

Major-General Patterson left a sick bed to share in the dangers and fatigues of the day; and after the surrender went forward to command the advanced forces towards Jalapa.

Brigadier-General Pillow and his brigade twice assaulted with great daring the enemy's line of batteries on our left; and though without success, they contributed much to distract and dismay their immediate opponents.

President Santa Anna, with Generals Canalizo and Almonte, and some six or eight thousand men, escaped towards Jalapa just before Cerro Gordo was carried, and before Twiggs's division reached the National Road above.

I have determined to parole the prisoners—officers and men—as I have not the means of feeding them here, beyond to-day, and cannot afford to detach a heavy body of horse and foot, with wagons, to accompany them to Vera Cruz. Our baggage train, though increasing, is not half large enough to give an assured progress to this army. Besides, a greater number of prisoners would, probably, escape from the escort in the long and deep sandy road, without subsistence—ten to one—that we shall find again, out of the same body of men, in the ranks opposed to us. Not one of the Vera Cruz prisoners is believed to have been in the lines of Cerro Gordo. Some six of the officers, highest in rank, refuse to give their paroles, except to go to Vera Cruz, and thence, perhaps, to the United States.

The small arms and their accoutrements, being of no value to our army here or at home, I have ordered to be destroyed, for we have not the means of transporting them. I am, also, somewhat embarrassed with the —— pieces of artillery—all bronze—which we have captured. It will take a brigade, and half the mules of this army to transport them fifty miles. A field-battery I shall take for service with the army; but the heavy metal must be collected, and left here for the present. We have our own siege train and the proper carriages with us.

Being much occupied with the prisoners, and all the details of a forward movement, besides looking to the supplies which are to follow from Vera Cruz, I have time to add no more—intending to be at Jalapa early to-morrow. We shall not, probably, again meet with serious opposition this side of Perote—certainly not, unless delayed by the want of transportation.

I have the honor to remain, sir, with high respect, your most obedient servant,

WINFIELD SCOTT.

P. S. I invite attention to the accompanying letter to President Santa Anna, taken in his carriage yesterday; also to his proclamation, issued on hearing we had captured Vera Cruz, &c., in which he says:—"If the enemy advance one step more, the national independence will be buried in the abyss of the past." We have taken that step. W. S.

I make a second postscript, to say that there is some

hope, I am happy to learn, that General Shields may survive his wounds.

One of the principal motives for paroling the prisoners of war is, to diminish the resistance of other garrisons in our march.

Hon. WM. L. MARCY, Secretary of War.

The consequences of this victory were felt at Mexico more immediately than any of the preceding triumphs, and caused Santa Anna to put forth, over the signature of one of his adherents, Manuel Maria Jimen, the following vindication of his tactics and conduct, which appeared immediately afterwards in the government organ, *el Diario del Gobierno:*

"The internal enemies of the country, the secret agents of our external enemies, those who are laboring to open to them the gates of the capital, neglect no means, however criminal, of fomenting dissensions and distrust among us, as more favorable to the designs of the invader is our own disunion than all the disasters we can suffer in combat. Hence the zeal and the bad faith with which they present to the public their accounts of the events of the war, disfiguring them in such a manner that the disasters of our army, as well in the north as in the east, may be attributed not to involuntary errors, but to treason.

"With a like motive do they endeavor to depreciate General Santa Anna, knowing, as they do, that he is the enemy whom the North Americans most fear, and that he once out of the way, they will have removed the principal obstacle that they have met with up to the present time, in their career of destruction and conquest.

"This idea predominating, these internal enemies of

the country have published various pamphlets, representing the triumph obtained by our arms at the Angostura as a loss. At the present moment they are doing the same thing in relation to the actions of the Telegrafo and Cerro Gordo, in both of which they censure the general-in-chief in terms so severe, that it only remains to accuse him clearly and expressly of treason.

"The editorial of the 38th number of the *Bulletin of Democracy* (whose authors are well known), is full of this kind of charges against Santa Anna, who is there accused of the loss of Cerro Gordo; the article saying that all the bad fortune proceeded from a want of foresight in the preparations, and from a like want of judgment at the time of the attack, and from bad arrangements. We are given to understand that he sacrificed uselessly a large portion of this force. And he is even blamed for not performing a miracle by raising, in a moment, a new army, just as if he were in France in the time of the National Convention. We need only read, with a little attention, the said editorial, to penetrate the depth and the wickedness of the design of its authors. Unjust men! your calumnies suffice to detect your partiality and your insane intentions.

"Without calling the attention of our readers to the documents published in the *Diario del Gobierno*, and in other papers, the *Republicano*, (which certainly cannot be taxed with partiality to Santa Anna), in its number of the 23d inst., gives a clear idea of what took place in this action—dissipates the rash imputations of our enemies—and depicting the conduct of the invader, his tactics, his numerical superiority, the advantages of his artillery, and all that contributed to facilitate his triumphs, demonstrates most completely, that our loss was the result of inevitable misfortune.

"In fact, our position was well chosen; it was fortified as well as circumstances permitted; its flanks were covered, and all was foreseen that was to have been foreseen in regular order, and in the usual tactics of war. True it is, that no expectation was entertained of the rare, bold, and desperate operation of the enemy, who, in the night between the 17th and 18th, broke through the woods, crossed a ravine up to that time never crossed, and taking in reverse the position which the main body of our army occupied, surprised it in the time of action, made a general attack on all parts at once, and cut off the retreat of the infantry, the artillery, and even a part of the cavalry. It is pretended that even the general ought to have foreseen this risk. But to this argument two sufficient replies may be made: First—that notwithstanding the old opinion, confirmed by the experience of the whole war from 1810 to 1821, that the road by which the enemy flanked us was impracticable, the general did not neglect it, since he stationed, in order to cover it, the greater part of his cavalry in the mouth of the gorge; and if this force did not fulfil the object of its mission, the fault should not be imputed to the general-in-chief. We do not intend here to examine and qualify the conduct of the chief or chiefs of the cavalry; the fact is, that the point which this force should have guarded was left uncovered, and that is more than sufficient to justify General Santa Anna.

"Secondly—a recent historical fact may serve for the second solution of the question. We refer to the passage of Bonaparte over the great St. Bernard, executed likewise at night, with such silence and despatch, that the Austrian general, deceived by the dexterity of the operation, said, on the following day, before he learned the result, 'that he answered with his life, that the French artillery had not passed that way.' And if this happened in Europe, in the midst of a war that had formed so many expert commanders, it need not astonish us that like events transpire among ourselves! Men are not gods!" * * * * * *

After enlarging upon the particular instances of patriotism displayed by Santa Anna, from the beginning of his career down to the present time, his apologist concludes by the following peroration :—

"Mexicans, be just! Do not suffer yourselves to be deceived by perverse and evil-intentioned men! Reflect that some of those writers, who to-day are so eager to lead astray your opinions, to the prejudice of our well-deserving president, have sold themselves to him for friends—have flattered him in the season of his prosperity, and now declare themselves his enemies when fortune is against him. Examine well the facts—compare, judge with attention and impartiality; and it is sure that your conclusion must be, that gratitude is due to Santa Anna, as one of the best servants of the republic, both before and since its independence.

(Signed)

MANUEL MARIA JIMEN."

Not satisfied with this explanation, Santa Anna attributed the failure to the misconduct of one of his officers, who replied; and General Minon, who had commanded his cavalry at Buena Vista, and on that occasion been similarly censured, also took occasion to reply, and charged the president with cowardice, and a catalogue of faults, the least of which was sufficient to cause his removal. That strife of words yet continues, and is not the least of the difficulties which oppress Santa Anna.

From the letter of Minon, the following extracts may not be uninteresting, and will serve to show the tenor of the whole document:

"In every battle which he has lost, and they are all those in which he has attempted to command in person, there was always some one who had caused the defeat, to blame; at Jalapa, in 1822, Sr. Leno, who was shot through the body and abandoned, failed in the combination; at Tolome, Landero and Andonaegui were culpable; at San Jacinto, Castrillon; and to-day, it is I. It is certainly sorrowful to see so celebrated a general always defeated and overcome, always and everywhere, by the faults of those he has with him. My astonishment arose from beholding the perfidy with which General Santa Anna had acted in regard to me, in seeking a pretext, and nothing but a pretext, to palliate the precipitation of which he had been guilty, and to liberate himself at the same time from the indestructible charges which had been made against him, for leaving San Luis in search of the enemy, without providing for anything—for having given battle to Taylor where he did—for the errors which he committed in the attack—for the absence of all directions during the battle, which might turn it to profit—for his retirement from the field without necessity—for his want of foresight—in fine, in providing for attention to the wounded, subsistence for the troops, and for their orderly retirement.

"The nation will know one day what that was which was called, without shame, the victory of Angostura. It will know that it had brave soldiers, worthy to rival, in ardor and enthusiasm, the best of any army whatever; that it had intrepid officers, who led them gallantly to the combat; but that it had no general who knew how to make use of these excellent materials. The nation will know that if, on those memorable fields, a true and splendid victory was not achieved, no one was to blame but him who was charged with leading the forces, because he did not know how to do it. According to the order of the attack, and with a knowledge of the positions occupied by the enemy, speaking in accordance with the rules of art, we ought to have been defeated. We were not, because the valor of our troops overcame all the disadvantages with which we had to struggle. The battle of Angostura was nothing but a disconnexion of sublime individual deeds, partial attacks of the several corps who entered the action. Their chiefs led them according to the divers positions taken by the enemy, in consequence of the partial defeats which he suffered; but there was no methodical direction, no general regulated attack, no plan in which the efforts of the troops, according to their class, were combined, that did or could produce a victory. General Santa Anna believes that war is reduced to the fighting of the troops of one and the other party, wherever they meet and however they choose. General Santa Anna believes that a battle is no more than the shock of men, with much noise, shouts, and shots, to see who can do the most, each in his own way. General Santa Anna cannot conceive how it happens that a victory may be gained over an enemy by wise and well-calculated manœuvres. Thus it is that he has everywhere been routed; and he always will be, unless he should have the fortune to meet with one who has the same ideas with himself in relation to war."

This opinion of Minon is perhaps justified by facts; Santa Anna at the head of the men of the tierra caliente, would be one of the most formidable enemies imaginable, but it may be doubted if, like his *Teniente*

Arista, he *is not* altogether incompetent to lead masses of troops. This is not an unusual failing, though the opinion of persons ignorant of tactics contravenes it; for more than mere courage is required by the soldier, the minutiæ of whose profession embrace details depending upon algebraic calculations and synthetical combinations, not easily intelligible to those who are not initiated by *practice* or theoretical instruction.

The internal condition of Mexico since the war became certain, has not been harmonious. Many revolutions have occurred, one of which has deposed Herrera, and a second substituted Santa Anna for Paredes, who has been driven into exile. While the president has been at the head of the army, contests have occurred in the streets of Mexico, where Gomez Farias, Valencia, Salas, and minor men have controlled the city, seemingly reckless of the fact that the best portion of their country was in possession of an enemy.

How Santa Anna was permitted to return to Mexico has been much discussed. It is not, however, denied that it was by the authority of the president of the United States; whether wisely or not, history will show.

Whether Santa Anna wishes to make peace or not, no one can tell, for he is so harassed with priests and *politicos* that he dares not now act openly.

The conduct of the clergy in all the political events has been below contempt. Fostered for ages by the Mexican people, they have refused to pay one dollar towards the expenses of the war, and have had power enough to cause the purest and most honest man in Mexico, Farias, to be stripped of his power as provisional vice-president, to which office he had been elected since the return of Santa Anna, and seem disposed to see the government crumble above them without being willing to sustain it.

A new constitution has, within the last few weeks, been *inaugurated,* and an election has been held, the result of which has not reached us as yet. So far the elections seem to involve no principle or policy, and it does not seem to make to Mexico or the world the least difference, whether Santa Anna, Eloriaga, Bravo, or Valencia be elected. In the mean time General Scott is marching on Mexico from the east, the western coast is controlled by the naval forces of the United States, General Taylor is master of the *provincias internas,* and General Kearney has no opponent in California. The lesson of the past is, however, utterly lost on Mexico, in which all patriotism seems to be extinct.

The Mexican forces have been uniformly defeated in every battle; and horse, foot, and dragoons have given way before the charge of the American army. In the stirring events which have occurred, hundreds of men, previously unknown in the United States, have acquired fame and honor; while in Mexico, no star has arisen to penetrate the gloom which obscures her prospects. In this hour of distress, the country turns from her army, which long has weighed on her like an incubus, to find salvation in the right arms of her people. She has appealed to that feeling, which in the United States made Marion triumphant; which enabled La Vendée to set at defiance, for a series of years, the best armies of republican France, and enabled the Switzers, after winning their freedom from Austria, to maintain it against the attacks of Burgundy.

To triumph in this manner, a people must be virtuous;

and the success of the Spanish guerillas, under Espoz y Mina, Empecinado, and other chiefs, must be attributed to the fact, that while the rulers of the kingdom were corrupt and degraded as possible, the people and peasantry remained virtuous and brave, as they had been in the days when they beat back the Moors, and conquered Mexico and South America. Whether the people of Mexico can dare such a strife, history will show. It is, however, a hazardous experiment; and one which, if it fail, subjects the conquered to the woful condition of dependence on the mercy of the conquerors.

This book is now finished, and such as it is, is presented to the reader. The author has sought no eclat or praise, other than that of offering a fair view of men and things in a country of which the most erroneous opinions are now entertained by the mass of his countrymen.

THE END.

A Note About This Index

It has not been possible to locate the given names of some of the surnames in this index. It was a custom of the mid-19th century authors to use whatever name came handy, perhaps on the premise that in those days everyone knew everyone else. It could also be that the author simply didn't know the given name and was unable to find it out, or, it may have been, too, that the author was not ambitious enough to locate and use the first name associated with a last name. No matter. Where a given name could be supplied, we have supplied it. Where not, we have left a blank.

Wm. H. Farrington